# BRIDGING THE GAPS

## COLLEGE PATHWAYS TO CAREER SUCCESS

JAMES E. ROSENBAUM, CAITLIN E. AHEARN,
AND JANET E. ROSENBAUM

Russell Sage Foundation • New York

## The Russell Sage Foundation

The Russell Sage Foundation, one of the oldest of America's general purpose foundations, was established in 1907 by Mrs. Margaret Olivia Sage for "the improvement of social and living conditions in the United States." The foundation seeks to fulfill this mandate by fostering the development and dissemination of knowledge about the country's political, social, and economic problems. While the foundation endeavors to assure the accuracy and objectivity of each book it publishes, the conclusions and interpretations in Russell Sage Foundation publications are those of the authors and not of the foundation, its trustees, or its staff. Publication by Russell Sage, therefore, does not imply foundation endorsement.

**Library of Congress Cataloging-in-Publication Data**

Names: Rosenbaum, James E., 1943- author. | Ahearn, Caitlin E., author. | Rosenbaum, Janet E., author.
Title: Bridging the gaps : college pathways to career success / James E. Rosenbaum, Caitlin E. Ahearn, and Janet E. Rosenbaum.
Description: New York : Russell Sage Foundation, 2017. | Includes bibliographical references and index.
Identifiers: LCCN 2017007388 (print) | LCCN 2017026291 (ebook) | ISBN 9781610448680 (ebook) | ISBN 9780871547439 (pbk. : alk. paper)
Subjects: LCSH: Vocational education--United States. | Higher education--United States. | College graduates—Employment—United States. | Labor market--United States.
Classification: LCC LC1045 (ebook) | LCC LC1045 .R773 2017 (print) | DDC 331.702/350973--dc23
LC record available at https://lccn.loc.gov/2017007388

Text design by Suzanne Nichols.

RUSSELL SAGE FOUNDATION
112 East 64th Street, New York, New York 10065
10 9 8 7 6 5 4 3 2 1

# BRIDGING THE GAPS

# Contents

# List of Illustrations

vii

# About the Authors

**James E. Rosenbaum** is professor of sociology, education, and social policy and research fellow at the Institute for Policy Research at Northwestern University.

**Caitlin E. Ahearn** is a PhD student in sociology at the University of California, Los Angeles.

**Janet E. Rosenbaum** is assistant professor in the Department of Epidemiology and Biostatistics at the School of Public Health at SUNY Downstate Medical Center in Brooklyn, New York.

# Foreword

IN 1988, THE William T. Grant Foundation released *The Forgotten Half*, a widely cited report that decried our national underinvestment in young people who did not attend college. "As young Americans navigate the passage from youth to adulthood," the report asserted, "far too many flounder and ultimately fail in their efforts. Although rich in material resources, our society seems unable to ensure that *all* our youth will mature into young men and women able to face their futures with a sense of confidence and security."[1]

More than a quarter-century later, James E. Rosenbaum and his colleagues published *The New Forgotten Half and Research Directions to Support Them*.[2] Part retrospective, part contemporary analysis, and part a prescription for the future in light of current needs, the authors pointed out that the "forgotten half" of today are no longer those who do not attend college, but rather those who do attend but do not complete—receiving no degree, no certification, no qualification, and ultimately little or no boost to their labor market prospects despite their college attendance. Today the vast majority of high school graduates attend some form of postsecondary educational institution, but nearly half are not rewarded for doing so because they obtain no mark of completion. In response, the authors laid down a set of recommendations for future research that could point toward ways to address the challenges faced by the new forgotten half.

It did not take long for Rosenbaum and his colleagues to follow their own advice. This book, *Bridging the Gaps*, represents an important step toward fulfilling the research agenda identified in *The New Forgotten Half*. It provides a clear-eyed examination of the challenges faced by students who enter postsecondary education ill-equipped to finish, not because they lack the talent or drive to do so, but because they face obstacles in a confusing, opaque system that does too little to support their progress. Yet such barriers are not inevitable. In *Bridging the Gaps*, the authors emphasize the potential of the community college sector to help their students succeed, especially through occupational preparation leading to specific job qualifications.

As is common in high-quality works of social science, the first contribution of this book is exposure: in this case, by uncovering the hidden story behind the lack of college success for the new forgotten half. What the authors dub "the new college reality" has emerged in a time of rising inequality: the income gains of the last three decades have largely been confined to the upper reaches of the labor market, and the wages of not only low-income but middle-income earners have fallen in real terms. A pervasive ideology of "college for all" has taken hold, and acceptance of this reality has led to high enrollment rates, but because too few students are able to navigate the transitions into college, through college, and into the labor market, completion rates lag. Moreover, whereas racial and ethnic differences in postsecondary enrollment are relatively small, the gaps in completion rates are large, and growing. In contrast to authors who cite students' lack of ability as the reason for their failure, Rosenbaum and his colleagues show how the institutional conditions of community colleges pose formidable obstacles to student success.

Most works of social science would stop there, having documented the extent, sources, and consequences of inequality. In *Bridging the Gaps*, however, the authors have merely set the table for the repast that is to follow. Community colleges can be part of the solution, they argue, but need to be structured differently so that students can make informed choices to secure their futures. The authors proceed to lay out specific, research-based plans for reorganizing community colleges to elevate students' chances of obtaining occupational certification and labor market benefits. Some of these ideas have been rigorously tested and others are more speculative, but all provide new directions for both research and practice. One reason that Rosenbaum and his colleagues are able to provide such detailed prescriptions is that they have spent many hours talking to the key actors—administrators, faculty, and students in community colleges—to better understand what they really need and what can feasibly be accomplished. The authors further recount two examples of community colleges that have reorganized in ways that are consistent with their recommendations, further fueling their claim that such reorganization is feasible and beneficial, not only to students but to the colleges themselves.

By moving beyond an account of where inequality comes from and why it matters to documenting specific *responses* to inequality, this book can serve as a model of public engagement for scholars in the social sciences. Often, researchers conclude a lengthy study of the nature of inequality with a concluding chapter that asserts, in essence, that if we would only cease the practices identified in the book that have generated inequality, we would have less inequality in the future. *Bridging the Gaps* shows the paucity of that approach and the value of a more in-depth analysis of measures to reduce inequality that are informed by an understanding of the contingencies faced by individuals working in organizations as well as by the needs and struggles of their clients.

One way to achieve such depth of analysis is by carrying out research studies in the context of a partnership between researchers and the institutional leaders who are at the forefront of change. More common in the K–12 sector, research-practice partnerships allow researchers and school district leaders to work together to construct a research agenda that answers questions that matter to district leaders.[3] For researchers, the partnership offers access to data and a real-world context for pursuing questions of practical import. For educators, the partnership expands their research capacity and provides an independent voice on program and policy effects. Extending such partnerships to the postsecondary level could foster analysis of the innovative ideas put forth in this volume.[4]

Of course, *Bridging the Gaps* is not the last word on the subject. On the contrary, its recommendations lend themselves to a new research agenda, one that focuses on a reorganized community college that achieves much greater completion rates than are typical today. Moreover, there remains much to be learned about the level of resources that will be needed for community colleges to reorganize effectively. Indeed, it seems clear that increased resources could well be justified by the increased efficiency documented in the success stories presented in the book. *Bridging the Gaps* thus presents a challenge and an opportunity for researchers as well as community college leaders to forge a new way forward.

ADAM GAMORAN, PRESIDENT,
WILLIAM T. GRANT FOUNDATION

# Preface

C OMMUNITY COLLEGES are pivotal institutions in society, and they shape opportunity for a large segment of the population. They exemplify American opportunity ideals, and they have created impressive college access. But they also show how traditional college procedures constrain our ideals. We tell students that college is the way to escape poverty, yet when they try, traditional college procedures and "college-readiness" rhetoric pose unnecessary obstacles at every step and block their opportunity. In the 2016 presidential election, when non-college voters reported that good jobs are out of reach, these views were partly due to perceived college obstacles. This study finds that those obstacles can be removed.

We tell all students that they must attend college, but we design college in ways that prevent most students from succeeding. People rarely imagine that colleges could be designed differently, but this study shows that they can. Extending our prior findings, this book provides a new paradigm that identifies the alternative options and procedures used by some private and public colleges to improve students' success. Instead of "moving the needle" on one dimension, this study identifies multiple pathways to success, multiple procedures that support students' success, and multiple job rewards that students can enjoy. Instead of blaming students or colleges, this research identifies the many alternative options and procedures that can enable students to succeed, despite initial disadvantages, and make "college for all" an approach that leads to more career successes for young adults entering the labor market.

We thank the many colleagues who provided thoughtful suggestions—Tom Bailey, Tom Brock, Steven Brint, Charles Clotfelter, Sheldon Danziger, Stefanie DeLuca, Regina Deil-Amen, Kevin Dougherty, Greg Duncan, Adam Gamoran, Sara Goldrick-Rab, Eric Grodsky, Maureen Hallinan, Davis Jenkins, Stan Jones, Takehiko Kariya, John Meyer, Mike McPherson, Richard Murnane, David Neumark, Aaron Pallas, Ann Person, Mike Rose, Mortimer Schapiro, Barbara Schneider, Jennifer Stephan, David Stern, Mitchell Stevens, Tom Sugar, Burt Weisbrod, and Chris Winship.

We offer our appreciation to each of the colleges studied for providing access to conduct this research. We also thank the many staff members and students who thoughtfully and candidly answered what must have seemed like endless questions. They gave generously of their time, shared insights, and impressed us with their dedication and commitment. We are particularly indebted to Judith Marwick at Harper College and Scott Evenbeck, Stuart Cochran, Tracy Meade, and John Mogulescu at CUNY. They took ideas from our writing and translated them into effective operational practices that embody those initial ideas. Researchers call that "implementation," but that term does not capture the creativity required to construct procedures that reflect the underlying ideas but also actually work in the local college context. As we were learning what they had done, their insights and designs repeatedly impressed us. It was thrilling to see how they translated our abstract ideas into real-world practices, which we have endeavored to describe in chapter 8.

We are indebted to Kelly Becker, Kennan Cepa, Amy Foran, and Pam Schuetz, who contributed in many ways—with project planning, data collection, and thoughtful insights in the early years of this study. We are also indebted to David Figlio, director of the Institute for Policy Research at Northwestern University, whose support was a great contribution to the project. Suzanne Nichols of the Russell Sage Foundation encouraged us when this book was just an idea, and she was helpful in all stages of the publication process.

We thank the Spencer Foundation and the Gates Foundation for their support. When conventional reforms repeatedly fail, it is wise to examine whether our traditional assumptions are faulty. These foundations made commitments to questioning traditional assumptions and learning how colleges actually work. We also appreciate suggestions from Hilary Pennington and Josh Jarrett, who were at the Gates Foundation, and Susan Dauber, who was at the Spencer Foundation. Their substantive comments significantly improved our research.

Special thanks go to Alexis Gable and Kennan Cepa, whose extensive and thoughtful comments greatly improved the entire manuscript. We must take responsibility for the remaining errors, but their comments improved every chapter of the book. Chenny Ng and Rachel Wolfe also made editorial comments on some chapters.

We learned much from Norton Grubb's enormous body of research, and he made valuable suggestions about our work along the way. He inspired many of our insights and improved our understandings, and it is to his memory that we dedicate this book.

# Chapter 1

## College for All:
## New Opportunities Through
## Community Colleges

THE UNITED states has embarked on a new educational goal in recent decades. The policy of "college for all" (hereafter CFA), which expands educational opportunity and encourages all youth to attend college, has dramatically changed the higher education landscape, with consequences that have reverberated across American society. National and state policies have been enacted to encourage increased college enrollment, including support from scholarships, grants, and loans. Reflecting the American ideology of equal opportunity, CFA encompasses both practical policy and our highest ideals.

To adults who believe that youth do not listen, the history of CFA provides a surprise: youth have in fact responded to the call to enroll in college. In 1960, only 45 percent of high school graduates entered higher education right after high school.[1] Since then, reforms have focused on encouraging more students to enroll in college, and these efforts have been a tremendous success. Each decade since 1960 has seen more students aspiring to college.[2] About two-thirds of high school graduates now enroll in college right after high school.[3] But by ignoring the many students who delay entry into higher education, even these oft-cited numbers understate the successes. By 1990, the rates of college attendance in the eight years after high school graduation were similarly high for whites, African Americans, and Hispanics (83, 80, and 80 percent, respectively).[4] More recent data find that 90 percent of on-time high school graduates enroll in college in the eight years after high school (see chapter 2).

Nearly all students have internalized the message that college is necessary for getting a good job—80 percent of students enter community college with the reported purpose of getting a better job.[5] Even students who report hating high school, students whose academic achievement is low, and students who are in jail express college goals. Some high school

1

graduates who had planned not to attend college change their minds after they enter the workforce (see chapter 2). College access has long been the major obstacle to upward mobility, but that is much less true today. College completion, however, remains a critical problem, especially in open admissions colleges. Although "over 80 percent of entering community college students intend to earn a bachelor's degree or higher, only 15 percent have done so six years after initial enrollment."[6]

## College Access Versus College Completion

Outspoken public leaders continue to debate whether policy should encourage college for all, and the answer is usually a simple yes or no, justified, respectively, by ideals or pragmatism. The question, however, is no longer whether we should strive for CFA; we have already achieved it to a large extent. The real question now capturing the attention of researchers and reformers has become: How can college access be turned into *dependable completion and job payoffs* so that more students benefit from the experience?

To answer this question, it is important to understand the new realities of higher education and the many alternatives to the traditional BA degree. The pressures of CFA policies to increase college access have radically changed both the types of colleges available and the types of students who attend. Besides traditional selective colleges, CFA has led to an increase in the number of open-access institutions—public community colleges, private occupational colleges (for-profit and nonprofit), and unselective four-year colleges.[7]

Community colleges are particularly important for increased access to higher education. Of the 17.6 million undergraduates in higher education, roughly 40 percent attend a community college.[8] The nation's 1,200 community colleges offer convenient locations, including satellite campuses near homes and workplaces. They offer flexible time schedules, including night and weekend classes, and low tuition (often under $3,500 a year).[9] Most important for American ideals, community colleges are nonselective—even students who barely pass high school can attend. Naturally, being so different in these ways from traditional selective four-year colleges, these institutions attract different types of students.

In the traditional college model before 1980, the typical entering student was a young, high-achieving, and affluent high school graduate. This is no longer the typical college student.[10] Colleges now serve both traditional students (young, affluent, and high-achieving) and nontraditional students (older, lower-income, and lower-achieving).[11] We cannot assume that what works for the first group will automatically work for the second, but that has been the usual strategy. Forced into a system not built for them, nontraditional students make enormous sacrifices to attend college and then face countless obstacles after they arrive.[12] It comes as no surprise, then, that nontraditional students drop out of college at higher rates, especially when pursuing traditional bachelor's degrees.

The enormous gains in college access are often wasted when students drop out of college without completing a credential. Students forfeit time and earnings, acquire new debts, and often get no earnings payoff. Instead of a useful degree, they leave college with nothing except diminished resources and shaken confidence. Instead of offering a dependable transition to productive adulthood, many colleges offer coin-toss odds of success, with some research showing abysmal degree completion rates, often less than 20 percent.[13] In losing the potential of its youth to take middle-class jobs, society also suffers from these failures.

Moreover, open-access colleges, particularly community colleges, fall seriously short of the goals of raising academic achievement, awarding bachelor's degrees, and helping students attain high-paid jobs. After decades spent trying to find remedial education programs that improve students' academic achievement, researchers have finally concluded that this approach shows no dependable successes.[14] Similarly, for ambitious students with BA plans, graduation rates are very low.[15] Readers of these reports can sense the authors' real disappointment, and sometimes even their anger.

Even if students manage to graduate, they have difficulty searching for work among unfamiliar jobs. Rapid changes in the labor market have created new jobs and new job requirements. Most youth (and many adults) do not understand today's middle-class jobs and have poorly informed ambitions.[16] For example, in one study, we interviewed a high school senior who planned to become a surgeon, with a backup plan to work at Starbucks. She did not know about all the occupations in between high-status professions and low-level service jobs—that is, the many rewarding mid-skill occupations.

Open-access colleges can prepare students for employment in a rapidly changing market. Associate degrees and certificates prepare students for vital mid-skill jobs—such as airplane mechanics, auto repair mechanics, computer technicians, HVAC services, manufacturing workers, medical aides, and elevator repair workers. The nation may be hemorrhaging jobs to low-wage countries and to automation, but many of these occupations cannot be offshored or automated.[17] They must be done in the United States, but they require specific college programs.

Our daily activities, and indeed our lives, depend on the skills of these workers. Several years ago, one of us (James Rosenbaum) went in for surgery. His anxieties initially focused on the surgeon's skills, but going through the process, he quickly realized that his life depended on the technical skills of an entire team, including twenty-year-old surgical tech assistants with one-year college certificates from open-access colleges. Students want jobs that can make a difference, but they rarely see these jobs that will enable them to make important contributions as young adults.

Open-access colleges, particularly community colleges, embody American opportunity ideals. They are pivotal to society's success in filling vital occupations and providing opportunity to nontraditional students. In studying these colleges, we have discovered not just the difficulties of providing that opportunity but also the ways in which open-access colleges nevertheless manage to provide it. These colleges offer many alternatives to traditional BA degrees, including alternative credential options with different qualifications, requirements, job prospects, and job rewards. Open-access colleges can also implement alternative procedures at every step of a student's college career, from revamping the college entry process to helping students discover and attain promising jobs.

Having already improved college access, community colleges can increase educational and employment opportunities that are essential for the welfare of the next generation and a strong middle class, which is the foundation of democratic society. But for this to work, we must find ways to create and expand alternatives that reliably lead to college completion and subsequent job payoffs. This book considers what can be done to increase students' success in the new college reality by examining alternative options for students and alternative procedures for colleges. In particular, we explore the alternatives that work well for nontraditional students, who often lack the time, resources, and family support demanded by traditional college programs.

## Exploring Alternative Options and Procedures

College for all is an ambitious goal that the United States has largely attained, but the even more ambitious goal of a bachelor's degree for all is rarely attained—for instance, only 20 percent of community college students obtain a BA in the eight years after high school.[18] We are not criticizing CFA, but we find that a single-minded "BA for all" focus underestimates alternative options and procedures that have real value, build the middle class, offer high odds of college and career success, and can be stepping-stones to a BA degree.

Students should be aware of the different credentials, qualifications, job rewards, and degree strategies now offered by colleges in order to assess which option is best for them. At the same time, colleges should use new procedures to assess students' academic preparation, create degree ladders, reduce transition obstacles, and support students' college progress and success. In addition, instead of blaming students for their failures, colleges could devise ways to reveal their previously unrecognized abilities. These new options and procedures could provide opportunity to new kinds of students who do not typically succeed in traditional colleges.

However, information about these alternatives and their job payoffs is hard to come by; even researchers and educators rarely have adequate information. We find that the changing array of credentials, requirements, and careers is poorly understood and underutilized. Addressing this lack of clarity on all the new options, our research has uncovered many alternative ways in which students can succeed in college and in their careers.

## Can College Solve Societal Needs?
## The College-for-All Gospel

Despite our deep-seated ideals about equal opportunity, American society is increasingly unequal, most obviously in income and material well-being but also in health, family support, food insecurity, and mental and physical health.[19] Indicators in each of these domains show increasing advantages for those at the top and increasing disadvantages for those at the bottom.

The stakes are broader than just education. Youth unemployment, job turnover, drug use, and political disaffection are strongly related to education.[20] Without a college degree, youth often get locked out of promising careers. In a society increasingly polarized between "haves and have-nots," college has come to define who has a chance at a decent life.

Although college can lead to good jobs, people who do poorly in high school often see college as an obstacle; indeed, a lack of college-level academic skills can lead to college failure, poverty, despair, and even political backlash. Even as they blame automation and offshoring for the loss of well-paid jobs, many non-college-educated men do not see college as an option, believing it to be unavailable to those who were not high achievers in high school. And if they do enter college, most who were low achievers in high school are assigned to noncredit remedial classes; there they see their college dreams die, and they soon drop out. Instead of offering opportunity, college often blocks opportunity, and no other options are seen or valued.

Community colleges seek to help youth escape poverty, but this is not easy. Poverty is a powerful foe: beginning early, it colors many facets of individuals' lives. In a recent study, the sociologist Jennifer Silva describes in rich detail the workings of poverty and its devastating impact on young adults' efforts to escape minimum wage jobs and get a college education.[21] Poverty poses many obstacles, making it difficult to enter college, to commute to college, to stay in college, to get a job, to keep a job, to dress appropriately, to speak appropriately, to pay rent and utilities, to stay healthy, to care for ill or disabled relatives, to eat a good diet, and sometimes to eat at all.[22] Even when young adults make good efforts to escape poverty by going to college, poverty stops them at every turn. Preventing poverty, moreover, is not just about helping the poor. The many middle-class students who drop out with no credentials and no job payoffs eight years after high school may be headed toward poverty, or at least a low-income life (see chapter 2).[23] We need to understand what colleges can do to help all students avoid the grasp of poverty.

"College" is a word with powerful, almost sacred, connotations. Norton Grubb and Marvin Lazerson have called the American approach to college "the Education Gospel"—a faith that education can solve societal problems.[24] Although skeptical about nearly everything and unable to agree about anything, Americans share a profound faith in education, particularly higher education, across party lines. Even now, as higher education faces increasing criticism for high costs and low standards, few doubt its importance to our society and the labor markets.[25]

The Education Gospel has turned into the college-for-all ideal. High school vocational education used to provide job skills, give students advice on career choices, and assist them in job searches, but now it has been replaced by more ambiguous college- and career-readiness programs. Under the umbrella of career and technical education (CTE), these programs promote college-going and career exploration, often at the expense of specific job preparation.[26] Many programs once found in high school vocational programs are now in community colleges and may require technical skills considered to be beyond the abilities of high school students. As high schools increasingly focus on test scores and college admissions, their capacity to prepare students for work has declined and colleges have become the primary means of preparing students for careers.[27]

The ideology and realities of CFA have even forced us to reevaluate our own views. In 2001, one of the authors (James Rosenbaum) wrote *Beyond College for All*, which showed how American society had shifted to urging all youth to attend college, how youth had responded, and the difficulties that resulted. He criticized the narrow CFA focus and described some avenues for occupational success that do not require college, such as good high school vocational programs. Since 2001, however, these noncollege avenues have been undermined and deprived of resources, while jobs have increased their skill demands. A living wage increasingly requires skills that come mostly from college programs.[28] Popular books with titles like *Success Without College* describe alternatives to college, but these are idiosyncratic niche opportunities that will not help many people.[29] College for all has become the reality, and college credentials are key to a living wage. The push for CFA may have made college essential.

But more is at stake than college degrees and earnings. As the classic "Forgotten Half" report showed, fully half of the nation's youth, not just those in poverty, are struggling in "the passage to adulthood."[30] Instead of blaming youth, this report found that the problem is rooted in society's failure to provide mechanisms that support youth's transition into productive adult work roles, which are crucial for the preservation of society. The report saw these problems as serious threats to society, but showed how society could build such transition mechanisms.

We see the same problem today. In 2015, almost 40 percent of young Americans (eighteen- to thirty-four-year-olds) were living with their parents or other family members—the largest proportion since 1940, according to the U.S. Census.[31] These numbers suggest not so much the "failure to launch" of massive numbers of individuals as a failure of societal transition mechanisms.[32]

The *Pathways to Prosperity* report contends not only that society needs to develop supportive transitions into productive adult work roles, but that no institution is now addressing that need.[33] This report suggests that society use existing institutions to perform this function, and it identifies apprenticeship programs that work with high schools, much as German apprenticeship programs do.[34] Yet college for all has prompted many U.S. high schools to ignore work and focus on test scores and college preparation, and CFA thus may lead employers to regard high school graduates as unprepared for work. Apprenticeship programs have promise, and turning U.S. high schools around to support such programs is possible, as recent reports have indicated.[35] Nonetheless, these efforts must overcome major obstacles.

Community colleges may be easier to adapt to apprenticeship programs than high schools. They already have ongoing occupational sub-BA programs with many valuable elements—experienced teachers, practical lessons, equipment, employer-advisory committees, work-site visits, internships, and job placement arrangements. They already exist in over 1,200 locations across the nation, and they are already doing some of what we would want apprenticeships to do, although unsystematically. If American society is to repair the institutional supports for youth aspiring to productive careers, we must understand what community colleges are now doing and how they can be adapted to better serve society's needs. Our goal is not merely to increase the education or credentials of young people, but to have community colleges create transition mechanisms that will prepare them to embark on productive careers.

Although community colleges serve all ages, this book focuses on youth because we want to examine how community colleges can become dependable institutional supports for youth seeking productive adult roles. Not only do youth and society desperately need such institutional supports, but as we shall see, many elements of such a role can already be found at community colleges.

Our society's prosperity depends on effective procedures for implementing CFA. American colleges already enroll millions of students, but too many students fail to obtain degrees. With a focus on the steps that students and colleges can take to improve students' odds of success, we hope that this study will contribute to that goal.

## The Critical Role of Community Colleges

The United States has been through educational revolutions before, having offered public schooling for all, high school for all, and expanded college access through avenues such as the GI Bill and community colleges.[36] In the past century, as high school became universal, it was radically transformed to serve all students and prepare them for a diversity of careers.[37] This history suggests that our preconceptions about college may be failing to match the new reality; perhaps we should now expect colleges to work differently as they expand and become universal.

Worldwide, the expansion of higher education has taken different forms. Some nations have only a single form, the highly selective university, which is expanding.[38] Some nations are differentiated, with some credentials rapidly expanding. In comparison, the United States is highly differentiated, with diverse institutions (public, private, two-year, four-year, and so on) and diverse credentials (certificates, associate degrees, bachelor's degrees, and so on). Like other nations, the United States has vastly expanded the number of less selective institutions and credentials.

Over the past forty years, college enrollment has increased, especially in two-year colleges. In 1973, 14.9 percent of recent high school graduates attended two-year colleges and 31.6 percent attended four-year colleges. By 2012, the former had nearly doubled (to 28.8 percent), while the latter had increased much less (to 37.5 percent).[39] Moreover, this is an underestimate, since students who attend two-year colleges often delay entry and many are over age twenty-five. With reduced barriers of time, distance, cost, and school grades, it is easy to see why so many students enter community colleges. These institutions offer valuable opportunities to any student, regardless of socioeconomic or academic background.

In 2015, the actor Tom Hanks wrote in the *New York Times* about his time in community college and how it launched his career as an actor.[40] Over seven hundred people responded, many with stories about how community colleges had opened up opportunities for them as well. Like Hanks, they reported having poor achievement and motivation in high school and said that community college had provided a second chance that changed their lives.

Yet even these enthusiastic reports seem to include a disturbing element of random luck, the sense that their positive experience with community college was a fortunate accident that contributed to their success. Clearly, not everyone can count on such luck, and many students do not have positive experiences at community colleges. The national data on degree completion indicate that the success stories are too rare.

Community colleges can serve as stepping-stones to successful careers, particularly for disadvantaged students. As a result of their open access and convenience, community colleges enroll students who are quite different from students in four-year colleges. Compared with four-year colleges, community colleges enroll more students with disadvantages— those with less-educated parents or single parents, public aid recipients, and students who are disabled, ex-offenders, or housing-insecure.[41] With their distinctive population, community colleges face unique challenges. Solving the problem of access creates the new problem of understanding how these institutions can help these students have more college and career success.

Unfortunately, while providing college access for many disadvantaged students, community colleges try to emulate traditional four-year colleges. They provide all students with the kind of information and procedures that were designed for traditional college students whose college-educated parents give them advice and financial support. To improve community college completion rates, we must consider alternative options and procedures to reduce their students' difficulties. Offering the same options and procedures to nontraditional students might look like equal treatment, but it is not equal because many of these students do not have the same resources as traditional college students and cannot benefit in the same way. This strategy backfires and leads to low success.

We find that students face obstacles in three transitions—in entering college, completing degrees, and entering careers. When they enter college, most students must take remedial courses that give no college credits, and when they choose their courses, they often mistakenly choose courses that do not count for their program. In addition, although 80 percent of students enter community college with the reported purpose of getting a better job, community colleges rarely tell them

how college is related to jobs or inform them about occupational programs.[42] Later, when students graduate, community colleges do not tell
BA-transfer students which four-year colleges will recognize their credits
in their intended major, and they rarely help graduates identify and apply
to jobs that will value their skills and compensate them appropriately.

However, community colleges also provide new opportunities for
success. Our own wide-ranging study uncovered multiple pathways to
newly important credentials, jobs, and job rewards with fewer obstacles.
We also discovered nontraditional institutional procedures that reduce
transition obstacles, offer new kinds of opportunity, and support success even for low-achieving youth. We found that many more students
can succeed than is commonly thought, and that many more can get
good jobs with more job rewards besides earnings. This book reports on
these findings in examining how community colleges can offer alternative procedures that help students cross the three college transitions.

## BA Blinders and Signs of BA Mania

From 1945 to 1990, going to a "real college" was mostly seen as pursuing
a bachelor's degree in a selective four-year college.[43] Since 1990, however,
broad-access college alternatives—nonselective four-year colleges, community colleges, for-profit colleges, and digital courses—have become
important postsecondary options for many students.

Unfortunately, policymakers rarely notice these alternatives. Having
attended four-year colleges and obtained BA degrees themselves, policymakers and educators often wear "BA blinders": they see the BA as the
best, truest, and often only credential worth pursuing. This view is widespread, and it operates literally as a blinder, preventing educators and
students from seeing alternatives that could improve students' success.

When we ask Internet search engines, "What percentage of Americans
have a college degree?" the answers are responses to a different question:
"What percentage of Americans have a bachelor's degree?"[44] An article
on the website salary.com, "8 College Degrees with the Worst Return on
Investment," considers only majors that lead to BA degrees.[45] Educators,
reformers, and the college-choice industry stress K–16 reforms and
BA goals, but say little about sub-BA credentials.[46] A "college results
online" webpage lists only four-year colleges.[47] Even researchers studying upward mobility sometimes consider the BA the only college degree,
ignoring alternative degrees when classifying education levels.[48] In an
important book, Barbara Schneider and David Stevenson warn about
students' unrealistic ambitions and advise parents to provide better
information for college planning, but they do not mention sub-BA credentials.[49] Almost all of us, it seems, wear BA blinders.

In this context, "college for all" becomes "BA for all." A society that worships higher education sees a BA degree as the only college degree. In the policy debate, BA-for-all advocates urge all students to seek BAs and ignore lower credentials.[50] According to one commentator, the BA degree is "the only sure route out of poverty."[51] Others worry about tracking less-privileged students into a non-BA path. In contrast, BA-for-all critics, arguing that many youth are unlikely to complete a BA degree, would encourage them to follow alternative routes to good jobs, including job training programs and high school vocational programs.[52] Both sides recognize that low-income and low-achieving students face major college and labor market obstacles. However, BA-for-all advocates urge policymakers to redouble their efforts against those obstacles, while the critics suggest that a BA-for-all approach is not feasible. This war is highly polarized and tends to go nowhere.

The BA goal has made its way into policy. Public school systems, the College Advising Corps, and many nongovernmental support organizations have policies to help all students apply to four-year colleges and seek BA degrees, regardless of their academic skills or occupational interests. Following the widely cited announcement that a BA degree has a $1 million lifetime payoff, educators urge all high school seniors to pursue BA degrees.[53] As they urge even low-achieving youth to have BA plans, they do not mention (and probably do not know about) the low odds of college completion, the ineffective remedial courses they will be required to take, or the wisdom of having backup options. Educators, policymakers, and other stakeholders fail to identify the disadvantages of seeking a BA degree—the low odds of succeeding, the long timetable for many students (it often takes a community college student six or more years to obtain a four-year BA degree), and the low earnings payoffs. Youth are told almost nothing about alternative credentials, much less their desirability.

High school students have listened to this idealistic encouragement: close to 80 percent of recent high school graduates have BA plans when they enter college. Even students who learn valuable job skills in the career and technical education (CTE) courses they may be taking in combination with their BA plans tend to dismiss their job skills as unnecessary to their future once they get a BA degree.[54] By 2002, 84 percent of high school sophomores expected to earn a BA degree or higher, including many students with poor grades who disliked school.[55]

The stakes are high. The BA is viewed as essential and worthy of any sacrifice. In pursuit of a BA, low-income students in particular make major sacrifices; they may not only suffer hunger, sleep deprivation, and stress but also acquire enormous debts that are not protected by the option of bankruptcy. Their efforts may not even lead to dependable earnings payoffs.[56] Many levels of policy and practice are affected. Policymakers urge free tuition for college; high school principals' pay depends on students' college enrollment; students say they must attend college to become respected adults; and high school counselors call in students who have not applied to college and bus them over to the local community college to sign up. A website warns that "simply put, a *college education is the gateway to opportunity in life,* and the sooner children understand, the more willing they will be to put in the hard work required."[57]

Going to college has become a pervasive and life-altering goal for American students from a very young age. Indeed, the BA pursuit sometimes resembles a kind of mania. Summer camps focus on college prep. Children's games claim to provide college prep. One kindergarten program canceled the school play so that children could spend more time on college preparation. Of course, the BA degree has real value, but these are disturbing signs of exaggerated claims and ignorance of alternative options.

## Traditional Procedures for Nontraditional Students: A Bad Fit

The word "college" conjures images of what are in fact many optional features of the educational experience—athletic teams, Frisbee on the quad, university seals embossed with Latin slogans, beautiful college campuses, dormitories with carefree students studying together, debating metaphysical issues, and completing papers after arduous all-nighters followed by sunrise epiphanies. As the sociologist John Meyer observed, we often define "college" by traditional institutional customs and practices that are irrelevant to producing functional skills.[58]

BA blinders can lead to excessively narrow traditional expectations that academic success will be pursued through the traditional procedures developed for the BA degree. Students, even those in community college, are expected to pursue BA degrees, take four years of full-time coursework, receive no interim credentials or payoffs, and explore many "general education" fields before choosing a major. They are expected to choose their courses from a wide range of options, and colleges often do not closely monitor their progress. When students take courses that do not count toward their degree, colleges tell them they are "broadening" their learning, knowing that the added costs will be absorbed by affluent parents.

However, traditional students are no longer the only type of college student, and these procedures designed for them pose serious obstacles for nontraditional students. With their BA blinders keeping them focused on options that are a poor fit for many students' needs, educators and researchers rarely notice broader college alternatives, so it is unsurprising that students fail to see the benefits to pursuing these alternatives.

Michael Kirst and Mitchell Stevens warn that "the remaking of college in the contemporary epoch has repercussions across society," and that "a variety of paths through college is risky for students."[59] We agree that changing college is risky. College as it stands, however, with the heavy emphasis on BA degrees, is obviously not working. This book extends Kirst and Stevens's argument to show desirable alternatives that are often ignored. Research often ignores "the variety, complexity, and agency of schools," but here we present research that recognizes these issues.[60] Although we agree that too many options can be overwhelming, we show how colleges can structure alternative options and procedures to reduce risks. We provide evidence that recent changes in higher education make it crucial that colleges offer new options and procedures.

Our understanding of "college" must expand so that CFA can dependably provide all students with the opportunity to succeed and prepare them for the diverse needs of a complex and fast-changing society. Our faith alone in college's ability to help society will not automatically make it happen. That depends on what form college takes and its ability to adopt alternative procedures that will pose fewer obstacles, provide more support, and help students discover their abilities, pass tests, form realistic plans, and make dependable progress toward degrees and desirable careers. In chapter 8, we describe two colleges that implement these procedures and provide some of the key information students need to form realistic plans that will lead to successful outcomes.

## Alternative Options for Students: Qualifications, Credentials, and Jobs

Policymakers and researchers usually focus narrowly on one-dimensional goals—attaining a BA degree, improving academic skills, and increasing earnings. However, the progress of many students toward one-dimensional goals inevitably falls below average. Ironically, even as reformers think that they are being idealistic, urging youth to see success as one-dimensional implicitly disparages the many students who end up in the bottom half of measures of academic skills and earnings. In fact, all three views of these goals—BA attainment, higher earnings, and better academic skills—are too narrow.

### What We Miss by Focusing on BA Attainment

BA blinders prevent us from seeing valuable sub-BA credentials: occupational certificates and associate degrees. Many open-access institutions, especially community colleges, confer these credentials and provide

**Table 1.1    Earnings Quartiles for Full-Time, Full-Year Workers Ages Twenty-Five and Older, by Gender and Education Level**

|  | Females | | | Males | | |
|---|---|---|---|---|---|---|
|  | 25th Percentile | 50th Percentile | 75th Percentile | 25th Percentile | 50th Percentile | 75th Percentile |
| High school | $21,100 | $30,000 | $40,500 | $27,300 | $40,400 | $56,500 |
| Some college | 25,200 | 34,600 | 47,000 | 31,700 | 47,100 | 67,200 |
| Associate degree | 26,900 | 39,300 | 53,400 | 36,000 | 50,900 | 71,900 |
| BA degree | 35,100 | 49,100 | 69,000 | 43,900 | 66,200 | 100,000 |

*Source:* U.S. Census 2012; Baum, Ma, and Payea 2013, 15.
*Notes:* The highest quartile of associate degree earnings is higher than 50 percent of holders of BA degrees. The lowest quartile of BA earnings is lower than 50 percent of associate degree earnings.

technical skills in a variety of occupations. Occupational associate degrees are not usually intended as a path to a bachelor's degree, although this is increasingly possible for applied BA degrees.[61] Occupational sub-BA programs mostly aim to prepare students for viable employment after graduation. These programs are growing, and now most associate degrees and almost all certificates are completed in occupational fields.[62]

Twenty years ago, BA blinders may have been warranted. Researchers found that sub-BA credentials offered little earnings payoff, so research focused on BA payoffs.[63] However, recent years have seen a change in this trend. After careful review of new evidence, Steven Brint reversed his prior verdict and reported strong indications that sub-BA credentials have significant payoffs.[64] Yet public discourse mostly ignores alternative credentials, which are considered the product of "low expectations" and a distraction from the only desirable prize—a BA degree. But this view is too simple. Although BA degrees confer higher average earnings than sub-BA credentials (certificates and associate degrees), there is a big overlap. The top quartile of certificate and associate degree graduates have higher earnings than most BAs, and the bottom quartile of BA graduates have lower earnings than most sub-BAs.[65] The BA degree is valuable, but it is not the only path to good earnings (see table 1.1).

In a comprehensive analysis of community colleges, Thomas Bailey and his colleagues probed deeply into the barriers that keep students from attaining their BA goals, and the remedies they suggest are insightful.[66] These researchers emphasize BA degrees because most students report having BA plans upon arrival at college, and they believe that colleges should be judged on how well they meet students' reported goals at entry. When we interviewed students, however, we found that they often did not understand BA degrees or their disadvantages. We also found that many students did not know about certificates and occupational associate degrees, how long it takes to earn these credentials, their requirements, or their career outcomes.[67] Like the student who plans to become either a doctor or a Starbucks barista, many students are unaware of the in-between occupations.

With 1,000-student caseloads, college counselors are hard pressed to provide detailed advising on these issues. In interviews with counselors, we found that few warned students about the challenges of the BA goal, the low (20 percent) success rates, or the fact that the "four-year BA" typically takes many community college students six or more years to attain.[68] No one tells students that a slower pace and interim successes can sometimes help them be higher-achieving and that sub-BA credentials offer less risky steps.[69]

Likewise, colleges do not provide clear descriptions of alternatives in catalogs, websites, or information sheets. Seeking to avoid what President George W. Bush called "the soft bigotry of low expectations," educators encourage BA goals for all students and do not feel authorized to burst students' BA dreams.[70] For many students, the BA degree is a high-stakes gamble: it has high costs in time and money, high academic demands, and low odds of success. Indeed, BA plans most often lead students to "some college with no credential" and no greater earnings than they would have had if they had never attended college (see chapter 2). In contrast, sub-BA credentials are rarely mentioned and poorly understood, but there are fewer obstacles to attaining certificates and associate degrees, and they come with higher odds of success, good earnings payoffs, and sometimes even later BA degrees.

We believe that encouraging students' poorly informed BA choices is not the best way to support their success. Entering college students, especially those who were low-achieving high school students, need to be informed about alternatives before choosing their first credential goal. Chapter 2 provides updated analyses of sub-BA completion, employment, and earnings.

## What We Miss by Focusing on Earnings

Policymakers often assess college outcomes by examining earnings, which are easily measured. Earnings and employment are important, but they are only one aspect of labor market outcomes; jobs can also provide autonomy, learning, and career futures. Chapter 3 examines whether young working adults value other nonmonetary job rewards, and which credentials lead to such job rewards.

## *What We Miss by Focusing on Academic Skills*

Reformers claim that students must be "college-ready" and have BA-level academic skills to benefit from college and progress to decent careers. Just as sub-BA credentials prepare students for specific jobs, they also have specific requirements. For example, students with poor academic skills often thrive after earning certificates as electricians and computer network technicians, sometimes earning over $60,000 by age twenty-six. In addition, students often later gain gratification outside of the realm of academic skills when they are recognized for their problem-solving skills working, for instance, as medical assistants, machinists, or technicians. Chapter 4 explores how sub-BA credentials provide students with low to average academic skills with opportunities for success.

## Alternative College Procedures for Navigating Transitions: Beyond Curriculum Pathways

Community colleges offer the promise of a degree that will provide a dependable escape from poverty, but they have difficulty making good on that promise. Now that the college-for-all standard requires all students to add college to their work-entry process, students must cross *three transitions*—college entry, degree completion, and career entry. Students report, however, that they cannot get traction across these three transitions—they get courses without credits, credits without credentials, and credentials without payoffs. As though stuck in a Kafkaesque nightmare, they take steps but make no forward progress and their efforts do not lead to the expected outcomes. Although students are blamed for their failures, their failures are in fact built into traditional college procedures, which are not built to help them succeed.

If students are to succeed, colleges must create procedures to help nontraditional students navigate these transitions. Our prior research showed that colleges can structure curricula to prevent student mistakes and failures. In 2006, we criticized the "cafeteria" model of higher education, which leaves students free to choose their courses but often leads to poor progress, and we noted the advantages of "dependable pathways" that give more structure to curricular choices.[71] Curriculum pathways remove some of the difficulty in choosing aligned coursework that will dependably lead to a degree. Since then, leading researchers and reformers have joined in criticizing the cafeteria model and elaborating curriculum pathways.[72] Although curricular pathways began in community colleges, Richard Arum and Josipa Roksa, two prominent sociologists, advocate for curriculum pathways in four-year colleges as well.[73]

Chapters 5 through 8 examine ways colleges can improve students' college progress, testing procedures can reduce remedial needs, degree-ladder procedures (streamlined sequential degrees) can expand paths to BA degrees, and college procedures can reduce transition gaps and improve student supports. Although most educators assume that the traditional barriers to college transitions are there for a reason, some colleges have redesigned those transitions to reduce the obstacles and support student success as they go through them. Moreover, even as reformers have begun to accept and advocate our ideas about curriculum pathways, our new research indicates that pathways can go beyond curriculum. Pathway procedures are institutional procedures that colleges, on their own, can devise to guide and support students' career progress in crossing the three transitions—delayed obstacles, quick successes, proximal incentives, incremental success, curriculum pathways, monitoring and mandatory advising, and career-entry support. This book reveals and questions the many taken-for-granted traditional procedures that block students' path to success, and it identifies alternative procedures, often not seen or appreciated, that community colleges can implement. We can help youth escape poverty by succeeding in college, but only if we notice and make use of these options.

## The Sociology of Ability

Americans believe that all youth deserve the opportunity to attend college and that all will benefit from this experience, gaining credentials, status, and job payoffs. CFA generates hope by encouraging every student to enroll, regardless of past experiences and academic records. The premise of this policy is that if students make an effort, they can succeed, and their prior achievement history will not hold them back. This attitude allows us to maintain the darker, often unspoken assumption that students who fail in college have simply not worked hard enough.

Much higher education literature focuses on students' failures and limited ability, but such a focus ignores the influence of social context on ability. In his book *Real Education*, Charles Murray assumes that high rates of college dropout are attributable to the low ability of some students.[74] Although Murray is correct that many students do not succeed in college, he draws the wrong inference. High college dropout rates reflect not only individuals' ability but also the *demands imposed by traditional procedures* on students with nontraditional backgrounds. Although students' problems are often blamed on their own academic deficiencies, our research finds that many of them do not complete degrees because they make non-academic mistakes related to course choices, time allocation, degree plans, and so on. We suggest that this happens in part because the traditional procedures in community colleges set students up for making such mistakes.

Students' "ability" to succeed in college can increase if they have better knowledge about alternative options and if institutions change their procedures to reduce arbitrary and culturally determined demands. A student who "fails" in the traditional college environment may be much more successful in a college that organizes its programs to reduce obstacles. In other words, we propose a "sociology of ability" and contend that "ability" is much stronger in a social context that poses fewer cultural obstacles and provides supportive, nontraditional procedures.

## College for All Changes Everything: Alternative Options and Procedures

Our usual commonsense understandings about college are narrow and misinformed—four-year BA degrees may take six or more years to attain, "college-level" academic skill requirements can be arbitrary and often unnecessary, and some job rewards are more satisfying than income. Colleges assume that remedial classes will fix students' deficiencies, that students know their own interests and abilities, that they can make good choices despite being uninformed, and that they will seek advice when needed. These commonsense assumptions are consistent with traditional college procedures—and *they are all wrong or misleading*.

College for all has changed everything. Under CFA, the concept of "college" has become broader than the traditional concept; "college students" are now more diverse, with more diverse qualifications; and "college success" has come to include newly important credentials with different requirements. In addition, being "college-ready" is now understood as including academic readiness for some programs that require only tenth-grade academic skills, and there are many more jobs and job rewards that lead to "career success" than indicated by the usual focus on earnings, including jobs with better career futures.

Although they have been around a long time, certificates and associate degrees are newly important options that serve new students, offer credentials in new majors, and lead to new jobs and job rewards. Instead of operating by traditional procedures, programs offering sub-BA credentials operate by new rules that avoid old obstacles (socioeconomic status, test scores), reduce traditional transition gaps, and support success for a broader variety of newly important careers.

This book presents new issues not covered in our prior book, *After Admission*.[75] It is divided into two parts: alternative options for students, and alternative procedures for institutions. Alternatives for students include sub-BA credentials (chapter 2), their job outcomes (chapter 3), and the alternative qualifications required by these programs (chapter 4). Like most research, our prior book did not challenge popular "college-readiness" rhetoric, and it ignored certificates and "some college," which are important and frequent college outcomes. Alternative procedures for institutions include remedial placement testing procedures (chapter 5), curricula incorporating alternative course structures that create steps on degree ladders (chapter 6), and procedures at both public and private colleges to reduce the transition gaps that impede student success (chapter 7). These alternatives were not recognized in our prior book. For the first time, we examine here how SES and test scores are related to completion of various credentials and to earnings within credentials, with surprising results. We also present new findings related to the sociology of ability and the discovery of unseen abilities. Nonmonetary job rewards from sub-BA credentials were neglected by most prior research, including our own.

Since *After Admission* was published in 2006, reformers have begun to implement our ideas about structured curricula, and in chapter 8 we describe how two community colleges implemented and extended ideas in that book. However, even as other researchers adopted our ideas about course pathways, we came to see pathways as procedures that change social contexts and reduce transition gaps. This book reflects our growing understanding that the college experience encompasses more than coursework.

If the bold stance of college for all is going to succeed, colleges must embrace a wide range of alternative ways to educate nearly all students. Our methods are designed to discover rarely considered alternative approaches, and an important goal of this book is to determine which ones are worth further exploration.

# PART I

## ALTERNATIVE OPTIONS
## FOR STUDENTS

# — Chapter 2 —

## Alternative Credentials: A Path Around the Usual Opportunity Barriers?

W HILE COLLEGES often tell students they must pursue one-dimensional goals (BA degrees, earnings outcomes, and academic qualifications), the next three chapters show that students can benefit from many alternative options—sub-BA credentials, nonmonetary job rewards, and nonacademic qualifications. Many options are not widely discussed, and we find they have advantages that are not usually examined, including fewer obstacles and new kinds of successes.

Although colleges aspire to provide opportunity for all students, they often reproduce initial disadvantages. Students with low socioeconomic status (SES) and low academic achievement have lower BA completion rates and worse employment prospects even if they complete BA degrees.[1] This chapter looks at one way to address these unsatisfactory outcomes: putting greater emphasis on sub-BA credentials.

Many programs leading to sub-BA credentials—that is, associate degrees (typically two-year programs) and certificates (expected modal time of twelve months)—are offered at community colleges. Indeed, the number of certificates and associate degrees awarded has increased fourfold since 1969, while BA degrees have only doubled. As a result, more students complete sub-BA credentials than BAs. In 2011, about 2 million students completed a certificate or associate degree, surpassing the 1.7 million students who completed a BA degree.[2] Much of this increase has occurred in recent years: the number of certificates and associate degrees conferred grew by nearly 80 percent between 2000 and 2012.[3]

This chapter uses recent national data collected by the U.S. Department of Education to examine sub-BA credentials as alternative options. We discuss which students complete these credentials—specifically

the rates of graduation among students who come from low-SES backgrounds and have low test scores. We examine whether sub-BA degrees
are worth pursuing: are they associated with employment and earnings
gains? Earnings vary greatly within each credential, with large earnings
overlaps among them.[4] If they attain these credentials, do students with
prior disadvantages face lower employment or earnings outcomes than
advantaged students?

## The Status Attainment Model

Sociologists use the status attainment model to describe the impact of
education on occupational attainment by examining the ways in which
social background and academic achievement (SES and test scores) predict years of education, which in turn predicts occupational attainment
(as measured by earnings or social status). The model has an intuitive
appeal, captures many of the important variables, and is strongly supported in empirical tests. But how does it operate in the college-for-all
environment? Having seen a dramatic increase in the number of certificates and associate degrees awarded in the past fifteen years, we
wonder whether this change has led to differences in the status attainment process.

The status attainment model may inadvertently ignore this question
because it usually measures years of education. Although this measure
made sense in prior decades, it may not work as well today. Big changes
in sub-BA credential attainment may be hard to detect in a simple "years
of education" scale, especially if students take longer to earn the degree
than it is designed to take. When, as is often the case, acquiring a two-
year associate degree takes four years and a four-year BA takes six
years or more, do we expect these students to earn more than those
who obtained the same credential in fewer years?[5] One can imagine
reasons why they would earn less for taking more years to get a degree
designed to take four years. Moreover, years of education may misrepre-
sent actual processes. As we show in this chapter, many students spend
several years in college and attain "some college" but no credential.
Attaining "some college" may take several years, but do those years of
education bring better employment or earnings in the absence of any
credential? We examine this issue as well.

According to the sociological status attainment model, students' individual attributes (such as family income, parental education, and academic achievement) predict years of education, which in turn predicts
job outcomes.[6] This model hypothesizes that students with low SES, low
test scores, or less ambitious educational plans will attain less education
and therefore lower earnings than more-advantaged, higher-achieving

students who are more ambitious. Moreover, the SES differences in the cultural values taught in homes may confer further advantages in school and work.[7] Other research supports these predictions.[8]

Although CFA encourages all students to attend college, the conventional findings from the status attainment model offer little hope for low-income or academically low-achieving students who enroll in college. If the status attainment prediction holds, they may receive little benefit from their time in college. Disadvantaged students currently enter college at high rates, but this model predicts that they will receive fewer college credentials and worse labor market benefits than more-advantaged students.[9] Even recent rigorous methods find reduced success for academically and socioeconomically disadvantaged students pursuing BA degrees and BA-transfer associate degrees.[10]

But colleges also offer many more sub-BA credentials that may work differently. Do students from disadvantaged backgrounds have higher odds of academic and employment success if they pursue sub-BA credentials? Despite widespread policy rhetoric that students need "college-level" academic skills to benefit from college, is that true for sub-BA credentials?

Indeed, when we asked community college faculty this question, they reported that some sub-BA credentials and their associated occupations require only eighth-grade academic skills (see chapter 4). For example, computer technicians and medical assistants must calculate proportions quickly and accurately, but students enrolled in these sub-BA programs do not need to have mastered algebra II. Detailed analyses of community college curricula indicate that their courses rarely require twelfth-grade academic skills.[11] Although some high-status occupations require high-SES cultural capital, mid-skill jobs that demand technical skills and a work ethic may not require class-related cultural capital.[12] We tend to assume that problem-solving, an ability to take responsibility, and communication skills require high academic skills. Yet community college faculty reported that computer network certificates, for which students do not need more than tenth-grade math skills, require that students learn to solve problems, to take responsibility, and to persuade higher-level managers to understand procedures for preserving computer security. Thus, we must ask: Do sub-BA credentials always require high-level academic skills?

## The College Opportunity Structure

College-for-all policy has led to large-scale college enrollment, especially in open-access institutions like community colleges. By 2000, over 80 percent of on-time high school graduates were enrolling in college within eight years after graduation, and the rates were similar for whites (83 percent), African Americans (80 percent), and Hispanics (80 percent).[13] Updating these results, we find further increases in college enrollment, but the small race differences have been maintained (91, 87, and 90 percent, respectively).[14] Given the large racial disparities in college access historically, remarkable changes in college access have occurred in recent years.[15]

This chapter analyzes the Education Longitudinal Study (ELS 2002–2012), a survey of the high school class of 2004, who were followed for another eight years until 2012. Although the rate at which students enroll in college immediately after high school has remained stable in recent years, at about 70 percent (see table 2.1), that rate is much higher when we give students more time to enroll. We find that almost 90 percent of on-time high school graduates in the class of 2004 reported enrolling in college within eight years of high school graduation. College enrollment was lower for students with low test scores (80 percent) or low-SES background (81 percent), but still substantial. The overwhelming majority of on-time high school graduates followed in the ELS responded to the pressures of CFA and eventually enrolled in college.[16]

Educators used to believe that high school seniors who do not have college plans do not enroll in college, but today even high school seniors who plan not to attend college are changing their minds.[17] A full 50 percent of seniors who planned not to enroll in college in 2004 changed their minds and had enrolled by 2012 (not shown in table 2.1). In another study, we interviewed some students who did this. They reported concluding that, facing repeated barriers to desirable jobs in the labor market, college was the only way to escape dead-end jobs and poverty.[18] Although immediate enrollment numbers have remained steady at about 70 percent and are much lower for low-income students, large numbers enroll over the next eight years, including a higher proportion of low-SES and low-achieving students.[19]

We should be encouraged, but not lulled into complacency, by the tremendous increases in college access, which are the result of impressive initiatives that must be continued. Also, efforts must continue to increase the high school graduation rate and to help students who did not complete high school to find postsecondary training. But however impressive the high rates of college access, completion rates are a serious problem. Despite 90 percent college enrollment, many students do not complete a college degree within eight years. They have the experience of "some college" but do not acquire a credential, and this is the most frequent outcome for students entering community college and for students with low test scores who enter four-year colleges (see table 2.2).

**Table 2.1  High School Graduation and College Attendance, by Socioeconomic Status and Test-Score Thirds: ELS (2002–2012)**

| | All | Low Test Score[a] | Middle Test Score | High Test Score | Low SES[b] | Middle SES | High SES |
|---|---|---|---|---|---|---|---|
| High school graduation by June 2004 | 86.1% | 72.8% | 89.6% | 95.8% | 76.9% | 87.5% | 94.1% |
| High school graduates who ever attended college, 2004–2012 | 89.6 | 79.7 | 90.0 | 96.6 | 81.1 | 89.6 | 96.6 |
| High school graduates who enrolled in college by January 2005 | 70.5 | 47.3 | 70.1 | 87.0 | 53.5 | 69.1 | 85.5 |

*Source:* Authors' calculations from the Education Longitudinal Study (ELS), 2002–2012.
*Notes:* The sample includes all ELS respondents in both the base year (2002) and the 2012 follow-up. "High school graduates" refers to on-time high school graduation (by 2004).
[a] Test score is the composite math and reading standardized test score from 2002.
[b] Created by the National Center for Education Statistics (NCES) through the ELS, the SES variable comprises information on parents' occupations and parents' education.

**Table 2.2** Highest Credential Attainment in 2012, by First College Enrollment, by Socioeconomic Status and Test-Score Thirds: ELS (2002–2012)

| | All | Test Score | | | SES | | |
|---|---|---|---|---|---|---|---|
| | | Low Test Score[a] | Middle Test Score | High Test Score | Low SES[b] | Middle SES | High SES |
| On-time high school graduates in the class of 2004 who enrolled in college (N) | 7,155 | 1,725 | 2,435 | 2,994 | 1,915 | 2,448 | 2,792 |
| First college enrollment | | | | | | | |
| Less than two-year institution[c] | 3.7% | 8.9% | 2.3% | 1.3% | 7.1% | 3.8% | 1.2% |
| Two-year college | 36.9 | 61.1 | 41.3 | 19.2 | 51.0 | 41.2 | 23.3 |
| Four-year college | 59.5 | 30.0 | 56.4 | 79.5 | 41.9 | 55.0 | 75.6 |
| Attainment of students who started at a two-year college | | | | | | | |
| Some college | 46.3 | 51.3 | 42.6 | 43.6 | 49.0 | 47.0 | 41.2 |
| Certificate | 17.1 | 22.5 | 16.3 | 8.9 | 21.2 | 17.2 | 10.8 |
| Associate degree | 15.8 | 14.5 | 16.6 | 16.8 | 15.7 | 16.7 | 14.6 |
| Bachelor's degree or higher | 20.7 | 11.7 | 24.5 | 30.7 | 14.0 | 19.1 | 33.3 |
| Attainment of students who started at a four-year college | | | | | | | |
| Some college | 22.5 | 44.3 | 27.3 | 14.9 | 35.6 | 26.1 | 15.2 |
| Certificate | 5.5 | 12.1 | 5.6 | 4.0 | 7.4 | 6.2 | 4.3 |
| Associate degree | 5.4 | 8.9 | 7.5 | 3.5 | 7.7 | 6.5 | 3.9 |
| Bachelor's degree or higher | 66.6 | 34.5 | 59.6 | 77.6 | 49.3 | 61.2 | 76.7 |

*Source:* Authors' calculations from the ELS (2002–2012), weighted.
*Note:* The sample includes all on-time high school graduates who enrolled in college and were not still enrolled in June 2012.
[a] Test score is the composite math and reading standardized test score from 2002.
[b] Created by the NCES through the ELS, the SES variable comprises information on parents' occupations and parents' education.
[c] We exclude the outcomes of the students who enrolled in less than two-year institutions because so few chose to begin their education at these schools.

Popular rhetoric encourages students to form BA plans, and 80 percent of students beginning in two-year colleges report having such plans (not shown in tables). However, only 21 percent of two-year college students complete a BA within eight years of high school graduation. Two-year college students have additional sub-BA options in certificates and associate degrees, and more students (33 percent) complete these than BA degrees. The low BA completion rates are often reported by education reformers, but the relatively higher sub-BA completion rates are less well known.[20]

CFA encourages even students with low academic achievement to have BA plans, but some do manage to discover sub-BA credential programs, despite counselors' reluctance to recommend sub-BAs for them.[21] Because sub-BA credentials take less time than bachelor's degrees, costs are reduced and students face less risk that financial or personal crises will interrupt their schooling. Of students who begin in two-year colleges who score in the lowest third on tests, only 12 percent get BA degrees, while 37 percent complete certificates or associate degrees (table 2.2). In contrast, 31 percent of students whose test scores are in the top third attain BA degrees, while 25 percent receive certificates or associate degrees. Students with low test scores frequently choose sub-BA credential programs.

Students who begin at four-year colleges are more likely to complete a BA (67 percent) and less likely to finish a sub-BA degree (11 percent), which four-year colleges rarely offer. However, for students in the bottom third of test scores in four-year colleges, only one-third complete BA degrees and only another 21 percent get sub-BA credentials. For low-scoring students, four-year colleges do not offer high odds of either a BA or sub-BA. Most students who struggle in four-year colleges would be better off transferring to a new college and pursuing an entirely new credential, but that rarely happens.

Unlike prior research, we are considering more options than just BA degrees.[22] However, even with our expanded conception of success, almost half (46 percent) of two-year college students get no credential. Four-year colleges have better completion rates overall, but not for students in the bottom third of test scores. Again, almost half (45 percent) of students with low test scores in four-year colleges receive no credential at all. In other words, *millions* of college students have no credential after spending time, money, and energy on coursework. No less disturbing, students are rarely warned about these coin-toss odds of success.

For students who leave college with no credential, the most they get is "some college." Students we have interviewed in this category often expect some payoffs for attending college. Some entering students say that they do not plan to stay long enough to earn a credential, but do expect to glean some value from their college experience. As noted, research sometimes inadvertently makes the same assumption that "some college" is valuable by measuring "years of education." This measure implies that there is added labor market value for students who persist longer, even if they do not leave college with a credential.

We believe that understanding the full array of academic options is an important place to begin in the hunt for improved educational experiences. Among these, "some college" and sub-BA credentials are poorly understood options.

We can put these recent findings in context by comparing them with an earlier survey. While the ELS studied the class of 2004, the National Education Longitudinal Study (NELS) studied an earlier cohort, the high school class of 1992. The two surveys asked almost identical questions, so they are easily compared. We find that the class of 1992 was as likely to enroll in college, and enrolled in two- and four-year colleges at similar rates, as the class of 2004 (table 2.3). However, two-year college students in the more recent cohort were less likely to get "some college" and no credential, and more likely to get a certificate. Certificate programs, which expanded between 1992 and 2004, seem to have been discovered by students, especially those with low test scores.

## Employment and Earnings After Completion of Sub-BA Credentials

We next examine whether completion and economic outcomes for those attaining sub-BA credentials differ from these outcomes for those who earn BA degrees. We ask whether sub-BA credentials, besides opening up opportunities to pursue BA degrees, can create paths to desirable jobs and career futures that are less related to family background or test scores than BA degrees are.[23]

For the on-time graduating class of 2004, college access was close to universal, but college completion encountered major obstacles. Students with low test scores or low SES were at especially high risk of leaving with "some college" and no credential, even when given eight years to finish a credential. Moreover, while two-year colleges are criticized for lower BA completion than four-year colleges, this completion rate gap is greatly reduced if we consider sub-BA credentials. We use this finding as a starting point to discuss sub-BA credentials as viable alternative options to the BA for students who are unlikely to finish the more expensive and academically demanding BA degree.

In the 1980s, Steven Brint wrote that community colleges did great harm by diverting students to sub-BA credentials, which had little value at the time.[24] Since then, however, Brint has observed new evidence that

**Table 2.3  Highest Credential Attainment in 2000, by First College Enrollment, by Socioeconomic Status and Test-Score Thirds: NELS (1990–2000)**

|  | All | Test Score | | | SES | | |
|---|---|---|---|---|---|---|---|
|  |  | Low Test Score[a] | Middle Test Score | High Test Score | Low SES[b] | Middle SES | High SES |
| On-time high school graduates in the class of 1992 enrolled in college by 2000 | 80.0% | 65.0% | 82.0% | 94.0% | 62.0% | 79.0% | 93.0% |
| First college enrollment |  |  |  |  |  |  |  |
| Less than two-year institution[c] | 3.8 | 8.9 | 2.3 | 1.4 | 8.3 | 3.8 | 1.6 |
| Two-year college | 36.7 | 58.3 | 44.0 | 19.2 | 52.1 | 42.6 | 24.5 |
| Four-year college | 59.6 | 33.6 | 52.0 | 79.5 | 39.7 | 53.6 | 73.9 |
| Attainment of students who started at a two-year college |  |  |  |  |  |  |  |
| Some college | 58.8 | 71.4 | 56.5 | 44.7 | 65.0 | 61.5 | 49.3 |
| Certificate | 6.4 | 7.7 | 6.2 | 4.9 | 7.5 | 5.7 | 6.3 |
| Associate degree | 15.0 | 12.1 | 17.4 | 18.6 | 17.8 | 15.7 | 11.4 |
| Bachelor's degree or higher | 19.8 | 13.4 | 19.9 | 35.5 | 9.8 | 7.1 | 33.0 |
| Attainment of students who started at a four-year college |  |  |  |  |  |  |  |
| Some college | 25.0 | 47.3 | 29.7 | 18.2 | 42.9 | 32.2 | 16.6 |
| Certificate | 1.4 | 3.8 | 2.1 | 0.1 | 3.6 | 2.0 | 0.5 |
| Associate degree | 3.5 | 5.8 | 5.2 | 2.3 | 6.1 | 4.7 | 2.3 |
| Bachelor's degree or higher | 70.1 | 43.2 | 63.0 | 79.0 | 47.4 | 61.2 | 80.6 |

*Source:* Authors' calculations from the National Education Longitudinal Study (NELS, 1990–2000), weighted.
*Note:* The sample includes all on-time high school graduates who enrolled in college and were not still enrolled in June 2000.
[a] Test score is the composite math and reading standardized test score from 1992.
[b] Created by the NCES through the NELS, the SES variable comprises information on parents' occupations and parents' education.
[c] We exclude the outcomes of students who enrolled in less than two-year institutions because so few chose to begin their education at these schools.

indicates that some occupational sub-BA credentials result in higher earnings than in prior decades.[25] That conclusion is reinforced by more recent research.[26]

Reviewing many studies of earnings outcomes, Clive Belfield and Thomas Bailey find a research consensus that sub-BA credentials have significant earnings benefits.[27] They also conclude that the "earnings premiums to education have grown over recent decades."[28] Sub-BA earnings premiums may be on the rise because of labor market demand for those credentials, which often prepare students for high-growth job markets such as health and information technology.[29] These fields maintained strong demand even in the recent recession.[30] In fact, employers often report shortages of qualified applicants for mid-skill jobs. Joshua Wyner estimates that 2 million mid-skill jobs, which often require sub-BA credentials, go unfilled because of a lack of qualified candidates.[31]

## Employment Outcomes

Were sub-BA credentials associated with improved employment outcomes for twenty-six-year-olds in 2012? In table 2.4, we find that individuals with a certificate, associate degree, or bachelor's degree all had significantly higher odds of being employed, with those odds increasing the higher their credential (1.53, 2.07, 3.32), compared with high school graduates who did not enroll in a postsecondary institution. Our analyses find that young adults with "some college" but no credential (who were not included in prior research) were not significantly more likely to be employed than high school graduates who did not enroll in a postsecondary institution (1.17, not significant). Controlling for individual attributes, students who completed a sub-BA credential were more likely to be employed than high school graduates, but those with "some college" were not.

## Earnings Outcomes

We also examined earnings among employed workers at age twenty-five (table 2.4). Using linear regression, we controlled for individual attributes as well as weeks employed and hours worked. We find that earnings increase for holders of BA degrees by 34 percent, for those holding associate degrees by 22 percent, and for those who earn certificates by 13 percent. Earnings for all three groups are significantly higher than earnings for high school graduates. In contrast, the earnings of individuals with "some college" are no higher than earnings for on-time high school graduates who never attended college. Although earnings results do not include unemployed individuals with zero earnings, our results point to similar influences on both employment and earnings.

Table 2.4    **Employment and Earnings Outcomes Regressions Eight Years After High School Graduation**

|  | Logistic Regression of Employment Status, 2012[a] | Linear Regression on Log Earnings, 2011 |
|---|---|---|
| SES 2002[b] | 1.14 | 0.05** |
|  | (1.80) | (2.77) |
| Test score 2002[c] | 1.02*** | 0.01*** |
|  | (4.07) | (4.83) |
| Graduate degree[d] | 4.96*** | 0.46*** |
|  | (6.04) | (8.58) |
| Bachelor's degree | 3.32*** | 0.34*** |
|  | (8.19) | (8.83) |
| Associate degree | 2.07*** | 0.22*** |
|  | (3.89) | (4.37) |
| Certificate | 1.53** | 0.13** |
|  | (2.84) | (2.74) |
| Some college | 1.17 | −0.03 |
|  | (1.36) | (−0.73) |
| Hours worked per week in 2011 | — | 0.02*** |
|  |  | (23.92) |
| Weeks employed in 2011 | — | 0.03*** |
|  |  | (29.97) |
| Female | 0.37*** | −0.16*** |
|  | (−10.91) | (−7.52) |
| African American | 1.11 | −0.12** |
|  | (0.71) | (−3.23) |
| Hispanic | 0.82 | 0.02 |
|  | (−1.63) | (0.50) |
| Other race | 0.76* | 0.06 |
|  | (−2.01) | (1.84) |
| Constant | — | 7.49*** |
|  |  | (86.94) |
| N | 7,596 | 5,109 |

*Source:* Authors' calculations from the ELS (2002–2012).
*Notes:* T-statistics are in parentheses. The sample includes on-time high school graduates not still in college by the end of 2011 (employment) or by the end of 2010 (earnings).
[a] Employed (full-time or part-time) versus unemployed.
[b] Created by the NCES through the ELS, our SES variable comprises information on parents' occupations and parents' education.
[c] Test score is the composite math and reading standardized test score from 2002.
[d] On-time high school graduates are the comparison for credential coefficients.
*$p < .05$; **$p < .01$; ***$p < .001$

## Employment and Earnings After Completion of "Some College"

With seventeen prior studies showing that sub-BA credentials increase earnings compared to a high school diploma, here we are confirming a well-established finding.[32] However, our finding on young adults with "some college" is more contentious, especially among those examining the earnings of workers under age thirty.[33] Even in the most statistically sophisticated studies, findings conflict as to the benefits of "some college."[34] Any benefit is likely to depend on how much college students complete, which can vary wildly, as well as their prior experiences and social connections. "Some college" may increase employment or earnings for students who are in certain majors, who get credits in certain skill areas, who already have certain jobs or job contacts, or who get jobs that use their skills. These variables are rarely studied; thus, even though we can reasonably suspect that averages do not tell the whole story, we are unclear as to how, when, and for whom "some college" is beneficial.

Nonetheless, virtually all studies agree that "some college" has no benefit for students who earn few or no credits, as often happens among young students who do not get a credential.[35] The practical conclusion is that students at high risk of receiving no credential cannot count on "some college" to yield better employment or earnings than they would have with only a high school diploma. Instead, credentials are likely to confer a significant benefit. Although this payoff probably varies by occupation, on average even a one-year certificate has a substantial and significant payoff.

We do not find these sub-BA payoffs in the earlier cohort. Repeating the analysis presented in table 2.4 for the high school class of 1992 (NELS), we find that associate degrees and certificates were not significantly related to employment or earnings in 1999 (not shown). The dramatic increases in receipt of these sub-BA credentials in the last fifteen years may have resulted from the improved employment and earnings payoffs. Indeed, our analyses indicate large increases in the payoffs to these credentials since the year 2000.

### Are Students with "Some College" Less Qualified?

Are these findings due to a selection effect or to the lack of credentials of students with "some college"? Did these students begin with inferior qualifications or resources compared with students who got sub-BA degrees? Inspecting their attributes, we do not find that students with "some college" have inferior backgrounds: their high school performance is similar to that of those with certificates (sharing low grade point averages, low rates of homework completion, and a tendency to get in trouble and to skip school), they less often have a low-SES background, and they less often have low test scores. Indeed, they are much more ambitious—more of these students have BA plans than certificate holders and more started at a four-year college (table 2.5). Therefore, students with "some college" may be more focused on BAs and four-year college than certificate holders (and perhaps associate degree holders), despite similar high school performance.

Young adults with "some college" rank lower than BA completers on every positive attribute and higher on every negative attribute. Compared to students who complete BA degrees, their prior school performance is lower, but their school performance exceeds that of many individuals who get sub-BA credentials. Overall, students with "some college" fall somewhere in the middle of the sample—they are not as high-achieving, advantaged, or motivated as BA completers, but they are often higher on these attributes than certificate completers.

Of course, these variables do not measure all possible student attributes, but they cover a range of behaviors and backgrounds that are likely to be associated with credential completion. Based on these findings, we see no reason why students with "some college" could not have completed a certificate had they followed an alternative postsecondary route.

Two large differences between these individuals and certificate graduates—having BA plans and starting at a four-year college—may provide a clue as to why they did not complete certificates. Their BA plans and four-year college beginnings may have prevented them from seeing the desirable features of certificates. In addition, their advisers may not have provided information that would have encouraged them to consider attaining a sub-BA credential or leaving the four-year college because it did not offer sub-BA credentials. Many students who are likely to stop at "some college" because they are unlikely to complete a bachelor's degree may be capable of completing a sub-BA credential, but they may not know about these credentials or their desirability.

## Do Student SES and Test Scores Predict Attainment?

While many students who start in a two- or four-year college leave with just some college, many others complete a certificate or associate degree. Many students who are normally locked out of bachelor's degrees—those who are from low-SES backgrounds and have low test scores—eventually complete a sub-BA credential (see table 2.2). We examine which student characteristics, if any, predict completion of each college credential (certificate, associate degree, bachelor's degree, graduate

**Table 2.5    Characteristics of Individuals by Different Levels of Highest Educational Attainment: ELS (2002–2012)**

| | Some College | Certificate[a] | Associate Degree | Bachelor's Degree | Graduate Degree |
|---|---|---|---|---|---|
| Low high school GPA third, honors weighted | 36.0% | 34.0% | 21.0%*** | 6.0%*** | 2.0%*** |
| Usually had homework done in tenth grade | 71.0 | 72.0 | 78.0** | 84.0*** | 88.0*** |
| Got in trouble three or more times in tenth grade | 13.0 | 12.0 | 9.0 | 6.0*** | 4.0*** |
| Skipped class three or more times in tenth grade | 12.0 | 11.0 | 11.0 | 5.0*** | 5.0*** |
| Low test score third in 2002[b] | 34.0 | 45.0*** | 29.0 | 9.0*** | 5.0*** |
| Low SES third in 2002[c] | 36.0 | 40.0* | 33.0 | 17.0*** | 11.0*** |
| Had BA plans in twelfth grade | 62.0 | 50.0*** | 61.0 | 93.0*** | 98.0*** |
| Enrolled in college in first term after high school | 66.0 | 61.0** | 73.0*** | 92.0*** | 94.0*** |
| Started at a four-year college | 42.0 | 26.0*** | 33.0*** | 84.0*** | 93.0*** |

*Source:* Authors' calculations from the ELS (2002–2012).
*Note:* The sample includes on-time high school graduates who were not still enrolled in June 2012.
[a]Significance compared to "some college."
[b]Test score is the composite math and reading standardized test score from 2002.
[c]Created by the NCES through the ELS, our SES variable comprises information on parents' occupations and parents' education.
*p < .05; **p < .01; ***p < .001, using chi-squared tests of significance

degree) and compare students who acquire a credential to those who do not ("some college" students).[36]

The results are presented in table 2.6. We see that while females have higher odds of completing a credential, whatever the type, there are no other consistent findings for all credentials. However, one characteristic comes close: enrolling in college immediately (within seven months after high school). This characteristic increases the odds of completing every credential except a certificate.

BAs are the traditionally encouraged degree, and BA completion mostly reflects the traditional status attainment model.[37] The factors that the status attainment model finds can predict "years of education" (SES, test scores, and BA plans) all significantly predict BA attainment in our analyses.

In contrast, these factors do *not* increase the odds of completing an associate degree or certificate. Test scores and SES do not predict successful completion of sub-BA credentials. Indeed, higher test scores and BA plans are associated with a *decrease* in the odds of certificate attainment.

Table 2.6    **Multinomial Logistic Regression of Attainment, Compared to "Some College," Odds Ratios**

|  | Certificate | Associate Degree | Bachelor's Degree | Graduate Degree |
|---|---|---|---|---|
| SES 2002[a] | 1.00 | 1.06 | 1.67*** | 2.29*** |
|  | (0.03) | (0.68) | (8.48) | (9.50) |
| Test score 2002[b] | 0.98*** | 1.00 | 1.06*** | 1.11*** |
|  | (−3.60) | (0.12) | (11.03) | (12.36) |
| BA plans in twelfth grade | 0.67*** | 0.83 | 4.42*** | 11.26*** |
|  | (−3.84) | (−1.51) | (12.89) | (6.91) |
| Enrolled in college in first term after high school | 0.99 | 1.39* | 3.20*** | 3.48*** |
|  | (−0.07) | (2.35) | (9.52) | (5.89) |
| Female | 1.54*** | 1.43** | 1.48*** | 2.49*** |
|  | (4.14) | (3.17) | (4.88) | (7.83) |
| African American | 1.07 | 0.55** | 0.81 | 1.17 |
|  | (0.44) | (−2.89) | (−1.55) | (0.76) |
| Hispanic | 1.04 | 0.83 | 0.97 | 1.04 |
|  | (0.25) | (−1.07) | (−0.48) | (0.18) |
| Other race | 1.04 | 0.97 | 1.35* | 1.80*** |
|  | (0.23) | (−0.16) | (2.42) | (3.56) |

*Source:* Authors' calculations from the ELS (2002–2012).
*Notes:* The sample includes on-time high school graduates who were not enrolled in a postsecondary institution in 2012. T-statistics are in parentheses. N = 6,938.
[a]Created by the NCES through the ELS, our SES variable comprises information on parents' occupations and parents' education.
[b]Test score is the composite math and reading standardized test score from 2002.
*p < .05; **p < .01; ***p < .001

These findings suggest that, unlike BA completion, certificates and associate degrees present a more level playing field for individuals who are from low-SES backgrounds or who have low test scores. The lack of a test score effect is consistent with faculty reports that students do not need high academic skills to complete certificates or applied associate degrees in many fields (chapter 4), as well as with the doubts about the need for a mastery of algebra II for sub-BA success, as mentioned earlier.[38] Nursing is probably an exception to these findings, but nursing's competitive application process is apt to contribute to the predictive power of SES and test scores. Although many community colleges' associate degree programs require students to pass the remedial placement exam, these results indicate that, beyond these minimum requirements, increases in academic achievement are not associated with increased odds of associate degree (or certificate) completion. Contrary to the usual rhetoric about "college-readiness," these findings suggest that sub-BA credential success does not necessarily require college-level academic achievement, nor does high SES make a significant difference. Students do not need high test scores or high-SES backgrounds to be successful at completing associate degrees, and this is even more true for certificate completion.

## Employment and Earnings Within Credentials

Do social background and academic achievement increase the employment and earnings of individuals within each of these college credentials? Do low-SES and low-test-score students who complete a sub-BA credential benefit from that credential as much as their more-advantaged peers? Research often finds that low-SES students experience "cumulative disadvantages."[39] For instance, *Sesame Street* aimed to reduce inequality in reading skills, but despite the TV show's efforts, disadvantaged children benefited from it less than other children, an effect that ultimately increased inequality.[40] Even after low-SES students succeed at one stage, they may face greater disadvantages at the next stage that prevent them from getting the full payoff that others get from the same credential. For instance, besides valuing a graduate's credential, employers may prefer graduates who have high test scores, a high-SES background, or BA plans (perhaps a proxy for motivation), so these attributes may predict higher employment or earnings for graduates within each educational credential.

We repeated our prior statistical analyses to analyze employment in 2012 (table 2.7), but this time we looked at the results for each credential separately to see whether the relationships between various individual attributes and employment outcomes differ for different credentials. We

|  | Logistic Regression of Employment Status, 2012[a] | | | | Linear Regression on Log Earnings, 2011 | | | |
|---|---|---|---|---|---|---|---|---|
|  | Some College | Certificate | Associate Degree | Bachelor's Degree | Some College | Certificate | Associate Degree | Bachelor's Degree |
| SES 2002[b] | 1.47** | 1.22 | 0.72 | 0.97 | 0.08 | -0.06 | -0.11 | 0.08*** |
|  | (3.00) | (0.93) | (-1.06) | (-0.19) | (1.64) | (-0.81) | (-1.80) | (3.47) |
| Test score 2002[c] | 1.01 | 1.03* | 1.00 | 1.02 | 0.00 | 0.01 | -0.00 | 0.00* |
|  | (0.65) | (1.98) | (0.20) | (1.24) | (0.92) | (1.55) | (-0.04) | (2.02) |
| Had BA plans in twelfth grade | 1.26 | 1.12 | 0.90 | 1.90* | -0.01 | -0.01 | -0.09 | 0.20* |
|  | (1.43) | (0.42) | (-0.27) | (1.99) | (-0.14) | (-0.14) | (-1.15) | (2.36) |
| Enrolled in college in first term after high school | 1.87*** | 1.17 | 1.11 | 1.55 | 0.15* | 0.13 | 0.08 | -0.07 |
|  | (3.99) | (0.62) | (0.27) | (1.23) | (2.04) | (1.28) | (0.87) | (-0.65) |
| Hours worked per week in 2011 | — | — | — | — | 0.03*** | 0.02*** | 0.03*** | 0.02*** |
|  | — | — | — | — | (6.88) | (4.61) | (5.35) | (8.75) |
| Weeks employed in 2011 | — | — | — | — | 0.03*** | 0.02** | 0.02*** | 0.02*** |
|  | — | — | — | — | (8.44) | (3.31) | (3.59) | (7.18) |
| Female | 0.36*** | 0.40** | 0.33** | 0.39*** | -0.22*** | -0.38*** | -0.21* | -0.09** |
|  | (-6.54) | (-3.26) | (-2.86) | (-4.51) | (-3.59) | (-4.21) | (-2.48) | (-2.66) |
| African American | 1.13 | 1.23 | 0.89 | 0.88 | -0.22* | -0.13 | -0.04 | -0.07 |
|  | (0.53) | (0.54) | (-0.19) | (-0.33) | (-2.04) | (-0.70) | (-0.22) | (-0.81) |
| Hispanic | 0.90 | 0.88 | 0.44 | 0.74 | 0.09 | 0.06 | -0.03 | -0.01 |
|  | (-0.51) | (-0.35) | (-1.47) | (-0.99) | (1.13) | (0.52) | (-0.23) | (-0.16) |
| Other race | 1.22 | 0.59 | 0.35 | 0.89 | -0.12 | -0.17 | -0.23 | 0.02 |
|  | (0.75) | (-1.36) | (-1.85) | (-0.49) | (-1.02) | (-0.89) | (-1.27) | (0.50) |
| Constant | — | — | — | — | 7.34*** | 7.96*** | 8.23*** | 8.04*** |
|  | — | — | — | — | (27.94) | (16.22) | (18.59) | (34.29) |
| N | 1,845 | 671 | 536 | 2,652 | 1,142 | 417 | 346 | 2,087 |

*Source:* Authors' calculations from the ELS (2002–2012).

*Notes:* The sample includes on-time high school graduates who were not enrolled in a postsecondary institution in 2012. T-statistics are in parentheses.

[a]Employed (full-time or part-time) versus unemployed.

[b]Created by the NCES through the ELS, our SES variable comprises information on parents' occupations and parents' education.

[c]Test score is the composite math and reading standardized test score from 2002.

*p < .05; **p < .01; ***p < .001

find that SES does not predict employment for any credential (except those with "some college"). Similarly, higher test scores do not predict increased employment for any credential—except among certificate graduates, for whom this is just barely significant ($t = 1.98$). In addition, BA plans predict higher odds of employment for students who complete BAs, but this factor is not associated with higher employment rates for those who complete any other credential. In sum, SES, test scores, and BA plans appear to pose few obstacles to employment for most credentials.

Turning to earnings, the status attainment model predicts that more-advantaged students will have higher earnings than others with the same credential. Indeed, we find that, for students who complete a bachelor's degree, SES, test scores, and BA plans all predict significantly higher earnings. However, sub-BA degrees do not follow the same pattern. None of these traditional predictors of earnings predicts greater earnings for those who attain a certificate or associate degree. Moreover, regressions that analyze high- and low-SES and test-score thirds also support this finding. Although SES, test scores, and BA plans predict higher earnings for holders of BA degrees, they are not predictive for those with certificates or associate degrees. We find the same results with dummy variables for SES and test thirds. Sub-BA credentials offer good employment and earnings payoffs that are not diminished for students with lower SES backgrounds, lower test scores, and no BA plans.

## Alternative Job Realities

The findings reported in this chapter conflict with a common assumption—that academic demands for higher-paid occupations are higher than for lower-paid occupations. If that were true, then we would expect high test scores to predict higher earnings within credentials. This assumption fits our findings for holders of BA degrees, but not our findings with respect to sub-BA credentials. To better understand our findings we looked at some of the specific occupations for which ELS respondents pursued a certificate.

Some certificate occupations support the assumption about academic demands. Medical assistants need to know some science and beauticians do not, and the pay in these two occupations shows comparable differences.

However, many certificate occupations do not fit this pattern. We examined the certificate occupations held by those in the ELS sample that were higher-paying according to Bureau of Labor Statistics (BLS) median annual earnings data: heavy truck driving ($40,260), HVAC ($45,110), machinists ($42,110), welding ($38,150), auto mechanics ($37,850), and airplane mechanics ($58,390). Most ELS respondents in these occupations had low test scores (bottom third), but the BLS descriptions of their jobs do not suggest the need for academic skills. These certificate occupations pay more than the median for male certificate holders who worked full-time ($35,000), and they illustrate our statistical results.[41]

HVAC services is a good example. When the furnace in one of our homes stopped working on a February Saturday night, we paid $300 an hour to have an HVAC person come fix it. He had only a one-year certificate, but we did not ask to see his test scores. His furnace repair skills were of high value, and we gladly paid for them. High academic skills are not always required for certificate occupations that pay more than median earnings, such as truck driving, HVAC services, and welding. Instead, BLS occupational descriptions suggest that these jobs demand perseverance, attention to quality, and an ability to get along with others, not academic skills. Those who take these jobs may learn problem-solving in practical contexts (such as delivery logistics, or trouble-shooting furnaces) without learning algebra. These certificate jobs illustrate the kinds of certificate or associate degree jobs for which academic test scores do not predict earnings.

Our descriptions of certificate occupations are illustrative only. ELS data cannot easily analyze job differences systematically because of the small number of individuals in each occupation. Systematic analyses of occupations require an enormous data set—like the 145,545 students in the entire state of Florida available for Louis Jacobson and Christine Mokher's study of educational pathways to higher earnings for low-income students.[42]

However, our major findings do not require detailed analyses of occupations. First, on average, certificates and associate degrees have significant payoffs for employment and earnings, which was not true in a similar earlier cohort, the NELS of 2000. Second, while test scores and SES predict higher BA completion and higher earnings among BAs, they do not predict completion or earnings for certificates or associate degrees. These patterns may not be true in some occupations, but they are true for most sub-BA graduates.

## Social Reproduction's Diverse Forms

The social reproduction hypothesis suggests that higher-SES students have greater odds of completing a credential than low-SES students and that they also have increased earnings within the credential. Some of our findings support this hypothesis, and some do not. SES background does predict BA completion, which leads to significant earnings payoffs over other credentials, and SES also predicts large impacts on earnings within BA degrees. But other findings do not support the social reproduction hypothesis. High SES does not increase the completion odds for sub-BA credentials, and it does not increase earnings within a sub-BA credential. We suspect that this difference is due in part to the fact that "middle-class cultural capital" is not required in sub-BA programs or in many sub-BA occupations, like truck driving or welding. Given the pervasiveness of social reproduction elsewhere in society, it is noteworthy when we find instances where it does not operate. Sub-BA credentials represent such a place. We suspect that lower-SES students may be encouraged to know that they are not disadvantaged in sub-BA programs, neither for credential completion nor for earnings.

Of course, we should note some caveats. All of our findings may be affected by the economic recession that was still lingering in 2012 and by the young age of the respondents (twenty-six). We do not know what will happen later, when the economy improves and the respondents get older. Yet these findings are important. For many individuals starting families in their twenties, earnings at age twenty-six are important for family support at a crucial time. Although BA degrees reproduce background inequalities, inequalities are not being socially reproduced within sub-BA credentials.

## Increasing Later Degree Options

This chapter has indicated that, despite the usual emphasis on BA degrees, students can consider alternative credential goals. Yet another alternative is also possible—students can combine several degree goals. Critics may worry that encouraging students to pursue sub-BAs looks like "cooling out": lowering students' ambitions and setting their sights on less prestigious goals.

Cooling out was a reality in the 1960s, when sub-BA credentials had little value, and indeed that was still true in our analyses of the 1990s NELS data.[43] Yet if cooling out students' ambitions often played out in the past as a kind of swindle, with no payoff and no recourse, now those encouraged to seek sub-BA credentials can attain significant earnings payoffs as well as higher degrees.[44] Instead of dampening students' aspirations, certificate holders are 22 percent more likely than high school graduates to aspire to an associate degree, and 13 percent more likely to aspire to a BA, according to the National Longitudinal Study of Adolescent Health (Add Health) (see also chapter 3).[45]

Many adults have multiple degrees. About 47 percent of BA graduates also have an associate degree.[46] Moreover, even certificates are not dead ends. Nineteen percent of adult certificate holders also have an associate degree, and an additional 12 percent have a BA degree.[47] If certificates represent a cooling-out, it is a temporary one that can be surpassed later.

The usual either/or argument for degree attainment—either a sub-BA or a BA—poses a false dichotomy. Students can plan to combine degrees, seek high-odds certificates, and then later get an associate degree or a BA degree. Indeed, colleges can assist students with these plans by offering degree ladders. These ideas are explored in the second part of this book.

First, however, having shown that sub-BA credentials lead to higher earnings, we go on in chapter 3 to examine whether these credentials lead to nonmonetary job rewards. And since, as this chapter has shown, these credentials are not related to social class background or academic test scores, chapter 4 examines the qualifications that they do require.

# = Chapter 3 =

## Money Isn't Everything:
## Do Sub-BA Credentials Lead
## to Nonmonetary Job Rewards?

RESPONDING TO students' difficulty in getting useful information for making their college choices, President Barack Obama, in his 2013 State of the Union Address, promoted a "College Scorecard" that parents and students could use to compare schools based on simple criteria related to "where you can get the most bang for your educational buck."[1] The scorecard would give students key information such as college graduation rate as well as employment rate and average earnings in the year after graduation. The scorecard's information on employment and earnings outcomes would certainly be useful, but what about other aspects of job outcomes?

In focusing on earnings, policymakers and researchers may be taking too narrow a view, ignoring many other job dimensions on which young adults evaluate their jobs. Jobs differ in many respects besides earnings, and various nonmonetary job rewards—such as autonomy, benefits, working conditions, and future careers—may be important indicators of good jobs. Analyzing the 2008 National Longitudinal Study of Adolescent Health (Add Health), this chapter examines whether various nonmonetary rewards are more strongly related to job satisfaction than earnings.

This broader focus may be especially important for evaluating sub-BA credentials. Although researchers have found that sub-BA credentials have significant earnings payoffs, doubts remain about whether they lead to good jobs and offer career preparation.[2] In some popular stereotypes, sub-BA jobs entail repetitive, low-autonomy tasks and offer poor future careers. But do they offer nonmonetary job rewards that cannot be discerned with a narrow focus on earnings outcomes? This study examines whether young adult workers view nonmonetary job rewards as satisfying and if so, whether various sub-BA credentials (and college attendance without credentials) are associated with higher nonmonetary rewards than high school diplomas alone.

44

## The Limitations of a Focus on Earnings

Research often analyzes earnings outcomes, and so it is not surprising that national policymakers would propose rating colleges on earnings outcomes. Thus, the rationale behind President Obama's College Scorecard is that colleges should be sanctioned if graduates do not receive better earnings, since that is students' reason for attending. However, this argument can be criticized on several grounds.

First, economic theory suggests that starting pay is not everyone's highest priority. Some individuals will sacrifice pay to gain better training in their early jobs, and some qualitative research indicates that young employees are aware of this trade-off.[3] This finding suggests that low starting pay may sometimes signal that a job offers better training and a more promising career.

Second, college occupational faculty report that they advise graduates to look for career-relevant jobs that use their skills and provide opportunities for job advancement. They also advise graduates to seek jobs that will provide them with the autonomy and responsibility needed to develop their skills. In contrast, some occupational faculty discourage students from taking highly paid jobs because they are often dangerous, physically demanding, or dead-end. Graduates who take such jobs may see the earnings advantages disappear ten to twenty years later, particularly if they are less willing to tolerate the job conditions as they get older or after suffering an injury.

Thus, earnings may not correspond to whether or not a job is "good" or satisfying to the individual who holds it. This chapter extends prior research to examine whether young adults' ratings of various nonmonetary job rewards are more related to job satisfaction than earnings are. We also seek to determine which credentials lead to better rewards.

## Job Satisfaction and Nonmonetary Job Rewards

Jobs vary on many attributes other than earnings that may be relevant in evaluating college payoffs. In organizational psychology, job satisfaction is the usual indicator of job quality, which is related to five core job characteristics: skill variety, task identity, task significance, autonomy, and task feedback.[4] Other research indicates that reasonable workload is an important determinant of job satisfaction as well.[5]

Analyzing a 1974 survey, Joanne Miller showed strong associations between job satisfaction and various job conditions—autonomy and occupational self-direction, job pressures, organizational structure and position, job uncertainties, and rewards and protections.[6] One recent review of U.S. research concluded that a good job is one that provides relatively high earnings, potential for earnings and career growth, adequate fringe benefits, autonomy (self-direction over work), flexibility to take care of nonwork activities, and relative security.[7]

Using national survey data, sociologists have found that adults' job satisfaction is less related to earnings than to nonmonetary job rewards. Research has found a wide array of nonmonetary job rewards that are related to job satisfaction, particularly autonomy and career relevance. Indeed, the effect of these nonmonetary job conditions on job desirability has been found to be twice that of earnings in studies of adults of all ages.[8] However, the diverse-aged adults in these samples began their careers in different labor market conditions, some of which no longer exist, so these surveys may not be useful to current students.

Because objective indicators of job rewards require researchers to make coding judgments that can raise doubts, researchers have placed considerable confidence in respondents' subjective ratings, despite concerns about respondents' subjective judgments of job rewards (for example, career relevance).[9] Many job attributes that individuals value are hard to measure objectively, and individuals' subjective ratings (including job satisfaction) provide indicators that are "closely related to other, more complicated objective measures."[10] We concur with researchers who have concluded that subjective ratings are valuable indicators of aspects of jobs that are otherwise difficult to measure and that subjective ratings are the best indication of individuals' own reactions to their jobs.

## Autonomy and Career Relevance

Although we examine many nonmonetary job rewards, we follow prior research in focusing on autonomy and career relevance. In research on national samples, these two job attributes have been strongly associated with job satisfaction, although we do not know if today's young adults respond in the same ways as older adults in the samples of prior decades.

Autonomy refers to how much control an individual has over his or her daily work life. For John Goldthorpe, autonomy is the central feature of middle-class jobs, because these jobs confer decision-making authority.[11] Similarly, Joanne Miller identifies occupational self-direction as an important influence on job satisfaction.[12] Perhaps the largest impact is noted by Michael Marmot, who finds that autonomy strongly predicts health outcomes: "Autonomy—how much control you have over your own life . . . plays a big part in producing the social gradient in health."[13]

Autonomy is important at all ages, but it may have special importance for young adults because it provides them with opportunities to demonstrate their judgment and ability to take responsibility, attributes that have been linked to career advancement.[14] Using the 1988–2000 NELS data, Anh Ngoc Nguyen, Jim Taylor, and Steve Bradley have found that perceived autonomy predicts five dimensions of job satisfaction for young adults: satisfaction with pay, satisfaction with fringe benefits, satisfaction with promotion prospects, satisfaction with job security, and satisfaction with the importance of their work.[15]

Career relevance—how closely one's job is related to one's future career—is also important to young adults. Parents, counselors, and mass media tell students to attend college to get a career, and students often say that they are looking for a "career, not a job." In pursuit of a career, however, young adults are often confined to jobs that offer no opportunities for career development.[16]

Autonomy and career relevance may be particularly important for the midlevel jobs that require sub-BA degrees. In recent years, Michael Piore contends, increased skill requirements in the labor market have led to a greater need for career-relevant skills.[17] According to this view, many jobs demand increasing training, career expertise, and autonomy over time.[18] Jobs in medical assisting, paralegal work, airplane mechanics, manufacturing, computer networking, and medical technology require sub-BA credentials, yet research has not examined whether these credentials lead to autonomy and career relevance for recent graduates. While some have criticized sub-BA credentials as offering narrow training and limited careers, and many others have ignored these credentials while advocating BA degrees, we examine whether sub-BA credentials lead to jobs that tend to offer autonomy and career relevance.[19]

Our study contributes to existing research in two ways. First, we examine how young adults' job satisfaction is related to some of the job rewards emphasized in organizational behavior research, especially autonomy and career relevance. Looking at how these young adults (ages twenty-five to thirty-two) rate their jobs on various dimensions, we also examine which dimensions are most closely related to their overall job satisfaction.

Second, we examine the various nonmonetary rewards of jobs attained through three educational credentials. In particular, we examine whether sub-BA credentials lead to some of the same nonmonetary job rewards as BAs. If young adults place high value on nonmonetary rewards, and if certificates or associate degrees lead to jobs with these job rewards, then they may find these jobs desirable even if they have low earnings. In that case, today's college students should consider pursuing these credentials, and policymakers' assessments of colleges—their "college scorecards"—should rate such outcomes.

## Studying Young Working Adults' Job Rewards

We analyze data from the National Longitudinal Study of Adolescent Health, a nationally representative sample of students who were in grades 7 through 12 in 1995. Precollege variables were measured in in-home interviews in the 1995 wave, when respondents were ages twelve to nineteen. Educational status, workplace conditions, and job rewards were measured in the 2008 wave, when they were twenty-five to thirty-two. This research extends prior studies that analyzed job conditions as mediating health outcomes in these data, but that did not examine job conditions as outcomes.[20]

### Various Dimensions of Good Jobs

How many young adults get jobs above the median earnings? The obvious answer is 50 percent.[21] Yet if we expand the definition of "good jobs" to those with either above-median earnings or above-median career relevance, then 59.9 percent of young adults have above-median jobs on one of these two dimensions. Adding a third dimension, autonomy, we see that 81.5 percent of young adults are above median on at least one of these three dimensions. The point is obvious, but the numbers are impressive: 80 percent of young working adults have jobs that are "good" on at least one of these three dimensions.

### Associations Among Job Rewards

Inspecting the entire correlation matrix for all job rewards (not shown), we find very few substantial correlations among young adults' ratings of their jobs. Add Health asks about three fringe benefits—health, vacation, and retirement—which are strongly correlated ($r$ between 0.68 and 0.72), and ratings on career relatedness are mildly correlated ($r$ between 0.37 and 0.48). Otherwise, there are almost no correlations larger than 0.15. Apparently, young adults rate these various job rewards separately, rather than seeing "good jobs" as positive on all these dimensions and "bad jobs" as negative on all dimensions.

## Associations Between Job Satisfaction
## and Job Rewards

The usual analyses implicitly assume that earnings are the only—or at least the most important—dimension that defines good jobs. However, we find evidence to the contrary. Five out of the thirteen variables we studied were correlated to job satisfaction (0.10 or higher): earnings, perceived status, autonomy, repetitiveness, and career relevance (table 3.1). In addition, these correlations do not change very much within different levels of education credentials (table 3.1). These findings, aligning with previous literature, indicate that a "good job" is multidimensional and relies on several factors.

Just as prior literature has emphasized, we find that career relevance and autonomy are consistently the most important correlates of job satisfaction. We also find these correlations persisting at comparable levels within education categories, which indicates that the relationships between job rewards and satisfaction are not mediated by education, even though education is associated with many job rewards (as we will show).

After controlling for background variables, we find that, with one exception, the five job rewards that correlate with job satisfaction also have significant coefficients in a regression explaining job satisfaction (table 3.2). The only exception is earnings, which is not significantly

**Table 3.1    Correlations Between Job Satisfaction and Job Rewards for Young Adults, by Educational Credential, 2008**

|  | High School | Certificate | Associate Degree | Bachelor's Degree | Post-BA | ALL |
|---|---|---|---|---|---|---|
|  |  |  | Highest Degree Attained by 2008 |  |  |  |
| Earnings | 0.11 | 0.17 | 0.07 | 0.10 | 0.02 | 0.10 |
| Perceived status | 0.21 | 0.20 | 0.22 | 0.22 | 0.11 | 0.21 |
| Autonomy | 0.29 | 0.37 | 0.32 | 0.33 | 0.33 | 0.32 |
| Not repetitive | 0.16 | 0.14 | 0.14 | 0.19 | 0.11 | 0.17 |
| Career-relevant | 0.35 | 0.36 | 0.35 | 0.38 | 0.37 | 0.37 |
| N | 4,470 | 938 | 1,058 | 2,838 | 1,155 | 10,582 |

*Source:* Authors' calculations from 2008 National Longitudinal Study of Adolescent Health (Add Health).
*Note:* Variables that correlate with job satisfaction at 0.10 or higher.

**Table 3.2** Regression on Young Adults' Job Satisfaction for Job Rewards and Background Variables

| Job Satisfaction | Coefficient | Standard Error | $t$ | $P > |t|$ | 95 Percent Confidence Interval | |
|---|---|---|---|---|---|---|
| Earnings | −0.0000347 | 0.0000406 | −0.85 | 0.393 | −0.0001143 | 0.0000449 |
| Perceived status | 0.0138824 | 0.0010829 | 12.82 | 0.000 | 0.0117599 | 0.0160050 |
| Autonomy | 0.0541544 | 0.0018498 | 29.28 | 0.000 | 0.0505286 | 0.0577802 |
| Not repetitive | 0.0455918 | 0.0058925 | 7.74 | 0.000 | 0.0571417 | 0.0340419 |
| Career-relevant | 0.1041264 | 0.004153 | 25.07 | 0.000 | 0.095986 | 0.1122600 |

*Source:* Authors' calculations from 2008 Add Health.
*Notes:* Adjusted $R$-squared = 0.2291, $F$ = 214.61, Prob > $F$ = 0.0000. Control variables: demographics (race-ethnicity [African American, Hispanic, Asian], gender); educational factors (grade average, test score, grades not reported by respondent); acculturation (nativity, parent nativity, speak English versus another language at home); and parents' SES (parents' self-reported educational level, household income, and whether they have enough money to pay bills.)

related to job satisfaction in this regression, and indeed it is only barely significant ($p = 0.045$) in a regression with the other four job rewards variables and no other controls. Not only are earnings not the most important determinant of job satisfaction, but we may doubt that earnings are important at all.

## Nonmonetary Job Reward Payoffs for Each Education Credential

We now analyze whether different levels of education lead to different nonmonetary rewards. We examine five credential groups: graduates who received a certificate, those who received an associate degree, those who received a bachelor's degree, those who earned a master's degree or higher, and nongraduates—those students who got "some college," but no credential. We find that every credential is associated with many nonmonetary rewards (compared to high school graduates), but that only a few nonmonetary rewards went to individuals with "some college" but no credential, and then at very modest levels.

Table 3.3 shows how various college credentials are related to each job reward, after many controls (listed in the table note). The table is complex; the asterisks show which job rewards are significantly related to job satisfaction.

### Payoffs from Some College but No Credential

Compared to high school graduates, students with "some college" reported a few rewards. In terms of career-related variables, they were slightly more likely to report that their jobs offered career preparation, but they also said that their jobs were *less* related to their career. Both relationships are weak. Students with "some college" were significantly more likely than high school graduates to report that they got benefits (health, retirement, vacation) and that some of their working conditions were better (they had a desk job, they had perceived status, they supervised others, or they were less likely to work hard physically). They were mostly similar to high school graduates in terms of autonomy and variety (but not with respect to repetitive work).

Overall, although they got some nonmonetary job rewards, they received fewer job rewards, at more modest levels, than for all groups with credentials. Moreover, they reported having jobs less related to their career as well as statistically similar amounts of autonomy and career relevance. Thus, merely attending college without getting a credential seems to have relatively few and weak benefits.

Table 3.3    Multivariate Nonmonetary Job Rewards Associated
with Education Levels, After Controls

|  | Some College | Certificate | Associate Degree | Bachelor's Degree | Graduate Degree |
|---|---|---|---|---|---|
| **OLS regression** | | | | | |
| Job satisfaction | 0.01 | 0.05[†] | 0.03** | 0.02** | 0.06[†] |
| Job autonomy | 0.01 | 0.07[†] | 0.04** | 0.06[†] | 0.08[†] |
| Job repetitive | −0.01 | −0.03** | −0.06[†] | −0.14[†] | −0.20[†] |
| **Poisson regression (IRR)** | | | | | |
| Job relates to career | | | | | |
| Preparation | 1.15* | 1.45[†] | 1.17* | 1.27*** | 1.23* |
| Career-relevant | 1.07 | 1.49[†] | 1.40[†] | 1.64[†] | 1.96[†] |
| Benefits offered | | | | | |
| Health benefits | 1.24[†] | 1.22[†] | 1.36[†] | 1.42[†] | 1.45[†] |
| Retirement benefits | 1.24[†] | 1.24[†] | 1.44[†] | 1.49[†] | 1.52[†] |
| Vacation benefits | 1.20[†] | 1.18[†] | 1.35[†] | 1.36[†] | 1.39[†] |
| Job conditions | | | | | |
| Day shift | 1.01 | 0.97 | 1.10** | 1.26[†] | 1.25[†] |
| Irregular hours | 1.03 | 1.16 | 0.90 | 0.82** | 0.90 |
| Hard physical work | 0.86* | 0.71** | 0.44[†] | 0.26[†] | 0.11[†] |
| Desk job | 1.70[†] | 1.50[†] | 1.90[†] | 2.51[†] | 2.08[†] |
| Supervise others | 1.15** | 0.99 | 1.09 | 1.03 | 1.07 |

*Source:* Authors' calculations from 1995–2008 Add Health.
*Notes:* N = 10,582. The sample is restricted to high school graduates who were employed full-time in one job in 2008. The entries correspond to the coefficient for each education level predicting each job reward. Rows 1–3 are linear regression coefficients; rows 4–13 are relative risks (incidence rate ratios). Control variables: demographics (race-ethnicity [black, Latino, Asian], gender); educational factors (grade average, test score, grades not reported by respondent); acculturation (nativity, parent nativity, speak English versus another language at home); and parents' SES status (parents' self-reported educational level, household income, and whether they have enough money to pay bills).
*p < .05; **p < .01; ***p < .001; [†]p < .0001

## Payoffs from Certificates

Compared to the jobs of high school graduates, the jobs of certificate holders had significantly higher career relevance, autonomy, variety, job status, and benefits. There were also more payoffs in terms of some working conditions for those with certificates (more held desk jobs, and less engaged in physical labor). However, their jobs were no better with respect to working day shifts or irregular hours than those of high school graduates. Although certificate holders reported increased levels of some job rewards compared to high school graduates, they still lacked the across-the-board reward increases that come with higher degrees.

## Payoffs from Associate Degrees

Compared with high school graduates, associate degree graduates reported more of almost all of the job rewards, with increases in career relevance, benefits, and working conditions. They also had slightly higher odds of finding jobs that offered career preparation and much higher odds of landing career-relevant jobs. They had higher odds of receiving all benefits (vacation, health, and retirement), and their working conditions were better than those of high school graduates (they worked day shifts, and they had much lower odds of having to do strenuous work and higher odds of having a desk job). They also had more job autonomy, variety (less repetitive), job satisfaction, and job status.

In sum, on most job rewards, associate degree holders have significantly higher payoffs than high school graduates and students with some college. Holders of associate degrees also enjoy a wider variety of job rewards than certificate holders and are generally on par with bachelor's degree holders.

## Payoffs from BA Degrees

Like associate degree holders, those with bachelor's degrees reported more of almost all nonmonetary job rewards than did high school graduates, across all categories—career relevance, benefits, working conditions, and job quality. Compared with high school graduates, BA graduates reported higher odds that their job had prepared them for a career and was career-related. They were also more likely to receive each of the cited benefits. In addition, they were more likely to work under nearly all of the desirable working conditions (but not that of supervising others, which no credential predicts). Finally, bachelor's degree holders also reported higher job quality—more job autonomy, variety, job satisfaction, and status.

Overall, bachelor's degree graduates, compared to high school graduates, were more likely to report having received almost all of the relevant job rewards. Although associate degree graduates' jobs were more wide-ranging than those of respondents with "some college" and respondents who had earned certificates, associate degree graduates got nearly all the same job rewards as BA holders, and sometimes at about the same magnitude.

*Payoffs from Master's Degrees*
*and Other Higher Degrees*

Like associate and bachelor's degree holders, graduate degree holders were better off in almost all respects than high school graduates. In addition, our analysis shows that most coefficients are as large or larger for graduate degree holders than for BA holders, with one exception: having a graduate degree did not get significantly lower odds of working irregular hours than having only a high school diploma. Overall, graduate degree holders reaped most of the same rewards that associate and bachelor's degree graduates did. However, their frequently larger coefficients indicate higher levels of rewards.

## Implications

The education policy community has neglected both nonmonetary job rewards as a measure of success and sub-BA credentials as desirable and worth striving for. In the colleges we studied, some job placement experts already warn students that there are often serious disadvantages to high-paying jobs. Some economists warn that "an overreliance on quantitative-and qualification-based measures has neglected qualitative evidence."[22] However, few students hear this message because most community colleges lack job placement staff and counselors serve 1,000-student caseloads. If we could somehow expose students to more "qualitative evidence"—for example, by adding nonmonetary job rewards to the College Scorecard—they would be more aware of important aspects of jobs that they will later value as young adult workers.

To start, quantitative or qualitative measures of nonmonetary job rewards could be created from Bureau of Labor Statistics descriptions and O*NET skill-level indicators. Graduates' ratings on follow-up surveys might be used. Research is needed to determine which indicators are more helpful to students in making their choices.

To its credit, the College Scorecard does acknowledge the value of certificates and associate degrees and presents them as options, yet its focus on average earnings may distract students from considering these sub-BA credentials. Students need to be aware of the nonmonetary job rewards associated with each credential. A one-year certificate could improve a student's autonomy and ability to find career-relevant work, even while continuing to pursue a BA degree.

This study's findings challenge the traditional narrow focus on earnings payoffs for young adults. Many jobs held before age thirty are "starter jobs": they may offer training and challenging experience in return for lower earnings.[23] In contrast, some high-paying jobs may not provide a good start or even predict high earnings in midcareer. Starter jobs are important because they provide training, job experiences, and career opportunities.[24] Just as Christopher Jencks, Lauri Perman, and Lee Rainwater have found for all adults, our findings suggest that young working adults are aware of the importance of nonmonetary job rewards and value them.[25] From our interviews, we have noticed that college students (and many college advisers) are often not aware of these job rewards and the sub-BA credentials that lead to them; therefore, they pursue earnings and do not consider whether jobs offer career preparation and autonomy.

This chapter also furthers research on the health implications of sub-BA credentials. As prior research has shown, certificates and associate degrees are associated with better health outcomes than those high school graduates get.[26] This chapter's findings build on that research by uncovering the specific job conditions that are associated with these credentials and that may mediate the relationship between health outcomes and job conditions (autonomy, variety, benefits, and career relevance). In addition, certificates, associate degrees, and BA degrees lead to jobs that make fewer physical demands, thus possibly reducing work injuries and other adverse health consequences.[27] Since many health outcomes are not evident until after age forty, these findings may understate impacts.

These analyses may also understate the payoffs of attaining higher credentials in the future. Although we analyze students' current credentials, many of them still intend to get higher credentials; if successful, they might gain even more nonmonetary job rewards.

Most important, these findings broaden our view of valuable outcomes beyond earnings and a single credential (the BA degree). Economic theory clearly warns about the risks of placing excessive emphasis on a single outcome. When everyone pursues a single goal (a BA degree, or high earnings), a worrisome consequence could be a "bubble mentality," as well as shortages of people getting other credentials and seeking other important job rewards. Policy that narrowly focuses on BA degrees and earnings outcomes may prompt too many students to pursue these goals, ignore many other desirable options, underestimate their successes, and distort college advising and priorities.

These analyses expand the possibilities for individuals to find jobs that are above average on some dimension. Not only can researchers help policymakers learn from the perspectives of individual young adults, but they can help these young adults anticipate the nonmonetary job rewards and career opportunities they will value when they enter the labor market. At a time when the U.S. Department of Education is considering making colleges accountable for employment outcomes, it would be unfortunate if federal policy pushed colleges and students to focus narrowly on earnings at the expense of career advancement.

American education is rightly proud of offering students choice and expanded opportunity, but it does a very poor job at informing their choices. The College Scorecard could provide crucial information if it avoided a narrow emphasis on a single outcome. If used only as a device for accountability sanctions, the College Scorecard risks creating incentives for colleges to steer graduates into high-paying early jobs, some of which may be disagreeable, dead-end, or dangerous. However, if also used as a means of providing information, the College Scorecard could make students aware of the diverse credentials and job rewards within their reach.

## Appendix: Measures and Analysis

Add Health asked a series of questions about respondents' current job in 2008. From their answers, we measured thirteen different rewards in four categories:

1. *Career relevance:* Whether the job was related to a career, prepared the respondent for a career, or was part of the respondent's career

2. *Benefits:* Whether the respondent received health benefits, retirement benefits, and vacation benefits

3. *Working conditions:* Whether the respondent worked day shifts or irregular hours; whether the job was physically strenuous, a desk job, or repetitive; whether the respondent supervised others or supervised managers

4. *Quality:* Whether the job brought the respondent status, autonomy, variety, or job satisfaction

Add Health asked about three fringe benefits—health, vacation, and retirement—and three career attributes. As noted later in this appendix, these two categories of variables are strongly intercorrelated, but other job dimensions were measured by a single item and were not highly correlated. Although creating factors for fringe benefits and career relevance might have enabled better measurements of these two dimensions, doing so would also have reduced comparability with the other dimensions. As a result, job rewards were all measured by individual items.

To examine the predictors of each nonmonetary job reward, we conducted ordered logistic regression with each nonmonetary job reward (measured on a Likert scale) using the Stata ologit function for the first thirteen items; we report IRR in rows 4 through 13 (table 3.3) for each education credential. IRR is a measure of relative risk, which can be discussed directly as a multiplier of probability (for example, five times as likely rather than five times the odds). For continuous variables, we used linear regression and report regression coefficients (rows 1 through 3). We verified model specification using the linktest, which was not significant, indicating that the model was correctly specified.

Because ordinary least squares (OLS) often gives distorted estimates for dichotomous outcomes, logistic regression is often used. Estimators from logistic regression are inconsistent, however, when the outcomes are not rare, as is the case for these outcomes. Therefore, we estimated relative risks using a Poisson working model, which yields consistent and unbiased estimators.[28]

# ═ Chapter 4 ═

## Beyond One-Dimensional Qualifications: How Students Discover Hidden Abilities

(in collaboration with Kennan A. Cepa)

> Whether portrayed as a cultural myth and empirical description, or a goal to be pursued, meritocracy is an important organizing principle of American society.
> David Bills, *The Sociology of Education and Work* (2004), 39

W HAT QUALIFICATIONS do students need to succeed in college and jobs? The answer usually focuses on "college-readiness," or college-level academic skills. College-for-all advocates often contend that college-level academic skills are necessary if students are to benefit from college and careers.[1] In turn, colleges emphasize remedial courses that make students "college-ready."

When society and institutions assign status to individuals on a one-dimensional scale of merit, scholars call this "meritocracy."[2] This model is embodied in academic theories. For example, the human capital model in economics and the status attainment model in sociology assert that academic achievement strongly determines life outcomes. Meritocracy is used by legislators when making policy, by counselors when advising students on their career choices, and by students when considering their career options. The meritocratic model continues to guide how we view selection into educational and labor market opportunities, and it reinforces our emphasis on academic skills.

In asserting that college-level academic skills are required for college and career success, prominent education reform organizations emphasize a one-dimensional meritocratic model. The ACT, a testing company that writes exams for selective four-year colleges and is a major contributor to policy discussions of college- and career-readiness, argues that academic skills are imperative for individuals' future college and career success.[3] Similarly, the controversial Common Core State Standards Initiative "focuses on developing the critical-thinking, problem-solving, and analytical skills that students will need to be successful" in "today's entry-level careers, freshman-level college courses, and workforce training programs." Although these are diverse goals, the standards developed have mostly focused on the traditional academic fields of English and math.[4] In other words, by emphasizing college- and career-readiness, Common Core contends that high academic skills are prerequisites to college and career success.[5]

Unfortunately, "college-level" academic standards seem out of reach for many low-achieving students, and the presumed solution, taking remedial courses, is rarely effective in bringing them up to this level.[6] How can low-achieving students conceive of having any career success in today's CFA society? Students are told that they can and should go to college regardless of their prior achievement, but their poor "college-readiness" suggests that they are unlikely to benefit from it.

Despite this widespread emphasis on the impact of academic achievement on employment outcomes, recent research has begun to look at the potential influence of non-academic skills.[7] Employers' hiring practices also raise doubts about the importance of academic ability. In fact, employers often deemphasize academic achievement and focus on non-academic attributes such as communication skills, teamwork, and work habits.[8]

Yet, although these non-academic skills are important in workplaces, they do not seem to be a part of the college experience. Nor do they seem to be of concern to college reformers, whose stress on the importance of academic skills for college and career success implies that these skills are the only qualifications needed.[9] Although Thomas Bailey, Shanna Smith Jaggars, and Davis Jenkins briefly mention non-academic skills, they mostly focus on the high academic skills required for BA degrees and improvements that would make remedial courses more effective in increasing academic skills.[10] Quantitative analyses indicate that some other school behaviors (good attendance, being well prepared for class) predict college success.[11] Aside from isolated cases, however, we lack a qualitative understanding of how these non-academic factors work in colleges and college programs; nor do we know whether and how occupational faculty take steps to develop them.[12] If workplaces value these non-academic skills, do college occupational programs stress them?

We asked community college faculty: What qualifications do students need to succeed in their occupational programs? And how do they develop these skills? Community college faculty often have occupational experience and employer contacts they can use to aid students in getting jobs.[13] As such, they are uniquely positioned to understand labor market needs, their students' needs, and how colleges prepare youth for work in their fields.

Occupational faculty reported that the one-dimensional focus on academic skills misses the enormous flexibility in occupational programs and even prevents students from seeing more options than are presented in the usual college rhetoric. Contrary to the assumptions behind the usual one-dimensional focus on academic skills, we find that:

1.  College-ready academic skills are not *necessary* for college or for jobs that require college.

2.  College-ready academic skills are not *sufficient:* non-academic skills are also demanded by college coursework and by jobs that require a college degree.

3.  The focus on college-ready abilities may obscure other student abilities.

As we see later in this chapter, occupational faculty reported that ability depends on institutional context. In the view of these faculty members, college-level academic skills may not be necessary or sufficient. Occupational programs may redefine ability as non-academic skills (people skills, ability to work with one's hands), not high academic skills, which many jobs do not require. Moreover, the different emphasis of occupational programs may in fact have academic benefits. Faculty often design assignments that help many students discover interests and abilities—even academic abilities—that were not evident in prior schooling and that perhaps they never knew they had. Indeed, even low-achieving students who see themselves as disengaged and "bad at school" can discover abilities necessary for the workplace and become enthusiastic about using them.

## Faculty Viewpoints

This chapter is based on semistructured one-hour interviews with forty-eight occupational faculty in six community colleges and two private two-year colleges conducted in 2012 as part of the Pathways Project. In each college, we interviewed teachers in the program areas that are the three largest nationally: health, computers, and business.[14] We cannot assert that they were representative, but we know no reason why they would have been atypical.

Although we rely only on reports from occupational faculty and do not have employer reports or student outcomes, these teachers were in a unique position to see how job search works and what skills employers expect in their field; indeed, they were often key players in the hiring process. As prior studies have suggested, many of these teachers reported that employers, because they have difficulty assessing new graduates, rely on faculty evaluations in hiring.[15]

These faculty were experts. Many had worked—and some continued to work—in the occupation that they taught, so they were knowledgeable about careers that few other people know. Their unique position as educators with relevant work experience gave them insight into industry demands and student capabilities, and they could see how their curricula taught the skills required in the field.

This study describes these teachers' reports of how they constructed occupational programs. Of course, they had vested interests, so we must be cautious in making inferences, and we cannot infer effectiveness from their reports. Yet our current knowledge is meager about what happens in these programs, and teachers' reports are an important first step.[16] Obviously, future research should consider other viewpoints and observe what actually occurs in classrooms, rather than relying on faculty reports. But observational studies are an enormous undertaking. In the meantime, faculty descriptions can alert us to a new perspective and identify options and qualifications besides the academic skills that are usually considered. We consider in turn each of the important insights that our interviews with occupational faculty uncovered.

## College-Level Academic Skills Are Not Always Necessary for College and Jobs

Although academic achievement matters for completing BA degrees, it may be less important for sub-BA credentials. Marc Tucker has found that occupational programs in community colleges do not require algebra II or high-level English literature skills.[17] Instead, they require facility with math and English at only a tenth-grade level or below. This is consistent with our prior finding (chapter 2) that test scores do not predict sub-BA completion or earnings.

Similarly, in our interviews, occupational faculty reported that *high academic skills are not needed for many mid-skill jobs.* This is particularly true for math, despite the fact that many colleges require associate degree students to pass algebra II. For example, computer networking faculty reported that their industry requires only basic eighth- to tenth-grade math skills. Similarly, an accounting instructor explained: "You would think math would be the problem in accounting but . . . the math part in accounting is really basic arithmetic. . . . There's no algebra. There's nothing beyond sixth-grade math." Another business faculty member reported that students with limited English skills can be successful as accounting clerks.

## College-Ready Academic Skills Are Not Sufficient for College and Jobs

Although mid-skill jobs do not require high academic skills, faculty reported that they *do* require alternative skills, both "hard" and "soft." Hard skills include knowledge of professional standards and mastery of occupation-specific technical skills, while soft skills include facility with analytic thinking, problem-solving skills, a capacity for teamwork, and communication skills.[18]

### Hard Skills

Employees must know the professional standards specific to their occupation and have the skills to meet those standards. Professional standards and responsibilities are prominent aspects of the occupations for which sub-BA programs prepare students, and knowledge of these professional standards is critical for career success. Professionals make decisions with legal and financial ramifications, and many sub-BA graduates take jobs with these important workplace responsibilities.

As defined by prior research, professional standards are rules based on knowledge in a professional field that guide decision-making.[19] These standards are often developed to improve performance, to avoid negative consequences, and to provide professional authority.[20] Even in stressful or ambiguous situations, professional standards define appropriate behaviors and areas of responsibility and authority.

We rarely consider the professionalism of mid-skill occupations, but these occupations have many of the defining attributes of professions, including "rigorous training and licensing requirements, clear standards for practice, [and] substantial workplace responsibility."[21] Thus, graduates of many sub-BA occupational programs need to know their field's professional standards and have the skills to act by these standards. Moreover, they often work in professional environments, interact with other professionals, and are expected to possess specialized, up-to-date professional knowledge and the skills to conform to professional standards. When a computer network fails, a patient needs preparation for surgery, or financial books must be legally compliant, colleagues, clients, and even supervisors defer to the professional judgments of networking technicians, surgical technicians, and bookkeepers.

In computer networking, for example, the ability to be in compliance with the laws that regulate the security of information requires computer networking expertise. Computer networking professionals not only install security software but must also explain and implement the procedures that preserve security. Computer networking professionals must be able to make decisions and instruct clients about important security issues. In allied health occupations, the ability of a technician to follow professional standards may mean life or death for a patient. Surgical technician faculty teach their students how to keep operating room equipment sterile, "because you *have* to be that specific . . . it either is sterile or it isn't. It's not 'oh well, that is sterile enough.'" As with other occupations, mistakes made by an allied health professional can have serious consequences. Students studying medical coding, for example, must have a working knowledge of surgical codes in order to record patients' medical conditions correctly so that the right procedures are done.

Besides a knowledge of professional standards, sub-BA students must also possess unique technical skills. Although the one-dimensional meritocracy model may suggest to BA graduates that they can easily fall back into mid-skill jobs if they fail at higher-skill careers, we find that having a higher-level education does not qualify them for these midlevel jobs. Many mid-skill jobs require specific technical skills that BA graduates do not possess. For example, faculty reported that medical assistants know how to run the business of a medical practice; many doctors and nurses do not have this skill. Similarly, computer networking specialists learn detailed procedures for protecting network security that computer programmers often do not know.

## Soft Skills

In addition to the job-specific professional standards and technical skills that students need to succeed at mid-skill jobs, occupational faculty also emphasized soft skills that traverse job boundaries. Students must have a capacity for critical thinking and problem-solving in order to apply their technical skills effectively. These are commonly demanded skills that employers often feel are lacking in job applicants.[22] Faculty reported that employers want students who can think critically about their work; facility with rote memorization is not enough. Students must be able to react appropriately given a specific set of circumstances and requirements. Although some may argue that academic skills promote such critical thinking, faculty reported that students learn best how to problem-solve in applied work settings.

Students also must develop communication skills to prepare for any occupation. In a national survey, employers reported that they valued attitude and communication skills above almost anything else; test scores and academic skills were some of the least important criteria for them.[23] As one faculty member reported to us, employers want prospective employees to have "the skills to communicate . . . and [they care] less about your GPA." Occupational faculty especially emphasized the importance of communication skills to success in the workplace. A computer networking instructor reported that, "thirty years ago, you could probably be the [isolated] technician in the corner . . . but now it's all about talking about the ideas, and explaining and interfacing [with] people." Faculty tell students that they will be more valuable to companies if they can work well with clients, not just work on computers. A computer networking faculty member explained that employers ask that the community college "not send them any more geeks." Faculty in our interviews also reported tangible payoffs to communication skills, saying that if a student can work with customers, employers will "pay them 40 percent more than a bench technician."

## Teaching Hard Skills

Employers highly value these non-academic skills, but they rarely know how to teach them.[24] We asked faculty how their classes helped students meet these labor market requirements. Most occupational faculty reported that they designed tasks that did not require high academic skills. Instead, tasks focused on the dimensions discussed here: learning professional standards, becoming technically skilled, and acquiring critical thinking and communication skills. Faculty chose "hands-on" instructional methods that relied on real-world experience rather than academic learning, and they entrusted students with real responsibility. This kind of coursework helped their students develop both technical skills and the soft skills the labor market demands. These teachers asserted that such activities motivate even students who have never been engaged in developing academic skills.

In each occupational field, faculty described how their programs taught students to conform to field-specific professional and technical skills and purposefully aligned coursework and activities with labor market requirements. These occupational faculty rigorously emphasized technical skills and industry regulations, as well as cross-disciplinary rules from multiple fields that were relevant to the profession they taught. A bookkeeping instructor reported that business students "have to know [that] there's a lot of law in accounting." In one business program, the faculty member early on taught students how fraud occurs in companies, even inadvertently. Taught that any business decision must comply with industry regulations, students had to learn "rules for everything, rules for recognition, rules for doing construction contracts using percentage of completion." As one faculty member summarized, "you cannot be a creative accountant. It gets you into trouble."

Laws create standards for professional fields, and program graduates must know the laws and how to comply with them. Computer networking students learn how to keep a company electronically compliant with the Health Insurance Portability and Accountability Act (HIPAA) and the Family Educational Rights and Privacy Act (FERPA) and how to ensure that the collection of credit card information follows data protection laws. A faculty member explained: "Security has become such an important issue right now. . . . When you start dealing with customer information, even in a small business environment, you have to start looking at some better protection and changing your practices." Mastery of professional standards can literally have life-or-death consequences in the health field, and these instructors imparted to their students the importance of this training. Graduates who later shared their employment experiences reported that their mastery of these standards earned the respect of those in authority.

Occupational faculty also told students that they would need to continue learning in their profession after college graduation. Professional jobs are distinctive in having "rigorous training and licensing requirements," and some fields require that students pass difficult licensing exams even after they meet degree requirements.[25] Moreover, in the fields we studied, the required competencies are constantly evolving. Bookkeeping rules and laws are amended, medical practices change, and technology evolves every few years. The need to keep pace with the dynamic demands of these occupations often makes professional training a lifelong commitment to continuing education in order to stay up-to-date on information and skills.[26] Computer networking serves as a perfect example of the fast pace of change in these fields. The computer networking faculty we interviewed told their students about the need to learn new software and techniques even after graduation and certification: "It's not like math or English or history, [where] you learn it once and it doesn't change." Instead, "what you learned in the first year is going to change completely in two years." New security concerns arise, and new software and hardware are created to address those concerns. As one faculty member said, "The day you stop learning about the new stuff coming out is the day that you better get ready to retire."

In later research, we interviewed sub-BA graduates who reported that their occupational program taught them how to learn and the necessity of knowing how to learn. Many of them did poorly in high school, but even they knew that they had to keep their skills updated so as not to let them become obsolete. Updating skills often builds on existing skills in many certificate occupations. Although skills sometimes change radically (such as with the shift to computer diagnostics in automobiles), updated skills rarely require college-level academic skills.

Technical skills and standards are crucial, but BA degree holders rarely learn them. Occupational programs are the main (and sometimes only) way to acquire these technical qualifications. As a faculty member reported, newly minted BA graduates come to his community college every year in June and ask "what [classes] they could take to get a job." Without the technical training, BA graduates often have difficulty getting jobs, despite their supposedly superior academic skills. Thus, many BAs subsequently enroll in certificate programs that enable them to do the same jobs that other certificate holders do without a BA (although we do not know if the latter have better careers later).

## Teaching Soft Skills

Occupational faculty reported that they developed classroom activities specifically to teach the soft skills crucial for employment—in particular, problem-solving and communication. In class and homework assignments, they set up problem-solving exercises that resembled real-world tasks and often included several layers of complications to which students had to respond and create solutions.

A surgical technician instructor, noting that employers want students "to be able to think . . . before they make a mistake [in surgery]," said that her exercises included multiple challenges that require students to decide how to apply skills and which ones to use. A business instructor reported teaching students that, "in the actual world, you have to be able to understand what you did and why you did it. Otherwise, you can't translate . . . that numerical answer to a business decision." An accounting faculty member provided a three-week project in which students did all of the business-related work for a fake company. Then the teacher gave students a test in which "ten more things happen to that company . . . so they've got to go all the way through the whole system, and they have to know all of the formulas to make all that work. So, you know, they're really doing the job." Other teachers asked students to make decisions in various scenarios. By using classroom tasks that taught students how to apply technical skills and solve problems with technical complications, these faculty developed new capabilities in students that would be crucial to their success in the field.

Occupational faculty also identified ways in which they developed communication skills. In one faculty member's field, completing a certificate signaled the acquisition of not only technical skills but also "good people skills." Faculty in different fields created class interactions and role-playing exercises that improved professional communication. In medical assisting programs, students role-played interactions with patients with various concerns. This exercise helped them develop critical listening skills and tested their knowledge of symptoms and specific patient needs. Students in computer networking programs role-played the situation of high-level managers ignoring procedures that would make their computer networks secure from hacking; students had to solve the technical problems this created and explain to the managers why the security procedures were necessary. Accounting assistant programs had students write memos about their findings from analysis of a department financial accounting exercise.

To build students' communication skills, faculty often gave homework assignments that included writing memos, responding to memos, interpreting instructions, anticipating difficulties, and understanding ambiguities. In addition, we found that some two-year colleges particularly emphasize public speaking skills.

## Giving Students Responsibility

Key common denominators between assignments that build hard skills and those that build soft skills are the high applicability to the real world and an emphasis on taking responsibility. Instead of merely learning to perform tasks, understand concepts, and apply them in a variety of professional settings, students learn that their actions have important consequences.

Many of the occupational programs we learned about used hands-on methods that specifically imitated real-world job tasks. In a computer networking class, students participated in one such activity: they were instructed to build LED displays and clap-light switches from a box of electronic components and could see or hear when they did it right. At another college, a faculty member showed students a computer simulation of the work he did for clients in his computer consulting business. Another computer course had students construct a website for a customer. A bookkeeping class visited an animal shelter, where students practiced balancing the books and conducting an audit. Another program culminated with a business strategies course that gave accounting, management, and marketing students cases to solve together, just as they would do in an actual office.

Students were also exposed to outside-the-classroom learning in the form of internships that immersed students in the field. One student intern wrote a computer program to track the number of golf cart rentals her company needed. When another student applied knowledge she learned in class to create a more effective inventory procedure for the national corporation where she was interning, the company adopted her procedure. Many health programs provided students with clinical experiences in hospitals, enabling them to practice their new skills in real environments with real patients.

In addition, occupational faculty reported assigning classroom tasks designed to give students responsibility and socialize them for professional adult roles. By the time students complete their occupational degree program, they must be prepared to assume duties that come with responsibilities, such as drawing blood, responding to medical emergencies, following legal accounting principles, and repairing vital computer networks to keep a company functioning. Occupational programs use instructional tasks designed to transform students into professionals who can handle professional roles and responsibilities and respond to challenges. This is similar to the German apprenticeship model, which enables young apprentices to develop a maturity and professionalism that American eighteen-year-olds are often thought incapable of handling.[27]

Following prior studies of how physicians are socialized, we have described elements of the process used by sub-BA programs to induct students into occupational roles, including training in professional standards and skills and simulations of occupational tasks.[28] The assignments and tasks involved in this process help to fully qualify students for institutionalized professional roles and authority. Although students with poor academic skills are often considered immature and irresponsible, their successful completion of these tasks in sub-BA programs shows that they are more than capable of filling professional jobs.

## Focusing on College-Ready Abilities May Obscure Other Student Abilities

Young students with low academic achievement are often perceived as unmotivated and lacking in ability, but the occupational faculty we interviewed reported that students often have more abilities than they realize.[29] This view of low-achieving students may result from the school context itself, which makes abstract demands that seem unreal to students. German apprenticeship programs, by contrast, are structured in a way that builds students' confidence and maturity by providing them with adultlike responsibilities in the workforce. American education, on the other hand, tends to make students passive learners with little authority.[30] Some students can operate well under this learning structure, but others—especially nontraditional students who may have less structure and guidance in their academic life outside of school—do not flourish in such a setting.

Thus, faculty reports that occupational programs can engage students and help them discover abilities and interests they did not know they had. This poses a serious challenge to the usual assumptions of the meritocratic model. When they first enter college, students base their course selections on incomplete knowledge of their own abilities. However, students in occupational programs, on the other hand, can be transformed by their occupational programs, and faculty reported their efforts to create curricula to facilitate that process.

For example, faculty reported that instead of asking students to choose a specialty in their occupation at the outset, they provide them with tasks and experiences that help them discover previously unknown interests and abilities. As one faculty member said, "One of the things that . . . [influences] students is . . . how [teachers] present things, how they get students excited about things and . . . how they draw out the talents they may have that they may not know about." Although those outside the field often characterize accounting as dull, these faculty reported that when students "get it, then it becomes fun . . . it's kind of like a puzzle." Exposure to a profession's goals and the use of professional skills enables students to see whether they enjoy the work. In accounting, for instance, they may discover an aptitude for solving problems in the business world.

In an introductory health course, students wrote case studies connecting complicated anatomy terms to different illnesses and symptoms, as if they were putting together clues in a mystery, and they learned whether to make medical inferences. In another health course, a faculty member taught phlebotomy students how to draw blood using a rubber arm. After mastering the technique, students advanced to practicing on one another. As students became more confident with this skill, this faculty member said, they became like "little vampires," eagerly asking to bring family members into the classroom so that they could practice and proudly show off their new skills. Our research team observed that students in this class exhibited obvious pride and confidence as their initial fear of the task turned into success with it and they discovered a new competency.

When students have successful experiences in occupational classes, they become excited about performing tasks that require the skills they have learned and can be confident that their new skills directly apply to real jobs. Faculty reported that their occupational programs, like German apprenticeships, transformed seemingly unmotivated students into work-ready productive adults.

Early hands-on successes motivate students further. In several computer networking programs, the first lessons involve taking apart a computer and putting it back together again. Even though at first this task seems daunting, with computer pieces spread across the work space, a faculty member described the course as "unthreatening, easy, and a lot of fun." He reported that his students were so engaged in these initial tasks that they became "hooked" and willing to put up with difficult assignments to build their skills. Such tasks, in showing students that they have capabilities they were unaware of, ignite new interests and make them eager to continue their studies—even those who did poorly in high school and have never been engaged in academic studies. In addition, many students are engaged by being given responsibility for the first time. Prior to college, many of them never had work duties with important consequences. In service jobs, their mistakes could alienate a customer but were unlikely to do greater damage. Their exposure in occupational programs to tasks with real-world consequences, however, transforms students who previously had no reason to be conscientious into serious professionals. Summarizing students' written reflections on a course they had completed, one teacher said that students' "experience in that classroom pushed them and . . . made them succeed in ways they didn't think they could."

We also have some examples from students' point of view. A faculty member reported that when he was a community college student in his twenties, he was disruptive in class and got in lots of trouble. His life was going nowhere, and he hated college. But after he discovered the medical assisting field, he learned that he had the ability to do it well, and he found the work personally rewarding. He now tells his students: "This field saved my life, and it can save yours too." We found this personal statement very moving, and we suspect that sharing his experience had encouraged many of his students.

We interviewed current students in some of these programs, as well as some graduates, for studies that have been reported elsewhere. They confirm the faculty reports cited here.[31] Students who had shown little interest in learning in academic classes reported that they now saw that the learning in occupational classes was vital, sometimes with life-or-death consequences or with other people's jobs depending on them. One community college student in medical assisting explained that this "experience was vital because this was the first time anyone has ever trusted me enough to allow me to demonstrate my work effort and diligence in a professional environment." These student reports resembled reports from German apprenticeships, which give youths the opportunity to "help make important decisions . . . in which others depend on them, [and] it can have profound effects on their sense of who they are and what they can do."[32] Community college students in U.S. occupational programs have similar experiences. As in apprenticeships, these students gain a new professional identity by making real-life decisions and discovering they have the ability to solve real-world problems.[33]

Indeed, students who had graduated seven years earlier reported that these programs transformed them into competent professionals. Many of these graduates had been regarded as "low ability" in high school and could not imagine any way they would ever do well in school, much less be interested in school. In occupational programs, however, they discovered that they could meet professional standards, master technical skills, and apply their knowledge to new circumstances that demanded problem-solving and communication. Within the occupational class-room, they succeeded in practical, non-academic activities and learned to handle responsibility. They also discovered interests that they had never anticipated. Perhaps most surprising to some of them was the discovery of interests and abilities in academic subjects like writing and math, which had been unimaginable to them in high school.

## Implications

Our societal emphasis on the benefits of the meritocratic model of education and one-dimensional rankings of academic skills can overshadow the importance of non-academic skills. The occupational faculty we interviewed described a variety of important skills that students can bring to the labor market and characterized part of their work as identifying each student's strengths along valued dimensions. According to these teachers' reports, occupational sub-BA programs recognize and develop many qualifications that can lead to a variety of desirable job outcomes. Students need such information about sub-BA programs, but colleges rarely notify them about these options.

Our findings also have implications for the current emphasis on remedial coursework. Remedial courses are largely ineffective at improving student chances of college success, but Bailey, Jaggars, and Jenkins have identified promising new remedial approaches that they hope will be more effective.[34] However those approaches work out, there is another possible approach, particularly for students with low achievement. The entire remedial process could be postponed or avoided if low-achieving students initially enroll in occupational certificate programs. These programs often do not require high academic skills or the passing of a placement test, they develop competencies valued in the workforce, and they allow students to postpone remedial coursework until they are ready to pursue a higher degree. If certificate holders decide to pursue associate or BA degrees—as more than 25 percent do—community colleges will probably require that they pass the remedial placement test.[35] (Four-year colleges may have ways to avoid this.) However, postponing this test until after a student earns a certificate may be a good strategy. Certificate courses may help students remember academic skills they have not used for several years, and the credential may give them confidence that will support their further ambitions.

The larger lesson in this chapter is that we must listen to the occupational faculty who shape sub-BA programs. Many of these teachers have spent considerable time in their occupational field, and they have thought more about the needs of their students and their occupations than anyone else in society. They give us a more complex view of the occupational world and its requirements than accountability schemes do. Moreover, they often have a better grasp of fast-changing labor markets than our statistics, which are inevitably lagging indicators. Developing accountability standards without consulting faculty is a recipe for misdirected standards that do not help students and do not serve these vital occupations.

For instance, one proposal is to examine earnings ten years after graduation—an appropriate time span for getting a view of career advancement. However, current outcomes for individuals who graduated ten years ago may not apply to the outcomes that today's graduates can expect in fast-changing occupations. Policymakers do not realize that using college scorecards to second-guess or punish occupational faculty carries great risks. However, college scorecards could provide useful information for faculty and administrators in designing programs and advising students on their program choices.

## Conclusion

Occupational faculty seem to have little use for the reform rhetoric about "college-level" academic skills; instead, they describe programs that demand only a modest threshold of academic skills and develop non-academic skills that employers want.

These faculty contend that low-achieving students are not necessarily destined for menial jobs but instead can get sub-BA credentials that develop alternative competencies and lead to significant earnings increases, nonmonetary job rewards, and gratifying jobs that serve vital societal purposes.[36] We might worry that these faculty are exaggerating, but their reports about job rewards are remarkably similar to our analyses of national surveys of young adults' outcomes (chapters 2 and 3).

College has enormous power to shape the careers of young people, but many have a poor understanding of how college can prepare them for work. Occupational programs shape students' plans by helping them see their own competencies, engage with their abilities, and develop new professional competencies. Some programs encourage sub-BA graduates to pursue further education opportunities in degree ladders within their occupation (see chapter 6). Instead of "cooling out" students' BA plans, occupational programs may lead to a quick sub-BA credential, new qualifications, earnings payoffs, and a new confidence to go on to earn higher degrees and have better careers, as many do.

Just as prior chapters showed that community colleges offer many more college pathways and many more desirable job rewards than is generally known, this chapter has shown that high academic skills are neither necessary nor sufficient for success, and that there are many, more desirable non-academic skills to develop that can improve students' college and career success.

## Appendix

Community colleges in California and Illinois were matched on enrollment size and student demographics. Our sample included colleges from high-, middle-, and low-SES communities, as judged by census tract data. The colleges in each state were in large urban areas. We chose accredited occupational programs (both private and public) that lead to jobs in high demand. Given our sample restrictions, these findings may not generalize to other colleges or programs. However, we offer new insights about occupational programs that may spur future research to consider new issues.

Our analyses merged faculty from public and private colleges because we detected no differences in their responses in systematic analyses. Indeed, some faculty taught in both types of colleges. In interviews, we asked teachers about their educational background, professional experience in the field, and how they helped students understand and develop qualifications for their program and jobs. In addition, we asked them to describe their occupational programs and the job-matching process.

# PART II

## ALTERNATIVE PROCEDURES FOR COLLEGES

# ═ Chapter 5 ═

## The Least Understood Tests in America: How College Procedures Shape Placement Test Results

W HILE TRADITIONAL college procedures were designed for traditional college students, the next four chapters describe traditional procedures and ways they create difficulties for students crossing important college transitions. We often assume that colleges must operate by traditional procedures, the only procedures we have ever seen. However, these chapters describe alternative procedures that allow community colleges to work differently and perhaps have fewer failures and more successes. Also, these chapters are about procedures that colleges can implement to help all students, not just those pursuing a sub-BA. The goal of these chapters is to show that college entry, progress, and career entry are likely to be strongly shaped by these procedures, which colleges can design to improve outcomes.

Procedures can affect testing results. If colleges give a "test" and students see no reason to do well on it, have students' skills been tested? This may sound like a silly question. Indeed, society usually makes information about tests so salient that virtually no one questions their importance. Everyone knows they must pass a test to get a driver's license, a privilege so coveted that even teenagers who are apathetic about school exams take the driving test seriously. Selective college admissions tests (ACT, SAT) are similarly well understood. In upper-middle-class high schools, where many students aspire to attend selective colleges, students understand the importance of college admissions tests, and a billion-dollar industry has emerged to prepare them for these tests.

Although just as important as the SAT and ACT, community college placement tests are often overlooked. These placement tests are crucial for admission into college credit courses, and thus for degree completion, but students seem apathetic about the process—an indication that they probably do not understand the stakes. What many also do not understand is that many community college courses are not college-level: they are remedial courses required because of their poor scores on college placement tests.

To maintain college-level standards, community colleges require students who were low achievers in high school to take remedial courses. These are high school–level courses in English and math that are intended to bring students' academic skills up to a "college-ready" level before they begin credit-bearing coursework. Colleges place students in remedial courses using placement exams—a standard part of community college enrollment in which students take English and math tests that cover topics they should have learned in high school. (In some community colleges, students can also place out of remedial courses by achieving certain scores on the ACT or SAT.) Most community college students do not do well on these placement exams, and as a result, over 60 percent of students in our nation's community colleges take at least one remedial course. In some urban community colleges, over 90 percent do.[1] These remedial courses consume students' time and money, but they provide no college credits and their record in improving students' academic skills is poor.[2]

To avoid discouraging students, colleges often are ambiguous when they describe remedial courses and their consequences.[3] This ambiguity begins with how colleges administer the remedial placement tests. To better understand students' reactions to these tests, we observed some students as they took a placement test.

After devoting several hours to waiting in lines and filling out registration paperwork, with her six-month-old baby in her arms, Emma learned that she had one more task to do before she would be done: without explanation, she was told that she had to sit at a computer terminal and answer questions.[4] With her baby fretting on her lap, Emma rushed through the questions, since her ride was waiting outside in the hot sun.

Although she was not told this, the college considered this set of questions a remedial placement test. Emma may have saved several minutes by rushing through the test, but her subsequent low score may have added months or years of noncredit remedial classes to her time in college, with commensurate additional tuition bills. No one at the college managing the enrollment process that day told Emma about these consequences. If they had, she probably would have devoted more attention to this task. Was a test administered in this way really a test of her college-readiness?

Susan reported that, when she registered at community college, she was led through a series of forms to fill out over many hours, and then sent to a computer to complete the last task. She was told that this task would help with choosing her "course assignments," but she was not told that she was taking a test; nor was she warned of the consequences—a low score would land her in remedial noncredit courses, adding time and financial costs to her college plans. While she was taking the test, two other students arrived and quickly raced through the test. Although Susan was proceeding quickly, these students finished much earlier than she did. They did not use the worksheets provided for calculating answers to the math questions, and they often appeared disengaged, staring out the window and answering some questions without reading them.

Did these late-arriving students take a test? To all appearances, the answer is no: they did not read the questions and made no effort to calculate the answers to the math questions. What did their test score mean? Did their score reflect their "readiness to work with college-level academic demands"? Or did it signify only their cooperation when told to answer a lot of uninteresting questions in a task that had no discernible purpose?

These stories are not anomalous. In the Beginning Postsecondary Students Longitudinal Study (BPS), a survey of 4,400 community college students, two-thirds of the students did not realize that their remedial courses did not count for credit.[5] Even many second-year students still did not understand this. Some expected to receive a two-year associate degree at the end of the year, when in fact their time spent in remedial courses had kept them from earning enough credits for a degree. Moreover, even students who did realize they had taken remedial courses were unaware of the implications. The BPS found that as the number of remedial courses students reported taking increased from zero to three or more, their educational plans barely changed even as their actual chances of completing a degree plummeted.[6]

Many studies have examined the impact of remedial courses on academic skills and degree completion.[7] Despite this extensive research about test outcomes, the placement test process, which is crucial to the remedial experience, has largely been ignored by researchers. As we define it, the "remedial placement process" includes notifying students that they must take the test, prepare for the test, and attain a certain score if they want their "college enrollment" to include real college courses leading to college credits. Remediation directly depends on this process and makes unwarranted assumptions about students' understanding and motivation.

This chapter addresses the role of remedial courses and placement exams in the community college experience and the impact of the remedial placement procedures that colleges devise, often without much reflection. Despite extensive research on remedial outcomes, few studies describe actual college procedures that assess students and place students in remedial classes. College procedures are the rules and practices that colleges regularly use. The remedial placement procedures we look at here often go unnoticed, but they can have a strong impact on students' behavior and outcomes. In this chapter, we ask: At what point do entering college students become aware of remedial placement tests? Do they prepare for them? And how seriously do they take these tests? If students do not understand why they are being given these tests, have their skills been tested? We also examine whether test scores, besides measuring students' skills, are influenced by college procedures. Would students get different scores on the same test if colleges used different procedures?

We discovered remedial placement procedures that lead to mistaken assessments, excessively narrow options, and unnecessary failures. Doing well on a remedial placement test depends on more than ability; it also depends on understanding the test. When we examined community college websites and observed advising processes at community colleges, we found that colleges rarely provide crucial information about placement tests: the purpose of the test, why students should want to do well on it, how to prepare, when to take the test, whether and how to take it again, how to use the results for choosing degree goals, and the credentials that require passing remedial tests.

Students rely on colleges for information that helps them succeed in college, but we find that information on placement testing is hard to come by in community colleges. Better procedures might lead to more valid test scores, better prepared students, less need for remediation, and higher rates of credential completion.

## Poorly Understood Tests with Unseen Incentives

In a country obsessed with tests, the college remedial placement tests may be the least understood tests in America. Despite extensive research on remedial test outcomes, research has largely ignored the information that community colleges provide to students about the remedial test process, and we have found glaring omissions and distortions in that process that probably contribute to problems usually blamed on student deficiencies.

Open admission policies in community colleges have given students a second chance, even those with prior low academic achievement. The emphasis on remedial courses as the solution to students' achievement difficulties has consumed an enormous proportion of the resources of already cash-starved community colleges: total spending on noncredit remedial courses in college is in the billions of dollars.[8] Researchers have also devoted enormous resources to studying the outcomes of remedial courses, which provide one of the most visible predictors of students' success or failure in community college.[9] Research findings have been discouraging: most students assigned to the remedial sequence never complete it.[10]

There are often at least two levels of remediation: a higher level for students with modest deficiencies and a lower level for those whose placement test scores indicate major academic deficiencies. The higher-level sequence may consist of only one remedial course, while the lower level may require students to complete a series of semester-long courses before entering college-credit work. For those referred to the higher level, success rates are 50 percent, but that drops to 17 percent for students in lower-level math.[11]

Since remedial courses cover material that students are expected to have learned in high school, one may wonder why students do not come into college with these skills. Our prior research found that most high school seniors plan to get a college degree, but 40 percent of students believe that they can attend college without working hard in high school.[12] Like the National Commission on the High School Senior Year, we discovered that many students regard senior year in particular as a time to take it easy.[13]

Many high school students know about open admission policies at their local community college, and they know that, as long as they graduate from high school, poor achievement will not prevent their access to college.[14] These students are partly right. High school grades and test scores do not bar students from attending college, since anyone can enroll in an open-admission college. However, high school grades strongly predict whether students will benefit from college. Students in the lowest quartile of grades who plan to get a college degree have less than a 20 percent chance of completing a college degree in the next ten years.[15]

Students do not see these outcomes, so they have little incentive to work hard and take difficult courses in high school. This failure to see outcomes may explain the widespread problem of a lack of academic rigor in senior year.[16]

Ironically, the standards movement contributes to student complacency. Many states require that students pass exit exams to graduate from high school. Yet the standards for these exams are almost always lower than the standards set by community colleges. Most states pose low standards for exit exams in an effort to avoid creating low high school graduation rates, which would lead to criticism. Consequently, just three months after passing exit exams establishing their "high school competency," many students fail the college placement exams. Students are understandably surprised to learn that "high school competency" does not indicate "college-readiness."

New York State tried to avoid this dilemma by requiring that students pass the high-standards Regents Examinations in order to graduate from high school. However, they discovered that even with increased instruction, two-thirds of students failed to pass, and no official wanted to deny graduation to that many students. Today the Regents Exams are still given, but with much lower standards—and students who pass them often fail college remedial placement exams.

Despite the critical importance of placement tests and remedial courses, high school seniors planning on entering community college are rarely aware of them.[17] Moreover, prior research has shown that students do not understand remedial courses.[18] What this research does not examine is the information that community colleges provide to students about the remedial placement process. Regardless of a college's remedial placement procedure, students should be informed of their options and the college's requirements. In our minds, not informing students about procedures *is* a procedure, and one with consequences. If students do not have easy access to accurate information about taking and preparing for placement tests, we can hardly blame them for not understanding their consequences or for not exerting much effort on a test typically given at the end of long registration process. The following analysis will show that community colleges themselves are contributing to students' lack of motivation to work hard in high school or prepare well for college placement tests by poorly explaining those tests.

## Methods and Sample

Since student-counselor ratios often exceed 1,000-to-1 at community colleges, personal advising time is limited, particularly during registration sessions, a chaotic time when most students are seeking information. One result is that websites have become the main source of information for students at community colleges. Unlike printed course catalogs, websites can be easily accessed and immediately updated. Nearly all community colleges have websites that provide extensive information about all aspects of college activities and requirements, including placement tests and remedial courses. Because of their central role in disseminating information, we conducted a systematic analysis of a variety of community college websites to find out what information they provide about placement tests and determine whether they provide the crucial information that students need.

Our sample consists of the websites of nine public community colleges, four in Illinois and five in California, which we have named IL1–IL4 and CA1–CA5. These community colleges vary in size and demographic composition (see appendix) and were part of a larger study in which we interviewed faculty and staff and interviewed and surveyed current students (see chapter 4).[19] Our analysis here occasionally uses information gathered through that larger study to support our website findings. We later conducted similar analyses on additional community college websites—ten in Ohio and nine in Florida—and had similar results. Although we do not know how these findings apply to other states, the consistent lack of information we found across websites leads us to suspect that few states or institutions provide students with sufficient information about college placement exams.

# Findings

All community colleges in our sample required students to take a placement test. Although the website information they provided on this test varied, it was generally poor. We analyzed the ways in which community college websites presented information about five key issues: (1) what the placement test is, (2) why it is important, (3) how to prepare for the test, (4) when to take the test, and (5) how to reduce or avoid remedial requirements given poor performance on the test.

## 1. Purpose: What Is the Placement Test?

Simply finding out that the placement test exists is a struggle on many community college websites. Several colleges barely mention it, and others bury information about it deep within their site. Students who simply browse their prospective college's website for important information might not stumble upon it, and even those who actively search for it will have a tough time finding crucial information about it. For example, IL2 hid information about the test four clicks away from the homepage. In contrast, it took only one click to find the academic calendar. IL4 tucked information on the placement test into a long PDF that took additional time to download and had to be read thoroughly to find the key information. The only way a student could find the placement test page on CA4's website was by searching for "placement test," and even then it was buried as the seventh result. We attempted to navigate to the same page from the homepage after discovering it, but could not.

Four colleges—IL3, CA1, CA2, and CA5—made placement test information accessible with well-marked categories, and students visiting their websites could find it easily, if they knew to look for it. In addition, CA3 provided some information immediately after one click; however, it was a struggle to find information on the specific tests or any discussion of their implications for required remedial courses that would motivate students to prepare for and do well on them.

## 2. Incentives: Why Is the Test Important?

There is a key fact that every student should know: students who get low scores on placement tests are assigned to noncredit remedial classes that increase the time and financial costs for a degree. That statement seems simple enough, but it is rarely conveyed to students. Eight of the nine college websites did not explain this information, and the ninth college gave only partial information. In fact, we find that colleges actually do the opposite: rather than providing students with accurate information on the consequences of placement exams, they make vague and misleading statements about how students' scores are used.

None of these colleges provided the information that students needed to understand placement tests, from the impact of these tests on their goals to how their test scores could help them adjust their goals to match their anticipated timetables, budgets, and promises to employers and family members. Idealistic reformers and college counselors urge all students to aspire to BA degrees, but those who encourage students to set high goals do not necessarily warn them about the costs and risks they will face if they have low test scores.[20] The fact that remedial courses give no college credits and thus add time and financial costs to students' original degree plans was not stated on any webpage that we examined, but it is crucial information.

To avoid discouraging students by giving them the bad news about the connection between low test scores and remedial courses, colleges usually described placement tests in vague and reassuring terms without saying anything that would encourage students to strive to do well on them. The information they provided was rarely wrong, but it was rarely adequate. For example, CA3 stated that "placement tests are required for suitable course placement." In a similar, but more reassuring, spirit, IL4 stated that "the test is not pass/fail" but simply "assists in advising and course selection." That description, while true, is evasive. If we define "success" as admission to the community college, then technically students cannot "fail" the test. But in consigning students to remedial classes that do not count for college credit, a low score is expensive. Therefore, webpages that say the tests have no consequences or that they are not "pass/fail" encourage a false sense of complacency.

Several other colleges took this reassuring attitude one step further by implying that students would be placed in courses that would improve their chances of success and allow them to make the best use of their time. For example, CA5 stated that the purpose of the test was to "evaluate basic skill levels so that students can better coordinate their needs and abilities with course requirements, select appropriate classes, and improve their likelihood of success." The placement test at CA4, described as an "aid to determine course placement," would help to "ensure that students don't waste a semester." While CA4 was right to worry that low academic skills could be a problem in college courses, helping students avoid "wasting" their time seems disingenuous considering that few students who enter college in low-level remedial classes ever complete their degrees.[21] Although these descriptions were mostly accurate, they failed to explain that some courses did not carry college credit but still cost money. Without that knowledge, students would fail to understand the implications of their placement test score.

Some colleges, while saying nothing explicit about the negative consequences of poor placement test scores, did describe their use with more transparency. IL3, for example, told students that test results "govern placement into college-level courses." IL1 stated that the tests "will be used as requirements for most college-level courses" but later assumed a vague and reassuring attitude in telling students that the writing placement test was designed to place them in the "English composition course best suited to your skill level" and that it determined placement in "the appropriate developmental writing course."

While at times these websites came close, they never explicitly said that low test scores lead to placement in classes that give no college credits and impede timely degree progress. As a result, the students we surveyed in these same colleges rarely imagined that some of their college courses might give no college credits and that taking these courses would thus delay their progress toward getting a degree when they were expecting to. We must reiterate that in examining these websites we were actively seeking out information that, unlike most students, we already knew existed. If students are not aware that remedial courses are non-credit-bearing, or that "developmental writing" is a remedial course, they will not realize the importance of these messages and the added costs implied by them.

IL4, the college that assured students that the placement test was not pass/fail, provided somewhat more comprehensive, but still seriously lacking, information on the incentives to do well on the exam. This college gave students crucial information by providing a detailed booklet about its placement tests and how they were used. Nonetheless, the booklet did not explicitly state that low scores would lead to assignment to non-credit-bearing courses. In addition, the information in the booklet's complicated table indicating the scores required for certain courses could have helped students figure out the importance of the placement test but probably did not because it failed to state which courses did not give college credits. Students could have found that information from other sources, but they would have had to be organized and knowledgeable enough to do so. Furthermore, the booklet did not say that students' placement test results might influence their degree timetable or the cost of college. This booklet was a complicated way of conveying simple, crucial information.

Only one website alerted students to the possibility of being placed in noncredit classes. IL2 warned that "lower scores *may* (our emphasis) result in having to take courses that do not award college credit." However, it did not specify the circumstances under which this might occur, nor did it make clear that a "two-year" associate degree would take longer than two years and costs would be higher than they anticipated. Like the other colleges, this college did not provide the information that students needed to understand the incentives for passing the college's placement exam.

## 3. Preparation: How Can Students Prepare to Pass the Placement Test?

The substantial costs associated with remedial education for both students and schools make appropriate placement essential. However, students' remedial needs may be inflated by tests of forgotten skills that they first learned in tenth grade or even earlier, such as algebra or geometry. Many high school students do not take a math course in their senior year. In addition, research has shown that much of the SES gap in academic achievement occurs over the summer, with higher-SES students requiring less review when they return in the fall. This "summer gap" arises because low-SES students receive less academic stimulation when they are out of school.[22] Since most students take the placement test in the fall, after having been away from academics for the summer, a few days of preparation would be appropriate for all students to renew their familiarity with strange words ("trapezoid") and remind them of the unusual tasks (calculating when trains will meet) often required on tests. If a student has not calculated the area in a triangle or spoken English to native English speakers in the past three months, a poor score may only indicate that the student's neighborhood or family do not facilitate practice in these school skills. In interviews, many community college students reported that they did poorly on the placement test because they had not used the material in a few months or a few years.

Refresher activities would probably improve achievement. Several students we interviewed said that only a few weeks in the remedial class brought it all back to them, but they were still required to complete a full semester. The placement test's validity would almost certainly be improved if students were helped to pass the test by first being given a brief review of school language and tasks.

Placement tests are designed as achievement tests, meaning that they test specific knowledge and skills that are learned in school, in contrast to IQ tests, which are intended to measure personal intelligence. Students should not study for IQ tests, but they should study for achievement tests such as the ACT or remedial placement tests. However, despite the probable benefits of preparation, most of the community college websites we examined did not explicitly recommend that students study for the placement test. Some did provide study materials, but it is unlikely that most students used them in the absence of easy access and a reason to do so (which was not provided). Of the websites we examined, one even *discouraged* preparation. IL1 told students that studying was "not recommended." This is customary advice for IQ tests, but it is absolutely the *wrong* advice for achievement tests—especially tests that are usually taken at least three months after high school ended. This school was the exception, however; most of the other websites provided a few sample questions as well as links to additional questions on outside webpages. For example, IL3's website told students about free one-day prep seminars offered by the college on eight dates over the summer. IL2 also held a workshop for students who wanted to improve their writing abilities before the test, as well as access to a math test prep service, both of which charged a fee. Still, none of these websites explicitly recommended that students study for the placement test. Since students were not informed about what was at stake, it is hard to imagine that many students took advantage of any of these preparation offerings, much less resources that cost extra.

## 4. Timing and Retest: When Should Students Take the Test?

There are two important advantages to taking a college placement test at the end of the senior year of high school rather than three months later when college is about to begin. First, the test content will be fresher. Students who take the placement test while still in high school avoid the problem of the "summer gap," and their test score will be a better indication of what they know—that is, the knowledge and skills that otherwise would "come back to them" a few weeks after starting college.

The second advantage is that early testing gives students time over the summer for practice, targeted preparation, and retests, which have strong benefits in raising test scores. The selective college admissions tests (SAT and ACT) usually tell students about the value of early tests. Many students take the PSAT (or Aspire, ACT's middle-level test) in their sophomore year and the SAT (or ACT) in their junior year, then retake the test in their senior year if they are not satisfied with their scores.

In contrast, administrators at the community colleges we studied reported that most of their students took the placement test at the last moment—when they registered in the fall. Although most colleges offer the opportunity to retake the test, taking the test this late allows no time for retesting before classes start.

Advice on when students should take the placement test was largely missing from the websites we examined. It was typically described as a step to be taken during the fall registration period. To add to the confusion, retesting policies differed between colleges. Five community colleges (IL2, IL3, IL4, CA2, and CA3) gave students retesting information. CA1 and CA5 noted only that retesting was not allowed. IL1 and CA4 provided information about time frames for retesting, but their policies were diametrically opposed: IL1 required students to retake the test *within* thirty days of their first attempt, and CA4 required students to wait until *three months after* their original test date before taking the test again. If there is a logic to these rules, all we can say is that different colleges and different states seem to follow different logics.

## 5. Options: How Do Students Reduce or Avoid Remedial Requirements if They Score Poorly on Placement Tests?

Despite the reassuring claim by one community college that "the test is not pass/fail," pass/fail is essentially the *only* test outcome at most community colleges, including the one making this claim. In other settings, tests may be used to diagnose students' skill needs, to show which skills they need to improve or the body of knowledge they need to develop, or to advise them about potential difficulties they may face. The placement test had none of these purposes in these colleges. Interviews with students and advisers suggested that when students were being informed about their placement results, advisers did not even mention their scores or the fact that the students were being assigned to a remedial course. Advisers merely said, "These are the most appropriate courses for you to take to begin your college career." They avoided communicating any sense of stigma or shortcoming, and they never mentioned students' failure on these tests. But students who failed to qualify for college-credit courses were about to suffer important costly consequences. The test scores determined how many semesters of remedial coursework they were required to take and thus how long it would take them to complete their degree plans. This information was not given to students.

Moreover, all the websites we examined withheld a crucial piece of information—some sub-BA credentials do not require the usual pass level on the placement test. Besides BA degrees, students can pursue applied associate degrees that sometimes have lower pass levels or certificates that either have much lower pass levels or do not require the test at all. Medical billing and paralegal programs do not require full college-readiness in math, computer networking does not require full college-readiness in writing, and utility technician programs do not require that students meet full college-readiness standards in either academic area. Even if their test scores require remedial coursework to pursue BA transfer, students can avoid remedial coursework by pursuing certificates or associate degrees that do not have these test-score requirements.

Not only do websites rarely offer this information, but sometimes they even make it hard to obtain. Low-achieving students, who are unlikely to be successful on the remedial path, could be informed about the certificates or applied associate degrees that do not require strong academic skills and may not require any remedial courses. They can later pursue BA degrees, which will require the placement test. But websites do not inform students about this option.

## Conceptual Implications: The Impact of College Procedures on Students' Test Scores

The most important lesson in this study is that test scores are shaped by social context. College procedures could include fully informing students about the placement test and all of its ramifications and requirements. They could also give students more information about occupational certificates—the sub-BA credentials that may not require college-level academic skills and thus offer students with low scores a chance to earn job payoffs while avoiding remedial requirements. The importance of this information cannot be overstated. In its absence, placement test scores not only indicate individuals' achievement, they also indicate whether college procedures present crucial information when needed. Unfortunately, we find that this information is largely absent.

In this case, what students do not know does in fact hurt them. Students are failing to take actions that would improve their test scores and their chances of avoiding remedial courses. High school students are wasting their senior year, wasting the summer after graduation, and failing to prepare for the test. Spending just a few days reviewing high school math and English might improve their pass rates and help them avoid one or more semesters of remedial courses. Indeed, some students we interviewed complained that remedial classes are too easy. They had already learned the skills taught in these classes, even though they had not remembered them on the day of the test because they had not reviewed them. Obviously, test scores are poor indicators when the material is not fresh in the mind—for instance, when testing tenth-grade skills that most test-takers learned two years earlier.

In a survey of over 2,000 students, the vast majority of students reported that they would recommend that students prepare for the placement test.[23] Since college websites had not warned them about the test's consequences, many had seen no reason to prepare; we can be fairly certain that they recommended test preparation because some of them had suffered from their own lack of preparation.

There is a depressing irony to these observations. Unlike the SAT and ACT, placement tests are poorly described. The least knowledgeable students with the most uncertain college prospects must take placement tests about which little information is provided, and they receive no warnings about the consequences of not studying for them. Prior research suggests that high levels of remedial placement are the fault of low-achieving students, but the present analysis indicates that community colleges are not providing crucial information that would motivate students to refresh their knowledge and give the exam their best effort. These tests reflect students' poor understanding of incentives that are not being explained.

Community colleges have experienced radical changes, including an enormous influx of new students, which was bound to create discontinuities. Besides not being prepared for college-credit courses, many low-achieving students have little understanding of testing and do not know how to seek help and find information and resources. Our goal is not to blame colleges, but to identify the information that students need to know about placement tests. The community college websites we examined were seriously deficient in the information they provided, making serious problems for students that much more likely. However, after these shortcomings are identified, they can be easily remedied.

## Policy Implications

Despite the shortcomings of community college websites that we discovered, they are not intractable. These websites could easily provide students with crucial information, and remedies are as simple and inexpensive as updating the website and making improvements to advising. We propose practical steps for the five issues we identified.

1. *Purpose: What is the test?* Community colleges should notify students of the test's existence by disseminating information about it to local high schools. Students should not be responsible for finding out about whether or not the test exists.

2. *Incentives: Why is the test important?* Students should know that entering community college is no indication of "success" and that their low scores on placement tests will lead to remedial courses that award no college credits but do increase the costs, in both time and money, of getting a college degree.

3. *Preparation: How should students prepare for the test?* Colleges should let students know that a few days of preparation for the test could save them one or more semesters of remedial courses. High schools could also provide preparation targeted at students' needs.

4. *Timing and Retest: When should students take the test?* Taking the test while still in high school could reduce the time that students spend in remedial courses. Like admissions tests, students should be encouraged to take placement tests early, before graduation, while their high school skills are fresh. Early testing would also give students a chance to retake the exam.

   The community college process, including placement testing, could be institutionalized into the high school academic calendar. Just as selective colleges have a national decision day, nonselective colleges could also have a decision day—say, May 1. Students could change their choices later, but early college enrollment would help them learn about programs, register, and take placement tests. They could also get counseling about their choices over the summer, when college campuses are quiet, instead of being forced to make snap decisions during the chaotic registration week. As noted later (chapter 8), Harper College does this.

   With these types of structural changes, colleges could develop procedures that enable students to improve their academic skills and make informed community college decisions. Such procedures, especially the May 1 testing, would also help students who have been out of school for a year or longer by providing an earlier assessment of what they recall and giving them time to refresh their skills over the summer.

5. *Options: How can students reduce or avoid remedial requirements if they do poorly on the placement test?* Low-achieving students or students with short timetables can still choose to take remedial courses, but they should be informed about alternative credentials that require fewer remedial courses. Despite colleges' pride in offering students choices, too little is done to help them make informed choices. Websites should warn about the time and financial consequences of a low placement test score and inform students about alternative valuable credentials they can earn while still working toward a BA degree (see chapter 6). Students who are informed about the requirements of different programs are better able to choose other options and complete an occupational certificate that will improve their earnings and their confidence; working toward a certificate may also earn them some credits as well as valuable experience in pursuing further education. College staff understandably worry that knowledge of

the extended timetables caused by remedial courses will discourage students, but not warning them about these predictable consequences does them a disservice.

Students could also be given a post-test printout that not only informs them of their placement score but also details the skills they must work on and the anticipated time to complete the degree they want, given the number of remedial courses required. This information is especially important to students as they budget for college costs.

These suggested improvements may be relatively simple, but they are key to reducing remedial costs for students. They will not solve the entire remedial problem, but many students are likely to benefit from them. In fact, all of the options suggested here are already available, but students are not usually aware of them.

## Structural Changes to the Placement Test Process

Beyond suggesting improvements in the dissemination of information to entering students, we also propose the following structural changes in the placement test process:

### Alternative Uses of the Placement Test

If properly administered, the placement test score indicates a student's level of preparation—specifically, a student's level in reading, writing, and math. Early testing can inform students of how much they need to prepare to meet pass levels in each of these subjects. If well designed, tests can also provide diagnostic information that lets students know which specific skills they need to improve. Such information would enable students to know *how much* and *what kind* of preparation they need before taking the test again.

Moreover, placement tests can be designed to diagnose students' specific skill needs while they are still in high school. For instance, if a student's score reflects a general knowledge of algebra but lack of mastery of certain skills, those specific deficiencies can be improved so that the student has better success on future exams. A high school teacher, on his own initiative, might have his seniors take the local community college placement exam at the beginning of senior year. The teacher could examine the results and then plan lessons to address students' skill needs. Some schools, such as "early college high schools"—in which students enroll simultaneously in high school and community college—

do this type of differentiated instruction systematically. Indeed, these schools sometimes administer the college placement test in ninth grade so as to detect skill needs early enough to address them long before college begins. Such early diagnosis provides clear direction for students and can shorten the time required for remediation. Recent research is examining the use of the ACT for diagnosing skill needs, which is now commonly used as the eleventh-grade standardized exam in many states.[24] Indeed, if computerized remedial instruction could be synchronized with test results, instruction could emphasize the skills that each student needs to improve.

## Alignment Reforms

Alignment reforms can bring the college placement test into high schools. In Florida, one of the few states that uses the same placement test in all its state colleges, the state legislature created a reform in 2012 under which that test is now administered to most eleventh-grade students; those who do not pass are required to take a college-readiness course to repair their academic skills.[25] In effect, the Florida reform, *before students arrived in college,* notified them about the test, informed them of its importance, assessed their own readiness, and gave them ways to prepare for college. This reform effectively removed many of the shortcomings of open-admission colleges that we have noted in this chapter. Unfortunately, countervailing political pressures led the Florida legislature to undermine this reform, first by making the remedial test optional in colleges and then by making it optional in high schools. This quick reversal occurred while the program was just beginning, so it does not reflect problems with the reform itself. Legislators seemed to be responding to parents' fatigue with too much testing, given the massive demands being made by Common Core tests. We sympathize with test fatigue, but we believe that the college placement test is far more useful to students than any other tests they take and should not be dropped.

Aligning high school and college standards to help students prepare for college-level coursework can be done without state legislation. We discovered that one community college, Harper College (see chapter 8), accomplished the same goal by working with local high schools, while also avoiding some of the problems associated with Florida's state mandate. Harper's experience shows that by synchronizing standards, school systems can move past blaming students for their academic deficiencies and instead show them exactly the skills they need to improve in order to meet their career goals.

We should add that we are not wedded to high-stakes placement testing. As long as it exists, however, students need to be clearly and consistently informed about the implications of placement tests and given early notification that allows them to prepare in advance.

In sum, possible alternative uses of placement tests include: (1) informing students about the predictable implications for their degree timetable, (2) advising students' program choices to fit their goals and timetable constraints, and (3) diagnosing and helping to remedy students' skill gaps. Such uses of tests could reduce the number of remedial courses students need to take and reduce the time needed to repair skill deficiencies.

## Placement Test Preparation and Standardization

Many community colleges devise their own local tests. A study of California community colleges found that over 100 tests were given in the state's community colleges.[26] These local tests vary in quality, and they rarely have extensive validation or psychometric properties. Even more seriously, this multiplicity of tests implies a multiplicity of standards, giving high school seniors the message that standards are ambiguous and conflicting. Indeed, students might see this as an incentive to shop for lower standards, and the high number of students moving between community colleges suggests that this may be happening.[27]

Today the community college placement test is a serious impediment to college credit classes, and taking institutionalized steps to make information about the test more widely available will encourage all students to prepare and to take more difficult classes in high school. Placement tests are at least as important as selective college admissions tests, and they should be similarly standardized. In addition, colleges must do more than simply alert students to the advantages of preparing for placement tests; they should also develop preparation materials and make them easily available.

There are several stakeholders that could address these problems: states, the federal government, and the College Board. States would communicate much clearer standards if they decided on a single test for all community colleges, as Florida has done. Clearer standards would help students understand what is required of them at any community college and take much of the guesswork out of preparing for the placement exam.

The federal Common Core curriculum may help to standardize curriculum and standards in the long run. But this will take time. Some early textbooks claim to have Common Core material, but reviews suggest that these textbooks' early efforts need improvement. Common Core also requires appropriate instructional techniques, and changes in teacher education are just beginning. Moreover, it will take twelve years to produce seniors fully prepared through the entire Common Core curriculum. Meanwhile, Common Core has encountered some roadblocks: it has been turned into a political issue, its major feature is a long test that ties up schools' computers for weeks, and it has inspired massive parent resistance. The jury is still out about whether Common Core will persist long enough to be fully implemented.

The College Board controls the major placement test in the United States (ACCUPLACER) since the ACT recently stopped giving its Compass test. Thus, they have the most capacity for bringing order to this chaotic process. In designing the SAT—"the big test" for four-year-colleges— the College Board took extensive formal institutional steps to devise a standardized test for college applications that became ubiquitous.[28] Despite the test's imperfections, the College Board made the college selection process more meritocratic, thereby increasing access for some previously neglected groups—public schools, neglected geographical regions, and some ethnic groups.[29]

The College Board could assist community colleges in a similar way by drawing up guidelines and developing better preparatory materials. Also, besides providing a single score for placement decisions, they could work with faculty to determine which combinations of scores are necessary for students to succeed in certain programs. Community colleges may benefit from leveraging the College Board to create more consistent national standards and provide useful and accessible preparation materials. Although the SAT and ACT led to an enormous test-prep industry, this could be avoided if community colleges themselves provide preparation classes and materials. Money spent on remedial would be better spent on procedures to reduce remedial placements.

## Conclusion

The validity of placement tests depends on students' understanding of these tests, which often is lacking.[30] The present findings indicate that colleges are not telling students about the remedial placement process and, at most, are offering vague and incomplete information. Although there are many reasons to believe that students do not always listen when they are being given useful information, this does not appear to be one of those times.

Are these findings generalizable? Although we have analyzed a limited sample of community colleges, there is no reason to believe that they are atypical in the information they make available to students. Expanding our analysis to a random sample of nine community colleges in Florida and ten in Ohio has supported the present findings.[31] We suspect that the findings are too uniform to be an accident. The findings are remarkably consistent: nearly all of the college websites we examined provided limited, vague, and even misleading information about placement tests.

Community colleges have done an impressive job of creating open access to higher education. However, more information, improved testing structures, test standardization, and accessible test preparation would help students with this confusing process that too often blocks their access to college credit courses and degree progress. If we do not improve the placement process, we will continue to underestimate students' achievement and unnecessarily consign many of them to noncredit remedial courses.

## Appendix

The process for selecting colleges for the larger study (of which this website analysis is a part) involved an iterative process that drew upon Integrated Postsecondary Education Data System (IPEDS) data. Specifically, from the 2006–2007 universe of 110 California and 48 Illinois community colleges, IPEDS Peer Analysis System data were used to identify institutions that were located in nonrural areas and enrolled at least 5,000 students (in an unduplicated twelve-month head count for 2006–2007). Further examination of key institutional and student characteristics (including total enrollment size, full-time or part-time and degree-seeking enrollment status, student demographics, and award rates of associate and certificate credentials) led to multiple groupings that shared roughly similar characteristics. Four pairs of the best-matched colleges across the two states were selected for the larger study and this website analysis, and one more was added from California, even though it could not be matched in Illinois.

# Chapter 6

## Degree Ladders: Procedures That Combine Dependable Credentials and High Goals

(Pam Schuetz, Kennan A. Cepa, and James E. Rosenbaum)

C OMMUNITY COLLEGES are proud to provide opportunity, yet they are unclear about what opportunities they offer. Most community colleges have more than fifty degree programs conferring certificates, associate degrees, and transfer options.[1] Traditional students may not be overwhelmed by these choices if they are advised by college-educated parents, but these decisions often trip up community college students, especially if they are academically or economically disadvantaged. With so many options, students struggle to see which opportunities are best for them. These opportunities rest on students' understanding of the implications of their choices, which includes knowing program duration, which courses are required, and potential careers. These are key issues, but given the great variety of programs and the quickly changing labor market, few students or college staff are aware of all program intricacies.

Although we leave students free to make their own choices on these issues, few students have sufficient information for making informed choices.[2] As detailed in chapter 5, our analysis of the information provided by community college websites and course catalogs showed relationships between courses, certificates, associate degrees, transfer options, and employment opportunities that are rarely announced to students. Rather than expecting students to find this information on their own, community colleges could more clearly communicate existing program structures. Moreover, rather than forcing students to choose one credential, community colleges could use existing structures to allow students to combine credential goals and make informed course, program, and career decisions. In this chapter, we present "degree ladder maps" that community colleges could construct to describe opportunity structures in ways that can better inform students' choices and permit students to combine degree goals.

## Degree Ladders and Maps

The sociologist Seymour Spilerman (1977, 561) describes a career path as "an ordered sequence of jobs."[3] Similarly, a degree ladder is an ordered sequence of program credentials in which some credits from an early credential also count for later credentials. Certificates are often the first credential in a degree ladder, and in a well-designed degree ladder, short-certificate credits count toward long certificates, associate degrees, and even bachelor's degrees. Ideally, each credential on the ladder has labor market payoffs.[4] Reformers have proposed the creation of stackable credentials, or degree ladders, as a desirable ideal.[5] However, they have not described how they work in practice.

In interviews, occupational program faculty described the degree ladders that already exist in community colleges. They explained that "we've built the [associate] degree on top of a whole bunch of certificates." However, even when a program's curriculum has degree ladders, they may not be visible. Indeed, in our interviews, when college counselors reported that certificates are dead-end, they seemed to be unaware of ladders. Even if degree ladders are not explicitly known about or announced, our analyses indicate that they exist and that they represent real opportunities that students can pursue.

Just as a road map pictorially shows the user the routes to a particular destination, a degree ladder map is a visual representation of the routes to a particular credential. In short, degree ladder maps portray information about the routes (specific courses, program length, certifications and experience required) leading to desirable outcomes (labor market payoffs). Although rarely done, colleges could construct degree ladder maps to show opportunities that already exist within community colleges but are rarely seen.

Most students enter college to prepare for careers.[6] Thus, degree ladder maps can help answer key questions that students are likely to have, such as: How long will this program take to complete? What are the required courses? Are any professional certifications needed? How much do entry-level jobs pay, and what sorts of advancement opportunities exist? In answering these questions, degree ladder maps provide students and counselors with a comprehensive, structured picture of the opportunities available. They reduce the confusion of too many choices, and they describe efficient pathways to advance from lower credentials to higher ones.

# Prior Research

Classic sociological studies describe the constraints that limit occupational mobility. For instance, Peter Blau and Otis Dudley Duncan as well as David Featherman and Robert Hauser have presented intragenerational mobility tables that indicate the odds of mobility from initial occupations to later ones.[7] Similarly, analysis of personnel records in a large corporation showed that early upward mobility predicts subsequent advancements, but failure to advance in any three-year interval predicts subsequent deceleration or a plateau.[8] In addition, researchers have shown that certain low-wage jobs act as "stepping-stones" to higher-paid positions.[9] Research has described models of occupational mobility, but we know less about how credential pathways work in community college occupational programs.

Research routinely examines the impact of "years of education," but years of education does not always translate to credentials or credits earned.[10] In fact, eight years after high school graduation, only 8 percent of community college students in the National Education Longitudinal Study of 1988 (NELS:88) had attained an associate degree; another 10 percent had enough credits but no credential.[11] Similarly, tallying the number of credits earned in college inaccurately reflects education's impact in the labor market; Norton Grubb, for instance, finds that isolated credits rarely have as much labor market payoff as credentials do.[12] Thus, this chapter goes beyond years of education and number of credits earned and examines the relationship between specific occupational credentials and jobs.

Spilerman suggests that educational attainment shapes career advancement, but this happens only if students see educational opportunities.[13] Research shows that being presented with too many choices—like the numerous credential options in community colleges—leads to disappointments and frustrations.[14] In contrast, the program structures described by James Rosenbaum, Regina Deil-Amen, and Ann Person help students navigate through a multitude of choices.[15] Building on that work, Judith Scott-Clayton writes about the "structure hypothesis" and shows that a lack of structure has a negative impact on student persistence; she also warns of the disadvantages of limited choice.[16] Drawing on the structure hypothesis, we identify ways in which community colleges could illustrate the structures that link educational credentials to occupational options.

Prior research focuses on structures that exist in private occupational colleges but rarely in community colleges.[17] This chapter examines the structures underlying the relationships between two abstractions (years of education and labor market success) that already exist but are unseen. Our diagraming of these structures illustrates education pathways, occupational mobility, and the relationship between credentials and jobs for community college students.

## Method

We analyzed the websites and course catalogs of two community colleges matched on enrollment size and student demographics. Both were middle- to upper-middle-class, suburban, medium-sized community colleges. One was located in Illinois and the other in California. Focusing on programs in allied health and computer networking, we carefully examined program requirements and career opportunities to construct degree ladder maps. We make no claims about generalizability to other colleges or programs, yet these degree ladder maps do illustrate how other community colleges could construct degree ladder maps.

Although the maps in the two colleges differ in minor details, they are similar in their general features, and so we provide here only maps for two fields in one college: health information technology (HIT) and computer and support specialist. They show how degree ladders might work in different majors, and how they could be represented as degree ladder maps. We do not expect that every program's maps would resemble the ones presented in this chapter. However, these maps provide a blueprint for community colleges to follow in creating their own degree ladder maps.

## Findings

For students, picking programs and courses is a complex process that involves several steps. Before making decisions, students must know the various stages of the choice process and recognize how to proceed through each step. Without guidance, students often make mistakes, such as getting courses without credit, credits without credentials, and credentials without jobs. These mistakes cost students considerable time and money—precious resources they often cannot afford to waste. Counselors are the obvious solution to help students understand program options, but it is difficult to expect counselors to know all of the details of every program and the nuances among them or to be able to give students good information when their usual caseloads are over 1,000 students.

To make an informed choice among educational options, students need certain information: they must (1) quickly pick a major or program, since each program has a different set of requirements; (2) find out which courses are required for the program they pick; and (3) know which jobs they are being prepared for so that they can evaluate their career options as they move through their chosen courses. Students rarely have this information.[18]

Instead of compelling students to collect such information and synthesize it on their own, degree ladder maps provide them with this information. Degree ladder maps organize program options and structure credential choices into a coherent set of pathways to occupations.

## Picking a Major or Program

Most colleges claim to offer fifty or more programs, and some offer over one hundred. Although this multitude of choices provides students with many opportunities, it also complicates their decision process and indeed leaves many students bewildered. For example, students may be unaware of which certificate courses transfer to four-year colleges. In addition, students may struggle to understand the subtle differences between similar-sounding programs, such as "Computer Information Systems," "Computer Networking Systems," "Computer Applications for Business," and "Electronics and Computer Technology." More generally, students need a quick, reliable way to choose among the varied options.

By organizing options, degree ladder maps illustrate clear pathways. Instead of expecting students to choose among dozens of discrete programs, degree ladder maps arrange options within program areas, illuminating a choice process that has multiple decision points and a limited set of options at each point. For example, looking at catalog information without a map, students might feel compelled to choose between a medical billing certificate and a medical coding certificate. With a map (see figure 6.1), students can see that these are related certificates—the billing certificate can be acquired on the way to earning the coding certificate—and thus understand that they do not have to decide between the two.

Instead of choosing between all possible health-related certificates, students can use degree ladder maps to choose between a smaller selection of basic certificates first, and later decide between intermediate health certificates. Thus, students make many small choices among only a few options at each decision point. Moreover, degree ladder maps show them the short-term labor market payoffs from each program and the long-term opportunities for advancement.

Iterative decision-making reduces the chance of picking a dead-end program because the degree ladder map shows whether each choice leads to another option on the ladder. This is helpful not only for students but also for counselors, who may worry about advising students

**Figure 6.1    Degree Ladder Map for a Health Information
Technology (HIT) Program**

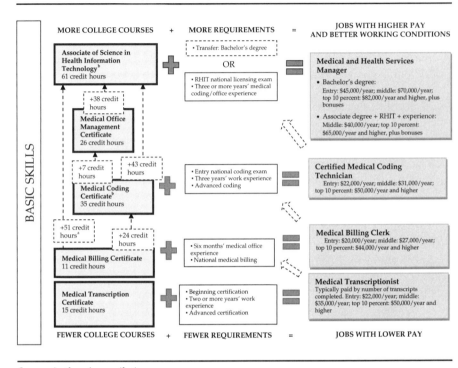

*Source:* Authors' compilation.

*Notes:* All HIT credentials at one community college are shown, but these are not the only possible combinations of experience, employment, and salaries. For more detailed information, see U.S. Department of Labor, Bureau of Labor Statistics, *Occupational Outlook Handbook*, available at: www.bls.gov/ooh. Basic skills are the foundation skills in reading, writing, and mathematics, learning skills, study skills, and English-as-a-second-language skills that are necessary for students to succeed in college-level work and future employment.

[a]To illustrate how to read the chart: a medical billing certificate plus 51 more credit hours earns an associate of science in health information technology. All eleven credit hours of a medical billing certificate count toward the associate degree.

[b]Limited enrollment program with prerequisites that include college-level biology, college-level algebra, and college-level English (or equivalents).

into a dead-end program. Degree ladder maps can help students and counselors understand the range and sequences of choices allowed in the college's program options. For example, the first column of degree ladder maps in figure 6.1 shows that seemingly isolated credentials in a course catalog can be stacked together to form a coherent program of related certificates. Twenty years ago, certificates were narrow and highly specialized, but that is no longer true.[19] Thus, an eleven-credit medical billing certificate is not a dead end but a qualification for an entry-level clerking job that pays better than minimum wage, as well as the first step on a path to an associate degree in health information technology. This ladder shows multiple steps all the way to a BA and describes specific incremental steps from a certificate to an associate degree or BA degree.[20] Thus, earning a certificate does not preclude students from continuing their studies, and degree ladder maps make it easier to plan a course of study that leads from an early certificate to a higher degree.

Increasingly, students need more than coursework to get a good job. Perhaps because the content of certificate programs can vary widely from college to college, many employers prefer prospective employees who have passed professional certification examinations or have some minimal experience for entry-level jobs. Colleges do not provide these examinations or experience, and students are often unaware that they may be at a disadvantage without them. The middle column of figure 6.1 illustrates this frequently hidden requirement. For example, a student who has graduated from a medical billing program will be in the best position to find employment if he has six months of experience anywhere in a medical office and has passed the national medical billing exam. Students who are aware of such requirements in advance are better positioned to get a good job.

Without limiting students' possibilities, degree ladder maps reduce their anxiety around decision-making by grouping similar majors together and showing how they can move between them and into employment. Instead of pondering isolated credentials that may or may not be dead-end, students can see pathways between credentials. Instead of picking one credential and program, students can see how credentials relate to one another and provide opportunities for advancement. In this way, degree ladder maps organize sequences of choices. Figure 6.2 shows a degree ladder map in another popular field—computer and support specialist.

Besides showing that picking a program does not commit a student to a lifelong decision, degree ladder maps bring order to what is otherwise a bewildering set of options that seem indistinguishable from one another. These maps benefit students by imposing a visible order and structure on college offerings.

## Selecting Appropriate Classes

The degree ladder map in figure 6.1 shows the pathways between HIT credentials but does not help students decide which courses to take. Given high student-counselor ratios at community colleges, students do not always receive guidance about course selection from counselors and

**Figure 6.2    Degree Ladder Map for a Computer and Support Specialist Program**

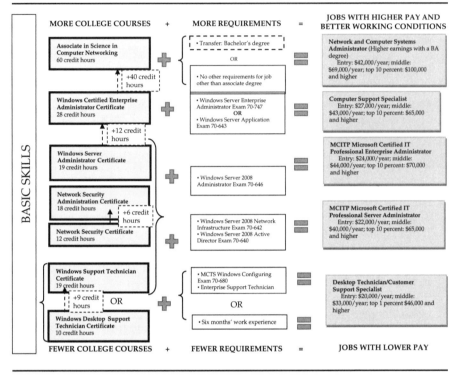

*Source:* Authors' compilation.
*Notes:* All computer support specialist credentials at one community college are shown, but these are not the only possible combinations of experience, employment, and salaries. For more detailed information, see U.S. Department of Labor, Bureau of Labor Statistics, Occupational Outlook Handbook, available at: www.bls.gov/ooh.

in fact tend to have great difficulty selecting courses that will help them make progress toward their credential.[21] This may not be a problem for traditional college students who have time and funds to take courses that do not count toward their major, but many students cannot afford to take additional courses that do not count toward their degree.

In interviews conducted at this college, students described their frustration over having to choose among confusingly labeled courses: some were called "credit" courses, some were termed "vocational" or "other" courses, and often courses were labeled with an indecipherable shorthand. When we tried to clarify these labels by calling the community college for assistance, we found that even staff members struggled to differentiate between the types of courses. This is not a criticism of staff, but simply an example of a confusing course selection process. As one student said, "It needs to be standardized. . . . I think there are too many options. . . . You can get lost." Another student worried that he had taken the wrong science class: "I've kind of figured [classes] out on my own, but I would hate to have figured it out on my own and then find out, 'Oh wait, you're forgetting something' . . . or [that] I should have taken that class instead of that one."[22] Consequently, students worry about every decision and have lingering doubts.

One student worried about a fellow classmate taking courses that would not help her progress toward the credentials she needed: "I told her if she doesn't know what [courses] she's going to take, she's going to be here forever." Another student said, "I took a class that I thought was the right kind of networking class, and it happened to be the wrong one to get. And I found that irritating."[23] Thus, it is important that students enroll in courses that count toward a first credential and understand how credits accumulate toward later credentials.

Students at this community college received course worksheets for liberal arts associate degrees, which they praised for organizing their options. One student described the associate degree worksheet as "a big list: you need a certain amount of classes from the arts, you need a certain amount of classes from the health sciences . . . and it is kind of like a checklist. . . . [You] just check them [classes] off until you have enough credit hours to get the degree." He found the worksheet to be "really convenient."

Nevertheless, even this system left crucial questions unanswered. Although students following the associate degree worksheets knew that they needed to take three science classes, they worried about which science classes would count. As one student said, "I asked for recommendations . . . [for] a science or something, and they [counselors] wouldn't really go through what would be a good fit." When students have to guess which courses will fulfill a requirement, their uncertainty can lead to costly mistakes.

We compiled detailed checklists of specific course requirements and electives for degree ladders in specific fields that students can use in tandem with degree ladder maps. Course checklists tell students exactly which courses count for each credential on the ladder, and whether courses required for one certificate also count toward later credentials. For example, figure 6.3 shows a course checklist for medical coding and medical billing certificates specifying exactly which courses students must take for each credential and which courses count for both certificates. Thus, if a student is not sure whether she wants a medical billing or medical coding certificate, she can first complete the courses that count for both, then decide as she gains more perspective. Course

**Figure 6.3    Checklist for HIT Courses That Count for More Than One Certificate**

|  | Medical Coding Certificate | Medical Billing Certificate |
|---|---|---|
| General education credits required | 8[a] | 0 |
| Core courses required |  |  |
| HIT 104 Medical Terminology 3 | Yes | Yes |
| HIT 105 Advanced Medical Terminology 1 | Yes | No |
| HIT 106 Classification of Health Data 3 | Yes | No |
| HIT 113 Coding for the Physician Office 2 | Yes | Yes |
| HIT 114 CPT Coding for the Physician Office 2 | Yes | No |
| HIT 115 Insurance Procedures: Medicare 1 | Yes | Yes |
| HIT 116 Non-Medicare Insurance 1 | Yes | Yes |
| HIT 120 Evaluation Coding in CPT 1 | Yes | No |
| HIT 121 Health Information Management 3 | Yes | No |
| HIT 123 Fundamentals of Medical Science 3 | Yes | No |
| HIT 125 Medical Billing Practices 1 | Yes | Yes |
| HIT 260 Reimbursement Issues 3 | Yes | Yes |
| HIT 270 Advanced Coding 3 | Yes | No |
| Total credit hours required for degree or certificate | 35 | 11 |

*Source:* Authors' compilation.
[a]In addition to core coursework, the medical coding certificate (but not the billing certificate) requires completion of two college-level English courses, two biology courses, two social science courses, one behavioral science course, and one fine arts course.

checklists clarify class choices for students and counselors because they are specific for each credential. Combining information from degree ladders (figure 6.1) and course checklists can help counselors support students in making quicker, more confident decisions about their immediate goals and timetables.

## Understanding Labor Market Options

Students want to know as soon as possible that there are labor market payoffs to their efforts, especially since their life circumstances may interrupt their college careers at any time.[24] Understanding the job market and knowing what jobs are available in each field is an important step toward student success.[25] Mid-skill jobs are often excellent options for community college students, but they are rarely understood. Even counselors know little about the mid-skill labor market, so they cannot give students reliable job assistance. When asked how students connect specific credentials to careers, one counselor replied, "I've got a ton of literature here that we go through, and I have things posted on bulletin boards." Such a process is haphazard and leaves some students unsure about the labor market value and opportunities for mobility in different programs. No trusted methods of learning about labor market payoffs are available to students, but degree ladder maps can show them and their counselors which jobs are associated with each credential.

Our degree ladder maps in two fields (figures 6.1 and 6.2) show the course pathways that students need to take to advance in a field and the jobs they can get with each credential. Instead of expecting students to discover the labor market payoffs of various certificates or degrees on their own, colleges can provide them with this information when they use a degree ladder map; the far right columns of figures 6.1 and 6.2, for instance, provide job information from the Bureau of Labor Statistics website. Students interested in the HIT field could use figure 6.1 to research the demand for medical billing clerks. Following the link to BLS, students could then learn what to expect in the job market with a medical billing certificate.

Finding a first job is important, but having a career also matters to students. One student said, "I can get a job. . . . But I don't know . . . if it's a *career.*" Degree ladder maps can answer that question. Figures 6.1 and 6.2 show that just as credentials can be described on a degree ladder, jobs can be arranged on a parallel "career ladder." Students can progress up the career ladder starting with an entry-level job with a short certificate.

Often occupational programs offer branching options for different types of jobs. For instance, a health program's diverse options might include certificates and degrees that lead to both work with patients and administrative work. In such a program, the degree ladder would resemble a tree with multiple branches, representing where these options diverge. Thus, even within a program, students can choose different types of work. Ladders illustrate the different opportunities available to students in a field.

Community college students report that they enroll to improve their job prospects and that they want to know that they are making progress toward that goal. Degree ladder maps can be an important resource toward this end: they show students both immediate job prospects with specific credentials and their long-term career options. Armed with critical information presented this way, both counselors and students can make more informed decisions about students' futures.

## Conclusion

Existing resources, like catalogs and websites, describe isolated degree programs but do not explain how they are related or how students can proceed from one to the next. Through painstaking analysis of course requirements in catalogs and websites, we discovered that these discrete degree programs can be put together to form degree ladders. These degree ladders reveal something that community colleges rarely mention in catalogs and websites: that they offer advancement opportunities in that some prior credits actually count toward later credentials. Moreover, degree ladders show that students, after attaining some credentials, have multiple options that could lead to alternative advancement opportunities into different kinds of jobs. In addition, degree maps often make it possible to project timetables and economic payoffs for each stage.

A remaining misconception about the worth of a certificate should be addressed. Twenty years ago, certificates were generally not required in any line of work and were often thought of as leading to narrow jobs that offered no advancement. Advisers did not learn much about them, besides these limitations. Unfortunately, our interviews indicated that some counselors still hold the opinion that certificates lead to dead-end jobs, but reality has changed in the last fifteen years. We certainly don't blame advisers; it is difficult to figure out how different credentials relate to one another as well as time-consuming to develop a representation of these connections in a simple diagram.

Although some colleges have aligned the course requirements between certificates and degrees, few advertise this to students. To guide students, colleges need to consider the numerous choices students face. If their choices were better documented and explained, students might make fewer wrong decisions and progress more effectively through the coursework. Degree ladder maps and ladder checklists can structure the choice process by limiting students' options and providing them with manageable steps to their goal.

College catalogs describe occupational credentials as discrete, stand-alone options, but here we have found that credentials can be combined to offer students multiple steps, higher degrees, and good jobs. Like physical ladders, degree ladders show the pathway from first steps to successively higher steps, although unlike a real ladder, students can "hop off" the degree ladder at any level along the way. Contrary to the stereotype that certificates and applied associate degrees are narrow and dead-end pursuits, degree ladders show the multiple pathways from certificates to associate degrees and even to BA degrees, especially applied BA degrees.

Degree ladders can offer multiple steps, smaller steps, tight stacking to make prior credits count, credential-to-credential fit to encourage further advancement, "career ladders" to better jobs, multiple pathways that provide alternative branches of study, job options and task variety, and sometimes paths to much higher degrees. In other words, degree ladders highlight many hidden alternatives that not only make students and counselors better informed about the options but also reduce the complexity of students' choices.

Degree ladder maps show the various options and timetables that colleges already offer but that students cannot easily see. Degree ladder maps may help students choose a program and form a credential plan by showing which credentials satisfy their interests and the most efficient way to combine credentials. Instead of assuming that students must choose their end goal before entering a program, degree ladders show that each starting place can lead to a variety of interim goals as well as end goals, which can be decided later as a student proceeds.

Students often worry that their early decisions lock them into a major or credential that determines their careers after college. Degree ladder maps show students the variety of decisions that can be made at any point, one step at a time, and indicate some of the options that remain open for later decisions. Rather than choosing a major for life, a degree ladder map allows them to pick only a starting place.

Degree ladder maps also illustrate opportunities to make midcourse corrections. For example, a student interested in working in a doctor's office might complete a medical office receptionist certificate in as little as one semester. If he finds, working as a receptionist, that he enjoys patient care more than front-desk work, he can apply some of his completed credits toward a related credential as a clinical assistant who gives shots or takes X-rays. To be a clinical assistant, he will need many of the skills he learned for the receptionist certificate, but the work will be more relevant to his interests. Like Spilerman, we refer to this type of midcourse correction as "branching."[26]

Additionally, program ladders can move apart and converge again at a later degree. Unlike most catalog descriptions, which portray every program credential as a separate entity, degree ladder maps illuminate connections among program credentials. In fact, ladders often show overlapping skill requirements (much like two intertwining tree branches) that allow for transitions between credentials and across programs.

The structure in degree ladder maps is valuable to colleges, which can construct cohorts of students progressing through the same courses.[27] Degree ladders can help colleges offer dependable schedules that do not include extraneous classes. Moreover, we suspect that degree ladder maps would be useful in designing future programs. They immediately raise questions about whether pathways can be made more predictable or tightly stacked, and include more steps and higher trajectories.

Remarkably, degree ladders already exist, but they are not generally seen, not even by college staff. Therefore, shifting to use of degree ladder maps would not require community colleges to restructure their programs, shuffle staff, or reconsider budget allocations. Instead, community college administrators would only need to map out the credentials and courses their college already offers. Faculty, who often know about labor market outcomes, could lend their expertise.[28] In comparison to other policy recommendations, constructing degree ladder maps is relatively manageable.

Besides having a functional purpose, degree ladders also create an opportunity structure. Structures are usually seen as posing barriers, but they also identify opportunities. Similarly, degree ladders show students many different opportunities as they make decisions and advance toward their goals.

# ═ Chapter 7 ═

## Beyond BA Blinders: Pathway Procedures Into, Through, and Out of College

C OLLEGES DEMAND a variety of culturally specific skills, knowledge, resources, and habits. Some are intrinsic to the purpose of higher education, but many are holdovers from old cultural traditions.[1] These demands are not a concern if colleges serve only traditional college students who understand these cultural traditions, and if the labor market demands only traditional academic skills. However, these demands may be outdated if colleges serve new groups of students or offer preparation for new occupations requiring other skills.

This chapter presents a general model of how colleges can construct procedures that support student success across the three transitions that pose difficulties in college. Contrary to Murray's assumption that high rates of college dropout reflect the low ability of some students, we show that student success largely depends on how colleges design their procedures.[2] Instead of blaming students for their difficulties, we examine whether their deficiencies arise partially from community college procedures and the demands they make on students.

Colleges often use traditional procedures that compel students to figure out what is required on their own. Here we examine how some private occupational colleges have constructed sociologically smart alternative procedures that match students' needs, pose fewer obstacles to student success, and even provide guardrails that keep students on track. College students experience many problems, we argue, not because they lack academic ability but because they lack cultural skills, information, and resources. Making students responsible for navigating this cultural gap is an unnecessary requirement.

In previous research, we emphasized curriculum pathways, which include organized courses, time schedules, and peer cohorts (who progress together in courses). However, now we see that pathways can be more than curriculum. In serving nontraditional students, colleges can use nontraditional procedures, among which, we discover "pathway procedures," which colleges, on their own, can devise to guide and support students' career progress at every stage in crossing the three transitions. Pathway procedures support college entry (delayed obstacles, quick successes, proximal incentives), college progress (incremental success, curriculum pathways, guardrails [monitoring and mandatory advising]), and career entry (four-year college transfer, job search). Although colleges can use other procedures to work with high schools, employers, and four-year colleges to align expectations, pathway procedures can be done by colleges on their own.

## College Transition Gaps: Courses Without Credits, Credits Without Credentials, and Credentials Without Payoffs

Reformers emphasize that colleges demand academic achievement, but colleges also require students to cross institutional transitions—that is, changes in their status as they move between institutions or within an institution. We often think of transitions as crossing a gap, moving from one solid place to another while facing the risks and challenges in between.[3] However, colleges can redesign these institutional transitions by both reducing obstacles and creating supports—like the bridge that helps a traveler traverse a ravine. We consider three specific college transitions:

1. *College entry* involves the transition from high school into college.
2. *College progress* involves the transition from college entry to credential completion.
3. *Career entry* involves the transition from community college to a job or a four-year college.

We usually envision any difficulties encountered during these three transitions as stemming from the problems of individual students in confronting an inevitable challenge, but in fact colleges shape these transitions in several ways, some of which create unnecessary barriers to students' successful transitions. We find that colleges can reduce transition difficulties by creating alternative procedures to handle transitions.

Students often report unexpected difficulties with all three transitions—they get courses without credits, credits without credentials, and credentials without payoffs.[4] In each case, students try to cross the transition, they seem to progress, but they often fail to advance. The challenges posed by each gap are not announced by the school or the larger society, and students cannot prepare for them—especially students whose family members or friends did not attend college. Instead of blaming students, we can see the roots of students' problems in the ways institutions design transition procedures.

First, the college entry transition poses challenges that make previously successful students (those who passed high school exit exams) unprepared for the college entry transition and often leads to their failure to pass the college placement exam just a few months later. This transitional failure occurs because high school standards are poorly aligned with college demands or because colleges provide poor supports—for instance, college advisers fail to warn students about transition challenges or to help them find preparation resources. As a result, students enter college buildings and pay college tuition, but find that they have registered for courses that do not offer college credits.

Second, transitions within college are difficult when students face hurdles without adequate supports. For example, students make bad choices because degree requirements are often complex or unclear. Required courses are overenrolled, not offered when needed, or offered at unpredictable times that conflict with students' other obligations. Colleges often encourage free choice, but take few steps to ensure that it is informed choice. As a result, students often accumulate credits that do not count toward their degree.

Third, career entry is difficult when institutions are poorly aligned and students do not receive good advice and information. BA-transfer students often cannot find a four-year college that recognizes their community college credits. Work-bound students may not know which jobs value their training, fit their needs, or have career potential. Nevertheless, some colleges have shown that it is possible to devise career placement procedures that inform, advise, and guide students through these processes (see chapter 8).

In short, before blaming students for failing to make these transitions, we should first examine whether colleges use procedures that pose obstacles or do not provide crucial information and supports.

## Procedures to Assist Students in Crossing Transitions

This chapter examines how some colleges have devised alternative procedures that radically transform the three transitions by reducing mistakes and failures, anticipating difficulties, and correcting difficulties quickly. We find that such alternative procedures can reduce obstacles, create quick successes, facilitate the three transitions, and offer students further opportunities.

The alternative procedures created by these colleges provide direction and dependable sequences of actions and supports that we call "pathway procedures." These procedures reduce obstacles and support students' progress across transitions. Institutional procedures can shape pathways in many ways besides determining the courses that students take: (1) how students use their time (dependable schedules, short vacations), (2) how students utilize space (nearby classes and advising), (3) students' social supports (peer cohorts, monitoring of their progress, mandatory advising, career supports), and (4) students' structured plans (incremental success, degree ladders, information on dependable career payoffs).

Comparing institutions can help us see beyond our usual views. Community colleges emulate four-year colleges in using traditional college procedures, but we find that nontraditional procedures designed to respond to student and labor market needs are used at some private occupational colleges. We begin our comparative analysis of these institutions by reporting analyses of national data that find that occupational colleges have dramatically better degree completion rates than similar community colleges, after matching comparable students.[5] Then we describe administrators' reports of seven procedures that might improve student success across college transitions, especially for disadvantaged students.

Although there is much talk of improving "institutional capability," we believe that the use of alternative procedures by college staff would reveal that such capability is already present.

## Why Study Private Occupational Colleges?

Occupational colleges—private colleges that offer career preparation in occupational fields, such as technicians, health care, and business—are accredited to offer college degrees and credentials (certificates, associate degrees, and sometimes bachelor's degrees), unlike the vast majority of private postsecondary career schools, which are not accredited. Occupational colleges are private, nonprofit or for-profit, but not selective, and they enroll large numbers of low-achieving and low-income students who are on federal and state financial aid. While some for-profit colleges are problematic and some even engage in fraud, we selected the best ones for our sample. Our aim was to learn more about their innovative procedures, which are rarely used in public colleges. Our sample represents isolated cases, and thus our findings are *not* generalizable to the entire sector. Our hope is simply to encourage public colleges to consider these alternative procedures.

Surprisingly, despite charging tuition that is five times higher than community college tuition on average, private two-year colleges nonetheless have larger proportions of low-income and minority students than public two-year colleges.[6] This is due not only to aggressive marketing by private colleges but also to the assistance they provide students in completing the complex paperwork required by federal loans and state and federal (Pell) grants. Most public colleges do not provide such assistance.

Contrary to the usual inference that poor success rates indicate that students lack the ability to succeed in college, occupational college outcomes suggest that alternative procedures reduce the perils and obvious barriers that nontraditional students usually face in traditional higher education and increase their chances for success. These observations suggest that the traditional procedures assumed to be necessary can in fact be altered.

## Findings: Comparing Completion Rates for Comparable Students

We first report studies of national surveys. In a previous study, we compared completion rates across four types of colleges using the National Education Longitudinal Survey.[7] As in prior literature, we compared student outcomes in two-year and four-year public colleges.[8] However, our analysis of the student body composition in these two types of colleges revealed that these colleges do not have comparable students, so we used the technique of propensity matching. This allowed us to compare students with similar social and academic backgrounds in different types of colleges.

We found that four-year public colleges have better completion rates than two-year colleges for students who resemble the typical four-year college student, but they have no better results for typical two-year college students.[9] In other words, if "community colleges are failing" the typical two-year college student, the same must be said for four-year colleges, which are no better at improving completion rates among these students. Simply getting community college students to attend four-year colleges will not solve the problem of poor completion rates. Similarly, getting community colleges to act more like four-year colleges will not solve the problem either.

Private occupational colleges have students who are similar to those at public two-year colleges; indeed, they are nearly identical in terms of the distribution of prior test scores, grades, and SES. Analyzing outcomes for comparable students at the two kinds of institutions, we find that students enrolled in a private occupational college are more likely

Table 7.1     Degree Completion Rates at Public Two-Year Colleges
and Private Occupational Colleges

|  | White | African American | All |
|---|---|---|---|
| Public colleges | 47% | 19% | 37% |
| Private colleges | 59 | 64 | 57 |

Source: Stephan, Rosenbaum, and Person 2009.

to graduate than those enrolled in a public two-year college, and this is true for the typical students from community colleges or occupational colleges (see table 7.1). In private occupational colleges, 57 percent complete at least an associate degree in eight years, compared with 37 percent in public two-year colleges.[10] The gap is even greater for African American students.

A more recent study found similar results. Using data from the Beginning Postsecondary Students Longitudinal Study (BPS), researchers compared for-profit college graduates and a merged category of community college and nonprofit college graduates, and they found that for-profit colleges have much higher completion rates for certificates and associate degrees.[11] Our earlier study examined a sample of students who entered college in 1992—right after new federal regulations led 1,300 private colleges to close.[12] By contrast, the BPS data were taken from a survey of students who entered college in 2004, by which time many new for-profit colleges had appeared, with new ways to evade regulations. Also, for-profit college enrollment had dramatically increased, and the students attending for-profit colleges may have been worse students than the cohort entering in the early 1990s. (Unfortunately, BPS does not have a good indicator of student achievement.) In any case, in two very different time periods, research finds comparable differences in sub-BA completion rates between private and public two-year colleges.[13]

Our goal is not to recommend these colleges, but to discover what we can learn from them. In the next section, we describe seven distinctive nontraditional procedures that private occupational colleges use to prevent some problems that students experience in community college and that may contribute to their higher completion rates.

## College Alternatives:
## Seven Nontraditional Procedures

How do private occupational colleges manage to have higher degree completion rates, even with comparable students? We analyzed program procedures in seven community colleges and seven occupational colleges in the six-county Chicago metropolitan area. Because our aim was to discover alternative transition procedures that might lead to increased student success, we purposely chose occupational colleges that we expected to be better than most, and so we must note that these colleges are *not* typical. From our close observations, interviews with college staff and students, and surveys of over 2,000 students, we discovered seven procedures used in occupational colleges that were devised to reduce specific difficulties that their students faced. Three procedures were aimed at improving the transition into college, three were aimed at improving the transition through college to credential completion, and one procedure was aimed at improving the transition into a four-year college or a job. These procedures were not followed by any of the community colleges in our sample. (See chapter 8, however, for a discussion of two innovative community colleges that have devised similar procedures.)

The three procedures to improve the college entry transition were: (1) delayed obstacles, (2) quick successes, and (3) proximal incentives. The three procedures to improve the transition through college were: (4) incremental success strategies, (5) curriculum pathways, and (6) monitoring and mandatory advising. The procedure to improve the career entry transition was: (7) career placement.

## Improving the College Entry Transition: Delayed Obstacles

Traditional college procedures frontload obstacles such as remedial courses and general education requirements. Because students are not told that many requirements can be delayed or avoided, many of them drop out of community college when they discover that they cannot master the initial challenges or that their courses do not give college credit.[14] By contrast, one nontraditional procedure is to delay these obstacles until they are required for earning a higher credential.

Although remedial courses are frontloaded in the hope that passing them will make later coursework easier, that is possible only for students who survive the remedial sequence—most students do not. Indeed, completion rates for students placed in the lowest-level remedial courses are terrible.[15] Yet students are rarely told that they are being sent on a low-odds path along which only 17 to 29 percent of students succeed. Nor are they told of alternative options with less-demanding requirements.

Contrary to the assumption that students need college-level academic skills to benefit from college, the faculty we interviewed reported that eighth- to tenth-grade academic skills are sufficient for a certificate in many occupational programs (see chapter 4). In recent research, Marc

Tucker and the team of James Stone and Morgan Lewis have found that community college courses require much lower reading and math skills than colleges typically require.[16]

Community colleges also frontload general education obstacles. Consistent with traditional college procedures, young students are told that general education is a good way to explore their interests. However, community college students report that general education does not help them explore their occupational interests. They are told that general education courses give credits for every major, but these courses do not count for many occupational majors. General education may have value on its own, but it is not without cost—taking general education courses demands time, money, and academic competencies that many students lack, thus often contributing to their failures.

In sum, college dropout occurs for reasons more complex than Murray's story about students lacking ability.[17] Largely because of cultural norms associated with BA blinders, students with low academic achievement are advised to take courses that then pose obstacles and set them up for predictable failures—all of which may be unnecessary for some sub-BA credentials.

## Improving the College Entry Transition: Quick Successes

Traditional college procedures delay students' success by requiring them either to have college-level academic skills or to take noncredit remedial courses. Nontraditional procedures do the opposite: students are offered quick successes that give them confidence that they have successfully made the transition into college classes.

Analyzing the BPS national survey that followed entering community college students over time, researchers found that 42 percent of students dropped out in the first year, 50 percent of them returned, and 53 percent of the returning students then dropped out again (and did not reenter over the next four years).[18] Despite dropping out, many students tried again, but *only 14 percent* of early dropouts ever completed a credential.

We call this the "fail-first" approach, and we contrast it with the "success-first" approach in occupational colleges, which place all students into college courses that enable them to succeed from the outset. These colleges reduce students' doubts about whether they belong in college by providing initial tasks that are engaging, career-relevant, and designed to match students' capabilities. As needed, these classes include short isolated remedial lessons, which are incorporated into occupational courses. Academic requirements increase gradually—after students gain confidence that they can succeed in college. Unlike the fail-first approach, all seven occupational colleges offered interesting and appealing tasks that gave students a quick success and quick confidence in the first weeks of college.

## Improving the College Entry Transition: Proximal Incentives

Unlike traditional college procedures, which pose a distant BA goal and provide uncertain incentives to achieve it, nontraditional college procedures offer quick credentials and job payoffs. In our community colleges, nearly all young students (under age twenty-five) reported that college advisers encouraged them to pursue the four-year BA degree and had little to say about other credentials they could be earning along the way. Our analyses of community college websites and interviews with community college academic advisers revealed a similar lack of guidance on interim credentials. Of course, advisers do not have to say much to promote BA plans, since students already get this message before they enter college—80 percent of high school graduates have BA plans.[19]

There was no lack of such guidance, however, at the occupational colleges we studied, which emphasized interim credentials that promised quick job payoffs. For students whose time, interest, and funds for college are limited and who are at high risk of dropping out on the way to a "four-year" BA that is likely to take six or more years, quick sub-BA payoffs are valuable. Moreover, the quick job payoffs from valuable quick credentials give them incentives to stick with their course of study.

## Improving the Transition Through College: Incremental Success Strategies

While traditional college procedures encourage a fail-first sequence, incremental success strategies do the opposite by encouraging students to earn interim credentials that will give them quick success on the way to a BA.

Cultural preconceptions lead community college advisers to encourage young students to pursue BA degrees, but they rarely mention alternative paths, even if they lead to the same BA goal. In addition, the counselors we interviewed reported that they did not mention occupational programs to young students (under age twenty-five)—and some even discouraged sub-BAs if students suggested them (but they did tell older students and returning dropouts about them).

Advisers rarely inform young students about the advantages of sub-BAs (quick, low academic requirements, and significant earnings payoffs). It is especially puzzling that low-achieving students are urged to seek BA degrees considering that these students have only 17 percent odds of completing remedial work.[20] The BA focus leads to predictable failures, while sub-BA credentials have higher odds of success and pay-offs, after which students can go on to higher degrees.

In contrast, these private occupational colleges equip all students with an incremental success strategy that will give them quick successes on the way to a bachelor's degree. Early courses are easy, engaging, and career-relevant. As much as possible, remedial lessons are delayed until after initial successes. Within twelve months, students can complete certificates in many fields that offer good jobs, and they can go on to work toward associate and bachelor's degrees. For students who have never done well in school, these successes provide a quick pay-off and give them confidence that they can succeed in college. After students achieve sub-BA successes, occupational colleges present them with more demanding courses and remedial content (which is often integrated into occupational courses).

Degree ladders may play a part in incremental success strategies by showing students which certificate courses count for the higher degrees (see chapter 6). Even if some credits do not count, the intervening credential they have earned assures students of job payoffs even if they do not finish the BA.

We should also point out that postponing a sub-BA credential as a backup option in case one's BA plans do not work out, though possible, is risky. After students fail at a BA plan, they have depleted their resources of time and money and are likely to have lost confidence as well. Prior research suggests that half of the students who try this "fail-first" strategy do not return to college.[21]

## Improving the Transition Through College: Curriculum Pathways

In contrast to the complex course choices navigated through traditional college procedures, nontraditional procedures offer clear curriculum pathways that structure a student's course choices, time schedules, and peer cohorts (who progress together).

Traditionally, colleges have encouraged students to "explore" and to take "electives." Instead of laying out the most efficient set of courses for their degree goal, community colleges let students make their own choices. Research shows that students who are encouraged to explore end up wasting a lot of time. In the high school class of 1992, for instance, 8 percent had earned an associate degree by the year 2000, while another 10 percent had enough credits for an associate degree (sixty or more) but no degree, and thus no labor market payoff.[22] Spending time on unnecessary courses may work well enough for traditional college students, many of whose college-educated parents can offer advice and pay for the extra semesters it takes them to finish their degree. But such latitude does not work well for the many disadvantaged students, including first-generation college students, who face time and money constraints in college.

Moreover, traditional college procedures set schedules on the assumption that classes can be offered at any time and that students will fit them into their daily schedule. Courses are plugged into a patchwork of weekly time slots that may require students to commute separately to campus for nearly every class. Course time schedules then change every semester, creating time conflicts with students' work or child care arrangements. Such conflicts rarely arise for traditional college students because college is their main occupation, not working a job or taking care of a family.

Curriculum pathways increase predictability for students as they manage their time, commute, and obligations outside of college.[23] We find that these private occupational colleges help students structure their time by offering courses in the same time slots every semester. Each semester students can fit their new courses into the weekly schedule they have already planned, and they can plan ahead across several semesters. Course offerings are also often offered back to back (so-called block schedules) to reduce students' commuting time. Thus, students do not need to rearrange day care or work hours every semester, as many community college students must do.

Curriculum pathways create positive social support by promoting peer cohorts—an entire cohort advancing together through the same courses in the same sequence, in the same times and places. In colleges that lack dormitories or robust student groups, peer cohorts provide a built-in support group. The students we interviewed at occupational colleges felt responsible to their peers in their cohort. One student reported that he had been thinking about dropping out, but he decided to stick with it because he did not want to disappoint his peers. Creating cohorts has big payoffs at little cost. One such cost, however, may be incurred for struggling students. Peer cohort support is so valued that occupational colleges offering curriculum pathways offer an additional tutorial course so that these students can catch up with their cohort. Peer cohort support is also reinforced by the frequent mandatory advising meetings for each cohort as a group.

Procedures that create curriculum pathways can quell students' fears that they will make bad choices and take extra time to complete their degree. Many community college students reported that their time in college had been prolonged because required courses were overenrolled or not available when they needed them, but private occupational college students did not have this problem, since their colleges guaranteed dependable course offerings for each cohort. If community colleges were not so preoccupied with urging all students to choose their own combination of courses, a cohort model provides predictable demand that colleges can anticipate and guarantee that required courses are available when needed. Chapter 8 describes one example of a cohort model in use at a community college.

The cultural norms of today's traditional colleges do not include curriculum pathways, but this "tradition" is actually relatively recent. Many of the most selective four-year colleges had many more requirements and even structured curricula thirty years ago. Even today's BA culture does not necessarily prevent structured curricula. The fifty-year-old Directed Studies Program at Yale University requires students to enroll in most courses together, and a few colleges (such as St. John's College in Maryland) are based on the "great books" curriculum, which specifies a fixed set of courses that all students must take during the first two years.

## Improving the Transition Through College: Monitoring and Mandatory Advising (Guardrails)

To avoid the mistakes and wasted time that often result from students making their own *free* choices, as emphasized by traditional procedures, nontraditional procedures construct guardrails—mandatory advising and monitoring of dependable progress to help students make *informed* choices.

Community college students make many mistakes that can waste their time and discourage them enough to drop out.[24] First-generation college students make mistakes because they are unlikely to receive advice from their parents, who did not attend college. Moreover, community colleges offer many courses and programs, and they have complicated rules about requirements. Students sometimes choose courses that are either too easy (adding nothing to their progress) or too difficult (risking failure), or courses that do not meet the requirements for their program, degree, transfer, or employment. They miss deadlines, they underestimate degree timetables, and some early credits expire if they do not progress quickly enough (in fast-changing fields like health services). Students do not ask counselors for advice because they are unaware that they have a problem (and also because counselors are hard to see).

Moreover, the rules are complex and confusing. The researchers in our studies, two PhDs who have been studying community colleges for many years, had great difficulty in understanding program requirements from websites and catalogs, and some of those requirements were beyond our comprehension, necessitating further inquiries. At least we knew that questions were needed and what questions to ask. The students we inter-viewed did not know that they needed to ask these questions.

Although community colleges offer advisers, students must initiate meetings with them. Many students, not realizing they have a problem, wait until it is very serious before trying to schedule a meeting. Moreover, with over 1,000 students for each community college counselor on aver-age, meetings are hard to schedule, must often be scheduled well in advance, and are brief and cursory when they do occur.

In contrast, occupational colleges implement frequent and mandatory advising (in group meetings added onto a course) and constantly moni-tor students' progress and problems. These procedures create guardrails that can dramatically reduce students' mistakes and prevent academic failure. Students are required to attend advising meetings several times each term, and since the meetings are in small groups with members of their program, the questions students ask may help the rest of the group as well. Occupational colleges also have monitoring systems that keep track of absences, grades, and teacher concerns. Using a computerized system, advisers contact any student whose record exhibits warning signs, before these problems get more serious.[25] Like pathways, these advising procedures are automatic. Also, occupational colleges locate advising offices in high-traffic areas that students pass through every day, so seeking advice is spatially simple.

Besides offering extensive academic advising, occupational colleges also offer social services to help students handle life crises. These col-leges have noticed that students are sometimes overwhelmed by major life crises, such as transportation, housing, work, and child care prob-lems, low wages, and health issues. Traditional colleges assume that such problems are rare and in any event are students' responsibility, but occupational colleges have figured out that providing social services is relatively inexpensive and cost-effective in helping students persist and complete degrees. Colleges typically pay a single staff person to provide advice about transportation (low-cost bus passes, carpooling contacts), housing (apartment listings, homeless shelters), and child care. Life crises can be overwhelming to individuals, but they are routine to social services staff, who can offer advice and resources for a quick recovery, freeing up students' time and energy for academics.

## Improving the Career Entry Transition: Career Placement

Traditional colleges expect students to search for jobs or four-year col-leges on their own, but those using nontraditional procedures provide career placement advice and assistance and form trusted links with employers and four-year colleges.

The assumption of traditional four-year college procedures is that college students do not have to think about jobs: a college degree guarantees them a good job when they graduate. That may have been true fifty years ago, but not today; nevertheless, many colleges still operate as if it were true. At the community colleges we studied, the career services office offered optional workshops in interviewing and résumé preparation. These workshops were neither required nor marketed, perhaps because the office was too small to handle many students. One career office even discouraged the student newspaper from mentioning them because the office could not handle more students. Community college career services offices rarely have connections with employers, and the only specific job information they offer is a bulletin board or website that lists miscellaneous job openings, often unrelated to program offerings at the college. In effect, the career services offered by community colleges operate under the traditional assumption that a college degree is a ticket to a good job, and college does not have to offer students anything beyond that.

One placement procedure sometimes used in occupational programs in community colleges is a mandatory internship, which they help students obtain. These internships, however, are generally not available to students in community colleges outside of the college's occupational programs. Mandatory internships contradict two traditional assumptions—that learning within the college walls is sufficient and that employers will hire students based only on their college degree. According to occupational faculty, internships offer vital professional training and provide valuable contacts so that employers get a chance to see students in action before making hiring decisions ("try before buying"). In many cases, an internship helps a student get a full-time job in the same workplace after graduation.

Private occupational colleges usually provide additional career placement services. Besides internships, some private occupational colleges make career placement services mandatory. Making these services "mandatory" is taboo in many community colleges, even though, as one faculty member said, "community college students don't do optional." In private occupational colleges, career placement services are not only required but structured in such a way as to comprehensively cover all aspects of the job search process. In contrast to community college career services workshops, which help students make prettier résumés, career placement staff in occupational colleges help students translate course titles into lists of work-relevant skills that employers recognize and value. Instead of assuming that students know how to search for and get a good job, career placement offices assume the opposite and provide extensive assistance to teach students how to find a job. Students are instructed to set up a telephone answering machine or voice mail, taught how to leave an appropriate message, told how to locate areas of strong demand relevant to their skills, and encouraged to consider a residential move, if strongly indicated, to improve their employment prospects.

Students are also told how to identify a good job, and some of the advice here surprised us. Placement staff we spoke with warned students to be skeptical of the highest-paid jobs because they often have bad job conditions (disagreeable workplace, physically demanding or dangerous tasks, few chances for advancement). Instead, these placement staff urged students to seek skill-relevant jobs that offer training because these are the jobs likely to lead to subsequent advancements. Indeed, job placement staff spend a lot of time making contacts with local employers who offer good skill-relevant jobs.

Although employers are usually skeptics, hiring managers trust job placement staff at occupational colleges because the students they send for interviews every year have a track record of becoming quality workers. Employers know that these placement staff will not mislead them about one year's group of students seeking jobs because that would undermine their credibility in future years. Although some faculty in community colleges have relationships with employers like these, they do not have time to use them very often.

Colleges can also provide support and direction for graduates seeking to enter four-year colleges. Even though some states have "articulation agreements" in which four-year colleges promise to recognize community college credits as electives, some departments in four-year colleges may refuse to recognize community college credits as credit toward their major. Students are expected to negotiate such complications on their own, but they have little information or bargaining power. In contrast, a community college we describe in chapter 8, Harper College, has pressured four-year colleges to clarify which Harper courses they honor, and Harper encourages students to attend the four-year colleges that recognize Harper's courses. Harper College has simplified the BA-transfer process by negotiating and identifying the best options for its graduates instead of expecting students to understand this complex process themselves with no assistance.

## The Sociology of Ability: Shaping Procedures to Reduce Obstacles

Contrary to Murray's one-variable model, which blames college dropout on students' limited academic ability, these private occupational colleges act as if they assume that dropout is caused by poorly structured transitions and that nontraditional procedures can improve them.[26] Even if we use Murray's language about ability, we would have to conclude that *traditional college procedures require students to have many other abilities besides academic ability*—the ability to persist long past four years to attain a college degree (when they expected it to take only four years), to withstand remedial coursework, to sort through a multitude of course offerings and figure out complex degree requirements, to know when they need counseling, and to understand and initiate a complex job search. Students may think that they know how to make college decisions, but that is rarely true, and their mistakes have serious consequences that they rarely anticipate. These occupational college procedures reduce the need for students to have these extra "abilities." Given the right pathway procedures, students do not need to endure the extensive and repeated dropout experiences that are built into community colleges' complex procedures.

Critics may argue that the attributes needed to meet these traditional demands are worthwhile, but we have never seen convincing evidence that the ability to decipher a college catalog predicts success in any occupational field (aside from perhaps college administration). Some may argue that these attributes are not really "abilities," and we would agree. These many attributes are "cultural competencies" that are strongly influenced by prior experiences, cultural know-how, cultural information, and the very specific skills learned in one's cultural upbringing.[27] The degree completion rates of occupational colleges show that colleges do not need to assume that students have these cultural competencies but instead can create systems to support students through a complex process.

More generally, we have proposed a "sociology of ability"—the idea that ability is an inference shaped by social context and thus can be changed by redesigning the social context.[28] For example, in remedial testing, the context is not immediately visible, but it includes students' "ability" to discern the incentives to do well, which colleges conceal (chapter 5). Since ability is regarded as an individual attribute that determines success in college, institutional procedures that affect college success will shape inferences about who has "ability." We find that community college procedures shape abilities in a negative way by posing unnecessary demands that impose disadvantages on individuals from some cultural backgrounds. When students encounter difficulty after difficulty, from remedial requirements to overenrolled classes to a lack of understanding of the labor market, they are likely to doubt their ability to succeed and be discouraged about trying harder or being more persistent. In contrast, as summarized earlier, Jennifer Stephan, James Rosenbaum, and Ann Person found that, among similar students, private occupational colleges have substantially higher completion rates than community college programs, and their degrees qualify them for comparable jobs.[29] It appears that occupational colleges manage to increase students' ability to succeed by implementing procedures that address specific student needs. In effect, *institutional procedures are shaping students' abilities to succeed.*

These occupational colleges not only act as if Murray's speculative concept of "ability" is less important than many other abilities (including cultural know-how), but they also make it unnecessary by using nontraditional procedures. Indeed, these occupational colleges, far from seeing "failures" as the result of individual students' ability, redesign college procedures *to reduce failures.* Instead of worrying about some unobservable student attribute (ability), they use procedures that reduce students' failures from college-imposed impediments, even making second chances automatic and penalty-free (see also the discussion of Guttman College in chapter 8).

Students might make better choices if they and their advisers were aware of these issues. Even in community colleges as currently structured, it is possible for students to create strategies to achieve quick wins and incremental success, to organize their course sequences, to seek out advisers' suggestions every term, and to use career services assistance. However, doing so requires heroic efforts on the part of individual students, and there is no guarantee that their efforts would be worthwhile if the college did not provide sufficient advisers. Rather than expect students to use their "abilities" to manage these hurdles, community colleges could adopt some of the procedures outlined in this chapter to make the process easier, more dependable, and more successful.

## Conclusion

We are impressed by occupational colleges' commitment to principles we believe in. They devise college procedures that pose fewer unnecessary obstacles to nontraditional students.

They also recognize that colleges themselves pose serious challenges as students approach college transitions, and they have designed pathways that provide structured methods of navigating college entry, credential completion, and career entry. They have improved these transitions by implementing many nontraditional procedures. Besides structuring course sequences, occupational colleges' pathway procedures can also structure students' time, use of space, advising experience, and social world.[30]

Occupational colleges design sociologically smart procedures that match students' needs. The policy emphasis on college for all has led to new kinds of students attending college. For students who did poorly in high school, college raises many doubts, and these students need a quick win to overcome their doubts. Given the desperate economic sacrifices many have made, they need a quick credential with an earnings payoff. Given their lack of clarity about college, these nontraditional students also need a clear curriculum pathway that helps them set a realistic goal and provides the most efficient curriculum sequence toward achieving it. Given students' family and work demands, these students need dependable time schedules, convenient locations, and frequent mandatory advising. Given the importance of social integration, commuter students need peer cohort supports that provide the social integration they cannot get otherwise.[31] Given the difficulty and complexity of job search and college transfer, they need aggressive college career services that guide them through difficult challenges. Occupational colleges have designed alternative procedures that respond to all of these student needs.

Occupational colleges understand that traditional college procedures are arbitrary and unnecessary to the college mission of preparing youth for productive roles in adult society. They also understand that social and economic contexts matter but are also malleable, so they design procedures to reduce barriers and improve incentives and success. Occupational colleges use ideas that underlie sociological theories, so it is inspiring and illuminating to see what happens when these theories are put into practice in real institutions.

Some caveats must be noted. We are not saying that all private occupational colleges operate this way, only that these specific colleges use alternative procedures that are rarely considered in community colleges and do not make the cultural assumptions typical of those who wear BA blinders. Community colleges are larger and more varied than occupational colleges, so they cannot offer private occupational colleges' single model exclusively. But they can use many of the procedures that occupational colleges have devised to support students' success and reduce the kinds of "abilities" needed to succeed (see table 7.2). Structured "package deal" programs would especially improve the chances of quick success for low-achieving students and provide them with a backup option if they have difficulty (as many will).

The BA degree remains an option for all students, but low-achieving students—who have only 20 percent odds of earning a BA—should be informed of their chances and told about backup options with better odds and quicker timetables for getting a first credential. Urging all students to focus on aiming high is not a benevolent policy when it forces students to fail repeatedly and still keep returning, while their time, money, and energy become depleted.

Table 7.2    Traditional College Procedures Versus Nontraditional
             Procedures Used by Occupational Colleges

| Traditional Procedures . . . | Nontraditional Procedures . . . |
|---|---|
| Defer payoffs | Lead to quick payoffs |
| Set up early obstacles (remedial courses) | Enable incremental success that delays obstacles |
| Are unnecessarily complex | Offer "package deal" pathways and preset time slots for courses |
| Leave students uninformed as they make course choices | Provide "guard rails" to help students make informed course choices |
| Encourage self-directed job search | Provide college-directed job choice and job search |
| Leave students uninformed as they make job choices | Provide job placement services to guide job choices and assist students with access to jobs |

*Source:* Authors' compilation.

In sum, for many students, community college is a long, treacherous road. Just as it makes sense to fill in holes on a dangerous path, colleges should improve their procedures by making college transitions less complicated for students. The amazing thing about our findings is that simple changes in procedures may alter opportunity structures, create clear incentives, remove obstacles, and give students confidence. After identifying the difficult transitions and the way traditional procedures work, any college can design alternative procedures that help its students succeed.

# = Chapter 8 =

## Innovative Colleges and
## Improved Transitions

C OLLEGES HAVE been around for a long time, and one of their many traditions now taken for granted is the assumption that satisfactory progress naturally occurs unless students' academic deficiencies are too great or their efforts too meager. Thus, as discussed in the previous chapter, when students falter in college transitions, the blame often falls on them, not on the institution.

Chapter 7 discussed promising procedures in use at some private occupational colleges. Here we discuss how two community colleges—Harper College in Palatine, Illinois, and Guttman College in New York City—recently redesigned procedures to guide students through the three transitions, demonstrating how public community colleges can use nontraditional procedures. Their new procedures resemble those identified as promising in chapters 5 through 7, but they have also innovatively adapted and extended those procedures. Rather than blame students for their problems, these colleges are now equipped to use nontraditional procedures to reduce their problems.

In developing pathways for students as they navigate college transitions, Harper and Guttman have devised different procedures for different settings, and that gives us a better view of their various approaches. The pathways we describe here may suggest actions that other colleges can take to improve student success by rethinking traditional procedures. Indeed, our primary goal in this chapter is to describe innovative procedures that community colleges have rarely even imagined.

Although we present a few isolated outcomes, we do not assess the effectiveness of most of these procedures. We mostly describe what was done, how new procedures were put into place, and what their purpose was. This account, we believe, will show that traditional procedures are not inevitable and will increase our awareness of alternative procedures. Although further research is needed to assess student outcomes, increasing awareness of alternative options and how they are implemented is a valuable first step. We have been impressed by how well designed these new procedures seem to be to address the kinds of student difficulties that we have seen in other community colleges. We are also impressed by these colleges' careful monitoring of student success and willingness to adapt procedures when they see difficulties. In our view, their efforts seem well conceived and well directed for supporting students through all three transitions.

## Harper College

Harper College is a public two-year college in Palatine, Illinois, that has implemented procedures to support students at all three college transitions. We spoke at length with the provost, Dr. Judith Marwick, to learn about Harper's procedures, and she commented on earlier drafts of this account. In addition, we interviewed ten advising staff members, and their reports support our descriptions of Harper procedures.

The college's president, Dr. Kenneth Ender, and Dr. Marwick have made dramatic changes to the college's procedures, basing many of those changes on prior research, including ideas described in our prior book.[1] Although we are not impartial observers, the following descriptions are straightforward reports of what we were told about Harper's recent efforts.

### The College Entry Transition

Improving college entry has been a priority for Drs. Ender and Marwick from the beginning. Capitalizing on Harper's unique position as one of the main colleges attended by high school graduates in the area, Dr. Ender met in his first week on the job with representatives from each of the twelve high schools that send graduates there. The agenda was broad and ambitious: to improve the transition from high school to Harper College by aligning standards, recognizing credits, and structuring the process to be transparent, streamlined, and dependable.

Dr. Marwick and other Harper leaders specifically sought to improve entering students' college-readiness by aligning high school curricula with the college placement exam. Instead of taking the usual approach of relying on college remedial courses to fix student academic deficiencies after they enrolled in college, these educators believed that local high schools could do a better job of preparing students for college if their academic expectations were aligned with those of the college. They believed that increased alignment between area high schools and the college would minimize the academic deficiencies that would need to be addressed when students entered college.

A critical, if sometimes difficult, component of the college's alignment efforts was including academic instructors from both Harper and the local high schools in all of these processes. When developing math preparation courses for local high schools, Dr. Marwick and her team initially faced resistance from Harper faculty, who were reluctant to work with high school teachers. After engaging with these teachers, however, and finding them to be dedicated and knowledgeable, a feeling of mutual respect and desire to improve student experiences emerged. Although the reforms took longer to implement because of the inclusion of instructors from both the college and the high schools, the results were ultimately stronger because faculty, who were largely responsible for the implementation, believed in the curricula.

*Aligned Standards*    Harper's efforts to improve college entry have taken many forms. Beginning with math testing and coursework, the college's leadership team developed a series of alignment reforms to improve entry into college-credit math courses.

*College placement exam in eleventh grade:* Harper College encourages local high schools to administer the college placement test in eleventh-grade classrooms, thus notifying juniors of how prepared they are for the Harper placement exam. Previously, high school graduates assumed that they were prepared for college after passing high school courses. However, the poor alignment of standards prevented them from knowing that passing high school courses would not automatically signal their college-readiness. By taking the college exam in eleventh grade, students and their school now know whether they are prepared for it, and if necessary, they can devote efforts in senior year to improving their preparation (see chapter 5).

*Mandatory math for all seniors:* Because only three years of math were mandated in order to graduate from high school, many seniors were not taking math. By the time they took the college placement exam, disuse had caused many of them to forget the math skills they learned earlier. They were then placed in remedial math to relearn the same skills they had mastered just a few years before. High school administrators agreed that they would best serve students by requiring math in their senior year, and they brought the percentage of seniors taking math up to 98 percent, where it is now. This and other reforms described here reduced remedial placements in mathematics by 27 percent—a huge improvement.

*Aligned courses:* The next step was to align twelfth-grade math course offerings with Harper's expectations of students' readiness for college-level courses. Working with local high school teachers, Harper math faculty developed senior year coursework that, when passed, signals placement into college-credit math coursework. Students who do not meet college-ready standards in eleventh grade do this coursework, which resembles the college's highest-level remedial math class, during their senior year. Moreover, to develop the best curriculum for the course, high school and college instructors are analyzing which students score highest on each mathematical concept; their schools will then be asked to share their curricula and teaching strategies for those specific lessons. All involved hope that this analysis will lead to a more standard and effective twelfth-grade math curriculum.

*Aligned-credit and dual-credit:* Students who meet college-readiness standards can take courses in high school that count for college credit at Harper. Some high school students do so through traditional dual-enrollment programs: they go to the college for class. However, Harper has implemented a dual-credit reform that allows qualified high school teachers to provide instruction for college-credit coursework. A review process that examines which math courses count for dual-credit in high school and college requires college faculty to work closely with high school teachers in designing appropriate and rigorous classes.

*New Specialist Role*    Entering college students need academic advising to understand requirements and develop course schedules. Reformers often assume that better advising requires hiring more counselors, which can be costly. Harper has found a less expensive way to provide additional advising supports to help students transition into college.

College counselors almost always have master's degrees in counseling, but many students who seek their assistance need specific program information, help with course selection, and scheduling advice, not psychological counseling. Dr. Marwick and her team realized that students' needs could be met by creating an entirely new advising role—what they call a "specialist"—that requires only a bachelor's degree. Harper counselors continue to help at-risk students with low grades, family difficulties, or emotional problems, but nine specialists now provide less intensive support for the many students who need it while the counseling department remains at the same size.

Harper specialists meet with all first-year students who are entering a degree program and provide them with basic information on financial aid, course requirements, and scheduling. Specialists must acquire detailed and specialized knowledge of the college's majors and courses, including their prerequisites, requirements, and career outcomes, and they must also be able to help students decide on their college goals and make plans to reach those goals. Unlike counselors, who work only during the academic year, specialists work through the summer and provide additional support to new students interested in getting a head start in college planning.

Advisers are often tempted to impress students with the wide variety of available college options, but this often leads to information over-load, confusing students and making it hard for them to make choices and develop a plan. In contrast, specialists help students develop clear college goals and plans. They are encouraged to provide "intrusive" advice—that is, to guide students toward making a clear college plan and toward anticipating the steps they will take in this plan.

*One-Stop Advising Center*    College procedures can structure physical space to improve student success. Following a national trend, Harper has created a one-stop, conveniently located registration and financial assistance center where students can go with all of their questions. Five specialists are located there to help with basic and procedural questions and to refer students who need further assistance to the appropriate office. This one-stop advising center is especially useful to entering students, but it serves all students throughout their time at Harper. The college also has plans to consolidate in one location a comprehensive center for career and academic advice and personal counseling. These one-stop centers are intended to avoid the confu-sion that arises when disparate student services are scattered across a college campus.

*First-Year Career Seminar*    Harper is now piloting a first-year seminar to help students develop career plans and detailed academic pathways to achieve their goals. Following a model developed in private occupational colleges, students with similar interests (health care, engineering, unde-cided) first take a class where they learn about a variety of career options, and then they create academic plans.[2] This process begins with a manda-tory session for newly enrolled students with a counselor or a specialist to discuss their career interests. In the seminar they are assigned to, students spend the semester completing exercises and listening to guest speakers as they learn about their various career options, about relevant college pro-grams, and perhaps more about their own interests. In some seminars, as with the course for prospective nursing students, students learn about the pathway's realities and the academic and bureaucratic obstacles (selective enrollment into health programs, long wait lists) that might confront them. Counselors and specialists visit the first-year seminar classes to advise students and create academic plans. Moreover, the course instructor, who may be a counselor or a faculty member in a specific occupational field, may informally become a point-person for students throughout their time in college.

Harper developed the first-year career seminar based on research findings that students who have created plans and specific career goals linked to their education are more likely to succeed.

In sum, Harper College seeks to reduce gaps in the college entry transition through improved alignment and advising. Alignment mechanisms allow high schools to administer the college placement test, align course standards, and recognize dual credit. The college has also improved support mechanisms by expanding advisory capacity, consolidating various advising centers, creating clear college plans for each student, and incorporating the college planning process into a full-semester course.

## Degree Progress

Like most community colleges, Harper proudly offers a rich variety of courses, but as often happens at most community colleges, students have great difficulty choosing the right courses to make efficient progress toward credentials.

Even students who are able to choose a major and who know the requirements often face obstacles. Required courses meet at times that unexpectedly conflict with other scheduled commitments. Students may have to readjust work or child care schedules every semester because of changes in course scheduling times. Faculty often do not realize that these conflicts exist and so cannot anticipate and reduce such conflicts. The new administration, noticing that students are often bewildered by the complexity of college offerings, implemented changes to address this confusion. Some of these changes—like the added specialists and the one-stop center—are beneficial for students at the college entry transition as well, as discussed earlier.

*Curricular Pathways*    Dr. Marwick and her team collected and analyzed data on student progress to credentials, then used these data to make faculty aware of the challenges to credential completion that students face, and their serious costs to students. Then, to improve college progress and credential completion in occupational programs, the school developed incentives to encourage departments to create curricular pathways for their course offerings. Some specialized technical programs have even developed simplified block scheduling (back-to-back course times), in predictable time slots every semester, which can help students prevent time conflicts well in advance. These changes seek to encourage departments to create procedures that foster dependable progress toward credentials by specifying up front, for each major, how full-time, part-time, day, and night students will move through the program.

In addition, programs with curriculum pathways are encouraged to streamline the coursework to emphasize the career outcome. As it is, the titles of many programs, especially in technical fields, are unclear because they do not align with the career for which they prepare students. Harper feels that even small changes like this can help students find the right program and progress toward credential completion.

*Early Alert System*    Harper has also implemented a new intensive advising system that identifies students whose progress might especially benefit from academic monitoring, such as students with poor prior academic records or students in special programs with GPA requirements they may not be meeting. Students are assigned to a counselor, and faculty give feedback to the counseling department. When a teacher notes that a student is not attending class or not performing up to standards, the teacher notifies the counselors, who reach out to the student and get to the root of the issue, long before midterm grades come in. These supports seem to be working. The college finds that students are 25 percent more likely to persist if they see a counselor when they are having difficulty.

Unlike critics who blame community college faculty for student difficulties—generating only resentment and no solutions—Harper College is using data to identify problem areas that are hard for faculty to see (for example, because faculty cannot track students' outcomes) and recognize systemic failures that cause breakdowns in students' progress. These systemic failures are rarely visible, but Harper has found ways to make them visible and addressed them by altering the systems. Many students' issues can be easily addressed, for instance, by modifying course schedules or increasing the monitoring of student success. At Harper, systems are altered or new procedures are designed to identify and address actual problems.

## Improved Career Entry

Community colleges offer two postgraduation options: jobs or four-year universities. Although students are responsible for guiding their own postcollege career, many have difficulty with both types of goals. Workbound students have trouble identifying jobs that value their training, and BA-transfer students have difficulty finding a four-year college that recognizes their community college credits. Alignment procedures can reduce career entry difficulties by identifying the requirements of specific jobs and four-year colleges and matching graduates to appropriate employers and colleges. Harper College has developed relationships with both types of institutions to provide guided transitions for all students.

Harper has placed the onus of identifying postcollege options on programs and majors, not just on students. If a department does not describe a program's career options, the college will not advertise it.

In this way, the college has created a strong incentive for programs to inform students about the jobs or BA-transfer options they can expect after graduating from the program.

*Jobs*   Harper's career services staff provide career entry support. Their specialized roles focus on helping students land the best jobs they can upon graduation. They also devote time to improving employer connections and developing a better understanding of what employers are looking for in job candidates. Although Harper's career services staff do not actively connect students to jobs, they work with students on résumés, interviewing skills, and appropriate job search strategies. They have developed such a strong presence on campus that students who have graduated from four-year universities come to Harper for assistance in searching for their first postcollege position.

Harper's leadership has also worked to make more connections between the college and local employers, especially the manufacturing industry. In conjunction with building a new manufacturing building on campus, Dr. Ender has worked with manufacturing employers to provide students with paid internships, which help graduates get full-time jobs.

Finally, most community colleges encourage teachers in occupational programs to help students find jobs, but Harper also gives staff time to develop relationships with local employers.

*Four-Year Colleges and Universities*   Many of Harper's students plan to transfer to a four-year college to finish a bachelor's degree, a transition that is often complicated by unspecified and changing credit acceptance procedures. The Illinois articulation agreement lists which community college courses count for degree credit at state four-year universities, but these universities have discretion to exclude these credits from meeting the requirements of specific departments. These departments can veto granting credit for any community college course that they judge to be not comparable to those in the major they offer. Because these decisions are often made anew each year, students and community colleges cannot predict what a department will decide. As a result, in spite of their efforts to plan their transfer goal and make sure that their coursework at Harper would be accepted by their next institution, many students were ending up with an abundance of general education credits, while lacking necessary credits in their major. Harper identified this as a serious impediment to student college transfer and took steps to rectify it.

Dr. Marwick and her team have begun telling four-year colleges that Harper will encourage students to apply to their college if they sign articulation agreements with Harper confirming their willingness to accept Harper graduates' credits in specific courses. In return, Harper advertises these four-year programs to their students, because it is more productive to encourage students to enter programs that honor their prior credits.

Harper's engineering program's collaboration with the University of Illinois at Urbana-Champaign (UIUC) is an impressive example of an agreement with a four-year college. Harper's engineering program is somewhat selective (but much less selective than UIUC), and it enrolls approximately fifty students who meet Harper's college-readiness standards. The program was developed by Harper's engineering faculty, who take great pride in it. Students follow a strict curriculum, are provided with extensive academic supports from faculty members, and are included in the early alert advising system described earlier. In exchange for maintaining a 3.3 GPA and meeting all course requirements, students are guaranteed admission in their junior year to UIUC's prestigious engineering program. Although a cohort has yet to complete the whole program, the first cohort of students has been highly successful in their junior year. Other community colleges have similar agreements with UIUC, and according to reports from UIUC, Harper's graduates are among the strongest academically.

Other examples of articulation agreements with four-year colleges include one that Harper has with Roosevelt University, which guarantees admission to pharmacy students with at least a 3.0 GPA in required courses. Northern Illinois University has agreed to accept Harper's graduating business students at junior-year status. These agreements are critical because they allow students to make dependable plans and they reduce the stress, failures, and wasted time students typically experience in the transition into a four-year college.

## Guttman College

Described by the *New York Times* as "a multimillion-dollar experiment in how to fix what ails community colleges," Stella and Charles Guttman Community College of the City University of New York (CUNY) is an entirely new community college. The design of its academic structure and curriculum was based on research on community college procedures. Guttman's goal is to improve students' chances of completing their associate degrees and entering the workforce or transferring to four-year colleges. To meet these goals, Guttman has developed reforms to improve all three transitions.

CUNY had already conducted one pioneering reform: its Accelerated Study in Associate Programs (ASAP), launched in 2007, is a comprehensive program designed to help more low-income students graduate and do so more quickly. Using many suggestions from our prior research, ASAP requires entering students to attend college full-time and encourages them to graduate within three years.[3] The program provides enhanced career services, tutoring, and comprehensive mandatory academic advising twice per month. ASAP offers back-to-back course schedules in the first year and a seminar course covering study skills and goal-setting. The program provides a tuition waiver and free MetroCards for use on public transportation, as well as free use of textbooks.[4]

In a random-assignment study, ASAP nearly doubled graduation rates, decreased dropout rates, and increased the credits earned (to forty-eight credits in three years, nine credits more than the control group). By the end of the study, 40 percent of the program group had received degrees, compared with 22 percent of the control group. At that point, 25 percent were enrolled in a four-year college versus 17 percent of the control group. At the three-year point, the cost per degree was lower in ASAP than in the control condition because ASAP generated so many more graduates, despite the substantial investment required to operate the program. ASAP's effects are impressive. The model offers a highly promising strategy, especially for educationally and economically disadvantaged students.

Guttman College took these reforms and added many more. Most colleges, like Harper College, are constrained by the need to create reforms within the existing college. This limits their options for innovation, and reformers must persuade faculty to consider the proposed alternatives. In contrast, Guttman was designed from the ground up, the product of a mandate to create a new college with substantially better degree completion and to use any procedures appropriate to achieve that goal. This mandate led to some fairly radical (for community colleges) administrative procedures and requirements. Advocates of traditional community college practices have criticized Guttman, but the faculty who chose to work there have been enthusiastic about its goals and procedures. Indeed, they have devoted extensive efforts themselves to developing and implementing Guttman's design elements.

Although Guttman's founders were afforded much freedom in the design of their college, it still must fit into the CUNY system. Operating in New York City, Guttman is one of many colleges serving the many city high schools and a vast variety of four-year colleges. As a single college within a large system, it lacks the leverage to change the practices of the high schools or four-year colleges, as Harper has done. Moreover, like other colleges in the CUNY system, Guttman and its staff are devoted to an emphasis on academic programs and BA transfer.

Like other community colleges, Guttman is nonselective, and it enrolls many students with poor academic records, including those who made bad grades in high school and even high school dropouts who later completed GEDs. Yet the admissions process makes sure that students are committed to the Guttman model, which requires that students be enrolled full-time, choose one of five majors, and accept a highly structured curriculum with short breaks. Guttman offers only five majors: business administration, human services, information technology, liberal arts and sciences, and urban studies. Students are organized in cohorts within each major. Entering students are also made aware of the college's distinctive features, as well as its possible benefits (block scheduling, peer support, close advising and monitoring).

Guttman is using many procedures we advocated in our prior book, and James Rosenbaum is on the Guttman advisory committee, so clearly we are not impartial; nevertheless, we have distinctive access to understanding what Guttman is doing. Moreover, we have a sincere desire to understand how these procedures work in practice, and thus our description is as objective as we can make it. In any case, our goal is not to evaluate but to describe Guttman's procedures and their implementation.

## A Radical Redesign of College Procedures

Guttman is distinctive in designing procedures to ease student transitions, particularly the middle transition—dependable progress through college. Like most community colleges, Guttman enrolls primarily students with low academic achievement. Most students had a C average in high school, and few are proficient in math, reading, and writing, according to the CUNY placement exam. Nearly all students are low-income and eligible for Pell grants. Like most colleges, Guttman seeks to teach higher-level skills (speaking, writing, analysis, critical thinking) and prepare students for professional careers.

As mentioned, colleges rarely have the luxury of starting from scratch, and most community colleges attempt to set these "college goals" by emulating traditional four-year college procedures. Moreover, even when administrators are eager for change, their existing institution is likely to be using traditional procedures. These procedures were not built for low-income students and students of color, who populate most community colleges, including Guttman and Harper. Harper must operate within the confines of these traditional expectations, but Guttman has had the freedom from the outset to question and reinvent many traditional procedures used by community colleges.

Guttman has created alternative procedures designed to reduce failures, especially for disadvantaged students. These procedures are unconventional, and they may contradict some observers' expectations of college. Yet they are consistent with the larger goals of higher education, and they may support greater completion rates.

## The Early Evidence

Early evidence is encouraging. An early study reports that 28 percent of the first cohort graduated within two years, and 49 percent graduated within three years, compared to an overall CUNY graduation rate of 4.1 percent within two years and 16.8 percent within three years.[5] The study also reports that Guttman's first-year retention rate was higher than that in all other CUNY schools.

Tracking students who transfer to CUNY senior colleges, Guttman has found that "86 percent of such students in its first cohort earned a C average or better. In a survey administered to students who graduated in August 2014, only a slight majority of graduates (58 percent) said that they spent more time at their senior college completing homework than they did at Guttman (which the researchers infer to imply roughly equal rigor)."[6] Anecdotally, researchers note that "the small number of alumni we interviewed report that the number and difficulty of writing assignments was greater in [first-year courses] than in their courses at the senior colleges they now attend."[7]

Here we describe many of the nontraditional procedures that Guttman has implemented. Like Harper, Guttman has grounded these procedures in our recommendations, including those described here with respect to private occupational colleges.[8]

Guttman's designers identified barriers that pose difficulties for students and designed nontraditional procedures that seek to reduce or overcome those barriers. Here our goal is to describe these nontraditional procedures and their underlying goals. These alternatives can help other colleges question their traditional procedures and consider ways to reduce barriers to student success. These nontraditional procedures are intended to create dependability and continuity and are largely aimed at improving graduation rates.

## College Entry

*Summer Commitment*     Students are required to attend a group information session and an individual information session in the winter before they apply. This ensures that they understand and agree to the Guttman model and its expectations.

After deciding to enroll by May 1, students pay a $100 commitment fee. Guttman has also created activities to keep students in the "academic mind-set" to reduce what researchers have described as "summer melt" (student attrition over the summer before college).[9] In May and June, Guttman organizes social events at the college, where students are encouraged to think about their college program and make social contacts. In July students attend an orientation meeting, and in August they attend the "Summer Bridge" program, which aims to provide them with skills, engagement, and short-term success on a group project. This activity develops a sense of involvement, accomplishment, and ability to succeed in college. Summer Bridge has been used by other community colleges and high schools and shown to be effective at engaging students early.

*Cohorts*   Students are randomly assigned to cohort groups before Summer Bridge, and these groups continue through the entire first year. Cohort members provide information and support to each other. "No one goes alone" is the goal of cohort groups, which gives students the message that everyone is in this together. Students report that cohort members provide important support, particularly in overcoming difficulties.

Cohorts, though common in graduate programs and some undergraduate programs, are not typical in community colleges. When community colleges do create cohorts, they often last just one semester, providing what seem to be only temporary benefits (like the "learning communities" at Queensborough Community College).[10] In contrast, private occupational colleges create cohorts that stay together for the entire progression toward a degree. Guttman's cohort structure falls in the middle: lasting for at least one year, it begins with the Summer Bridge program. At the end of the first year, students move into their major and form new cohorts with students who are in their program of study. Guttman staff, remaining aware of the possible discontinuities created by this transition, continue to refine this aspect of the model. They are particularly concerned with maintaining continuity of advising as students are handed off from first-year student success advocates to career specialists in the second year.

*Basic Skills Development*   As in most community colleges, many of Guttman's entering students do not meet all academic standards. Guttman avoids prerequisite sequential remedial courses, however, because of the extensive literature that shows it is not effective. Instead, basic skills development is integrated as needed into substantive college-credit courses. In particular, isolated basic skills lessons are added to a college-credit course in statistics and a course called "City Seminar I." Incorporated this way, these lessons seem more relevant to students' college coursework and career goals and less like irrelevant obstacles. Guttman's procedures for basic skills development are similar to procedures we have noted in private occupational programs (see chapter 7).

*Extensive Advising*    At community colleges, each counselor often serves 1,000 students or more, and so advising is often minimal. In contrast, Guttman reduces the student-counselor ratio (seventy-five-to-one in the first year) and mandates advising sessions, including ninety-minute weekly group advising facilitated by a student success advocate. This time counts toward a college-credit course called "Ethnographies of Work."[11] Given the crucial importance of the first days of college, advisers begin contacting students from the outset and continue doing so throughout the year.[12] Guttman also increases advising resources by encouraging instructors to serve as mentors and providing a peer mentor program.

*Career Planning*    Most community colleges do little to guide career planning, and even their minor efforts do not begin in the first year. Colleges typically assume that students will quickly and automatically figure out their career plans and the appropriate major. That rarely happens, however: college students often change majors many times before graduation. In four-year colleges, students may spend up to two years deciding on their plans. However, for two-year college students, who do not have the same luxury of time, such changes present important setbacks and add to the time needed to complete a program. Community colleges rarely allocate any staff time for assisting students with career decisions.

Guttman offers two first-year courses called "Ethnographies of Work I" and "Ethnographies of Work II" as part of the required first-year core curriculum (which also includes a statistics course and "City Seminar I"). "Ethnographies of Work" is designed to assist students in making career and degree plans. They learn about possible careers that might interest them, do research on these careers, visit worksites and interview people in the field, analyze what college programs lead to these careers, give a final presentation, and discover a variety of career options in listening to classmates' presentations. Most community colleges promote students' free choice but do little to assist their *informed* choice. Guttman's first-year course helps students make informed choices about careers and programs. Faculty report that students making choices after taking this course are more likely to stick to that choice for the rest of their time at Guttman.

## College Progress and Multiple Pathways Procedures

Guttman has focused on creating dependable college progress to degree completion with highly structured pathways, such as a preset sequence of courses.[13] Pathways also structure other aspects of college: structured time schedules (dependable time slots every term), structured space (first-year classes in one location, one-stop advising in a single nearby location), structured advising (regular mandatory meetings), structured social supports (peer cohorts), and structured progress (continual monitoring and support).

*Time*    Time is especially important in the Guttman model. Since many community college students have many potential time conflicts (from work or family) and time is scarce, structured procedures can help them fit college into their busy lives. Guttman constructed pathway procedures not only for specific courses but for structuring time in several ways.

*Short vacations:* The long college summer vacation is a sacred tradition, but it increases the risk of dropout, especially for disadvantaged students who have fewer resources and are more likely to be confronted with crises during breaks. Vacation is unstructured time that interrupts the continuity of studies and increases the risks of distraction and dropout. Shorter vacations reduce these discontinuities and their associated risks.

*Full-time enrollment:* Community colleges have traditionally encouraged part-time students, but Guttman requires full-time enrollment in the first year. Part-time studies can lead to unintended consequences that increase dropout risks, such as outside obligations that limit students' availability, and create a loss of momentum and continuity.[14] Moreover, a curriculum that includes part-time students is often scheduled in widely scattered time slots (early morning, late night, weekends) that make full-time studies difficult. Indeed, students who are free to commit to full-time enrollment may be under the impression that part-time study is just as good, not realizing the added risks. Despite common arguments that all community colleges should offer part-time studies, Guttman's designers believed (based on research) that part-time studies would reduce the continuity and engagement they were striving to create. Students who want to study part-time can do so at other CUNY colleges.

*Predictable course schedules:* Schedules that are consistent across terms and years enable students to anticipate their college time commitments and schedule life demands around them. With classes scheduled back to back and in the same time slots every term, commuting time is reduced and efficiency is increased. As one student reported, "The block schedule helps to organize the rest of my life."

*Structured Curriculum Pathways*    As noted earlier, Guttman offers only five majors—business administration, human services, information technology, liberal arts and sciences, and urban studies. These majors were carefully selected. Each program specifies its required courses for each semester. Unlike some other community colleges, Guttman never surprises students by requiring courses that are not being offered when needed or excluding students because they are overenrolled. Nor do Guttman students mistakenly enroll in a course that does not count for their program.

The usual free choice model with myriad electives does not give students enough information to make informed course choices, so they make mistakes that lead to extra semesters spent in school. As in private occupational colleges (see chapter 7), Guttman's structured course pathways essentially eliminate this possibility.

*Monitoring Students' Progress*    Guttman's "Starfish Early Alert" system enables advisers to reach out to students who are showing the first signs of difficulty. Three cohorts of twenty-five students are organized into a "house" of seventy-five students that shares the same instructional team comprising faculty, a student success advocate, library staff, and graduate coordinators. Using the Starfish Early Alert system—which was rolled out in the fall of 2015—this instructional team meets for ninety minutes a week (of faculty compensated time) to review the progress and challenges of students in their house. The early alert system enables and facilitates their communication with students who are at risk as well as with students who are doing exemplary work. In the first year, the student success advocate is the main point of contact, besides faculty, with students.

*Many Second Chances*    Giving students multiple second chances is a fundamental part of the Guttman culture. Students are told that their past does not matter and their prior grades are not an obstacle to high expectations—they will still succeed if they follow the requirements and make an effort. While most colleges offer tutoring, Guttman encourages the attitude that tutoring is a normal academic activity, and faculty and advisers are quick to recommend it. They seem to have succeeded in reducing the stigma around tutoring.

*Catch-up Term*    Like two other CUNY colleges (LaGuardia and Kingsborough), Guttman breaks up the traditional semester schedule of two fifteen-week semesters (with a six-week summer session) into two twelve-week semesters and two six-week terms. The short six-week terms provide a chance for students who did poorly in the first twelve-week term to master concepts they missed the first time and stay on track if they pass. This structure also encourages students to take courses over the summer (in the six-week spring II summer session), as over 80 percent of freshmen do. Finally, these shorter six-week and twelve-week sessions help students focus their attention on a few subjects. Breaking up the academic terms this way also has the advantage that if life events require a student to drop out, he or she forfeits less time and can more quickly return in a new semester.

This "second chance" short term is similar to the small makeup courses that occupational colleges offer to students who did not pass a course in the previous term. Having a "catch-up" term creates a culture of success for all. In such a culture, taking more time to succeed carries no stigma. Failure is quickly reversible, and students are given many second chances. Given the value that U.S. society places on second chances, especially in education, it is surprising that this kind of second-chance program is so rare.

## Career Entry

*Designing Programs to Meet Labor Market Needs*  Having restricted its offerings to only five programs, Guttman was careful to choose five majors that lead to careers with high demand and a good future. Careful labor market analysis takes time, and few community colleges have the resources to devote to this important activity. Although Guttman encourages all students to pursue BA transfer, it also strives to make sure the associate degrees it offers have value in the labor market. Guttman is not unusual on this point. CUNY and the New York State Department of Education require that all program proposals include labor market analysis and justification, along with a demonstration of student interest. By offering only a few programs, Guttman may be able to put more time into studying each one.

*Designing Career-Relevant Courses and Experiences*  Careers and the city are major themes in the Guttman curriculum. The Summer Bridge program focuses on urban issues, which often are related to occupations. Ethnographies of Work I and II are first-year required courses. Service learning and other forms of experiential education are valued and structured into the curriculum whenever possible. City and state work sites are common destinations for field trips, and the mayor's office is very supportive.

*Four-Year College Transfer*  As part of the CUNY system, Guttman has articulation agreements with several four-year senior colleges, and the fact that they are in the same system may facilitate alignment. The "Pathways Common Core" curriculum recently instituted by CUNY facilitates the recognition of transfer credits, both with and without a degree in the system. When in rare cases credits are not recognized, advisers warn students and suggest strategies for being prepared.

Guttman is striving to create cohort support—in ways similar to the national Posse Program in selective universities—in each of the major four-year colleges to which many Guttman graduates transfer.[15] Besides organizing peer cohorts among students entering Guttman, Guttman is also planning to organize new peer cohorts of graduates who attend the same four-year college in order to provide them with supports as they adjust to four-year college. This work is now in progress; foundation support and the cooperation of community and senior colleges in heretofore unique partnerships are likely to be required if this program of cohort supports is to succeed.

## Conclusion

In our prior book, based on our observations of private occupational colleges, we speculated that various procedures designed by these colleges to improve student success could also be implemented in community colleges.[16] Harper and Guttman Colleges have now implemented many of these procedures. The two colleges have very different contexts, and they have emphasized different procedures. Harper has taken extensive steps to improve alignment with high schools, employers, and four-year colleges, and it has taken some important steps toward improving college progress. Guttman has focused more on procedures to improve college progress, but it has also taken important steps toward improving college entry and career entry. Here is a summary of these efforts by the two colleges:

Harper College:
  *College entry:* Improvements in high schools' alignment with Harper (mandatory math for seniors, eleventh-grade pretest, aligned course offerings, aligned dual credit), new specialist role, first-year career seminar
  *College progress:* Incremental success (certificate–associate degree–BA), curriculum pathways, block scheduling, predictable time slots, intensive advising, monitoring progress
  *Career entry:* Aligned standards, career entry support, more solid connections between Harper and local employers, more articulation agreements with four-year colleges to recognize Harper credits

Guttman College:
  *College entry:* "Quick win" Summer Bridge program, avoiding remedial obstacles, mandatory full-time studies in first year, first-year career planning course

*College progress:* Multiple pathways procedures—prescribed course sequences, dependable time slots, peer cohort supports, short second-chance term, short vacation, frequent mandatory advising, monitoring progress, and incremental success

*Career entry:* "Ethnography of Work" course (observations and practicum work experiences, articulated credits), aligned standards, career entry support, articulation agreements with four-year colleges

Although each item listed here is a separate reform, all share the same process. They are designed to create dependable student progress across transitions by coordinating standards, time, space, and social supports to ensure that every step they take counts toward their goal, will have recognized value, and will be supported by peers and advisers. In its linkages with high schools, employers, and four-year colleges, Harper takes the lead in setting the standards and working with other institutions to ensure the success of its students. Guttman has developed unique structured programs that clarify and support transitions and reduce many opportunities for failure along all three transitions.

Some of these reforms, such as high school mathematics alignment, are fully operational and have shown some success. Other reforms are still being piloted or are in planning and development stages. The accounts given in this chapter show us how transitions can be either redesigned in an existing college or constructed from the ground up in a new college.

Joshua Wyner has described a few of these reforms, but his description gives the impression of isolated procedures aimed at different goals.[17] However, these reforms are likely to be more coherent, clearer, and more supportive of success if they are not approached in isolation but rather are treated as part of a larger reconceptualization and reshaping of the college experience. Unlike isolated niche reforms, which may not be integrated with students' prior education or their plans for future studies, the reforms at Harper and Guttman target all aspects of college and seek to create a seamless coherent pathway across all three transitions. Moreover, these colleges' efforts to integrate their reforms with surrounding institutions have improved transitions not only within the colleges themselves but also between high schools, the community colleges, jobs, and four-year colleges.

These various reforms all aim to reduce gaps in the three college transitions and create smooth structured pathways that lead to dependable progress and enable students to face fewer obstacles and make more informed choices. Transitions inevitably create challenges, but institutional procedures can reduce the gap and make successful transitions more likely.

## The Sociology of Ability: Changing the Rules on Failure

As discussed in previous chapters, when students fail in college, the usual inference is that their own "low ability" is responsible. Guttman and Harper Colleges use many procedures designed to reduce students' mistakes and prevent failures. These colleges take responsibility for failures, take steps to reduce them, and thus question the inference that failure is always a matter of low student ability. Many student mistakes are prevented by pathways, and any problems students are experiencing are caught quickly by frequent monitoring and advising before problems lead to failure. Academic shortcomings are addressed as needed to prevent failures. Time requirements are stipulated at the outset in predefined time blocks and do not change every term, and the requirement that students be enrolled for full-time study is intended to reduce failures from outside demands.

Most dramatically, Guttman and Harper *change the rules about failure.* As we have shown elsewhere, education often operates like a tournament.[18] As in a tennis tournament, a college failure eliminates the individual from the competition, with irreversible consequences: failures are final. Many students do not return, and those who do often enter different colleges or programs.[19] However, as in a tennis tournament, any success is tentative—individuals go to the next level of competition, where some will fail. Success at any stage may turn into failure at the next stage.

Guttman reverses this sequence. Unlike a tournament, where success is tentative and failures are final, at Guttman, *success is considered inevitable,* even if delayed, *and failure is tentative.* This is clearest in the design of the two-part semester, which allows a first-term failure to be followed by a second chance for success at the same course in the next term. The first failure is tentative, not final, and a second chance is immediately available. In Japan, school failure is not considered to indicate low ability, but only that more effort is needed.[20] The same is true at Guttman: failure indicates the need for more effort, and a new opportunity is immediately available.

Ability is an inference based on performance in a particular context. Guttman has designed a radically different context that makes failure temporary and subject to change. It gives students more chances to succeed. Because Guttman creates conditions that support success, ability becomes a more likely inference.

Harper College has taken another approach to changing the rules on failure. Harper strives to reduce college entry failures by clarifying expectations and helping high schools prepare students to meet those expectations. Instead of fixing academic failures after college entry, Harper has helped high schools prevent those failures before entry. Dual credit goes further by creating college successes before college entry.

Harper has also clarified the career entry process. Instead of leaving everything to the student and blaming them if they take community college courses that do not count for credit at four-year colleges, Harper strives to reduce those mistakes by clarifying which four-year colleges recognize Harper courses for credit in which majors. Choosing the right courses is a task of overwhelming complexity that no individual student should be expected to do alone. Harper has taken that task on itself. Similarly, Harper has worked with local employers to clarify their needs and how Harper courses can educate students to meet those needs.

These two colleges have implemented reforms that reconceptualize community college. Instead of assuming that student ability determines their college success, these colleges assume that students can show greater ability and be successful if college procedures are more support-ive. Instead of assuming that students must figure out for themselves the complex demands of employers or four-year colleges, these colleges have taken responsibility for imparting that information and devised procedures to specify what is needed.

These two community colleges have taken their responsibility for student success seriously and thoughtfully designed college proce-dures that create easy second chances, reduce confusing demands, and provide various kinds of support. These are not just isolated reforms; they broaden our conceptions and expand our awareness of alternative options and procedures.

# ═ Chapter 9 ═

## The New College Reality:
## Alternative Options
## and Procedures

AMERICAN SOCIETY is facing serious problems that an improved college-for-all policy could address. The middle class is being hollowed out by the offshoring and automation of jobs, and many youth cannot see pathways to productive adult roles. Blocked opportunities lead to desperation and political backlash among non-college-educated young adults and their parents. One likely cause of this discontent is a narrow vision of college that poses unnecessary obstacles to college success. In this book, we have presented a broader vision of the many possible paths to college success and middle-class careers.

In a series of studies, we have described how this broadened vision of CFA creates a new college reality by expanding access, warning students about the low odds of attaining a BA degree, offering valuable sub-BA options, creating degree ladders, avoiding "cooling out," reducing SES and academic obstacles, helping students discover their abilities, and providing alternative options and procedures that support degree success, good earnings, and valued job rewards. Indeed, by constructing pathway procedures, this type of CFA policy can reduce mistakes, and by emphasizing alternatives, it expands desirable options. These elements are new features in colleges, and they expand opportunity beyond traditional ideas of college success.

With 90 percent of high school graduates entering college, access is no longer the major problem. Indeed, college-going has become almost automatic, an expected activity for nearly all youth. Compared to prior decades, that is an impressive achievement. Yet, as it stands, CFA offers false hopes for many youth. The most frequent outcome for students who enter community colleges is no credential and no job payoff. Students sacrifice time, tuition, and forgone earnings, but with nothing to show for it, these sacrifices simply leave them further behind, with disadvantaged students being harmed the most. The new college reality can change these

151

outcomes and provide systematic ways to rebuild the middle class, meet skill demands, and help youth become productive adults.

## The New College Reality: Principles and Practical Actions

To reduce inequality, we must understand what college for all really entails. Instead of blaming students' difficulties on poor academic preparation, we find that students' problems also arise from widespread misconceptions and unsupportive institutional procedures. Looking at many of our findings, we find it incredible that these alternative options and procedures are not already standard practice. Instead of blaming students, there is so much to be gained by turning to these alternatives.

We find six principles that broaden our views of the new CFA reality. Each suggests practical actions that can improve students' college success and career outcomes.

## Alternative Options: Beyond One-Dimensional Success

CFA expands college opportunities by offering diverse options, but this diversity is poorly understood and poorly utilized. Contrary to traditional views, CFA may not always require "college-level" skills and progression toward a BA degree but instead can create quick credentials that lead to high earnings, nonmonetary job rewards, and even higher degrees later on. This view is bolstered by our interviews with occupational faculty, whose broad views of student competencies, credentials, and job rewards are rarely noticed (chapters 2 to 4).

In broadening requirements, rules, job outcomes, and credential sequences, CFA can go beyond "moving the needle" on success to offer many different successes, not just one. Instead of limiting our idea of "success" to one-dimensional academic skills, BA degrees, and earnings, we have seen that sub-BA credentials provide desirable alternatives to all three, and they do not favor high SES or high academic skills. The one-dimensional model is useful for research, but it makes a poor model for students and colleges. Many students see traditional college goals as out of their reach, and they are unnecessarily discouraged. They do not see the alternative credentials and significant job payoffs that they can dependably attain even with low academic skills. This book has shown that students can choose among many alternative options, combine credentials, create backup options, and choose incremental strategies that gradually lead to success, one step at a time, with less chance of total failure.

## Beyond BA Blinders

Educators should warn students about the low odds and long timetables (six or more years) associated with BA degrees and inform them about sub-BA backup options. The college advisers we interviewed did not inform young students of the value of sub-BAs, which have high odds of success, bring high earnings and job rewards, and enjoy high employment rates. Many of those with a sub-BA also go on to earn a higher degree.[1] The strongest argument for encouraging students to get a sub-BA is that nearly half of community college students have no credential and no earnings payoff eight years after high school, despite large sacrifices.

Incremental success strategies let students retain their BA plan, but combine it with other credentials. Students can pursue a high-odds sub-BA credential on the way to a later BA degree, reducing the risk of no payoff. Even if their college plans are interrupted before they complete their BA degree, students who have persisted long enough to attain a certificate or associate degree receive significant payoffs compared to how they would fare with only a high school diploma. The dramatic growth and increased value of certificates in particular could radically increase opportunity.

For students who anticipate academic challenges or high risks of interrupted schooling, a college certificate program makes a good career start in many fields. These programs pose few obstacles, have short timetables and low achievement requirements, provide significant earnings payoffs, and often lead to good jobs, including some with nonmonetary job rewards. In our society, low SES and low academic achievement significantly reduce an individual's odds of attaining a BA degree, but these disadvantages do not reduce certificate success or earnings among certificate graduates. Pursuing an incremental success strategy may increase the time it takes to attain a BA degree, but it greatly reduces the risk of getting no credential and no payoffs.

Americans already practice incremental success strategies in a variety of domains, most commonly in the workplace, where we talk about moving up a "career ladder" step by step. There is no reason to treat college differently. The growing numbers and value of sub-BA credentials make incremental success possible. In addition, applied BA degrees may make more streamlined incremental success possible in some occupational fields.[2]

## Beyond "College-Readiness"

College-level academic skills are helpful, but students do not need them to benefit from college. Although academic test scores predict degree completion and earnings among BA graduates, test scores do *not* predict completion or earnings among certificate graduates. In fact, occupational faculty reported that eighth- to tenth-grade academic skills are often sufficient. Rhetoric about the need for "college-level academic skills" gives many students a false sense of blocked opportunity when in fact they can benefit from college.

The myth that students must be "college-ready" to succeed in college leads colleges to assign many students to remedial courses that are unnecessary for some sub-BA goals. It is said that "developmental mathematics is where aspirations go to die."[3] We agree, but the harm may also occur earlier. The euphemism "developmental education" and its procedures prevent students from preparing for the placement test, understanding remedial courses, or avoiding testing and remediation entirely by starting with a certificate program. Remedial courses would be less of an obstacle to students if colleges used better remedial test procedures or informed students about sub-BA programs that did not require that they pass remedial exams.

## Beyond Earnings

Our society focuses on high earnings, but seeking high-paid jobs is often a poor strategy, since high pay sometimes indicates dangerous, strenuous, or unhealthy working conditions or a dead-end job. Although they may not anticipate this while still in college, young adults' job satisfaction is more strongly related to nonmonetary rewards, such as autonomy and career relevance, than to high pay. Educators should help students see that certificates and associate degrees can lead to nonmonetary job rewards, better career futures, and even better health (chapter 3).

Counselors cannot provide such information when they have 1,000-student caseloads. Alternatively, colleges can provide detailed career information in courses, as both Guttman and Harper Colleges do.[4] Also, policymakers should be wary of evaluating colleges solely on the basis of graduates' earnings; such evaluations create incentives for colleges to send youth to dangerous or unhealthy jobs just because they are well paid.

## Alternative Procedures and Structured Pathways

Society needs to provide dependable pathways into productive adult roles for each new generation, and youth want that also.[5] Apprenticeship accomplishes this important goal in other nations and in a few programs in the United States.[6] In this country, many of us expect colleges to prepare youth for productive adult roles, but colleges do not have dependable success with this. As it stands, college students face barriers at each of the transitions identified in this book: they get courses without credits, credits without credentials, and credentials without payoffs.

Although reformers like choices, many students told us that they wanted, not more choices, but dependability—of access, progress, and career payoffs. Besides crafting courses, pathway procedures can also design supports across the three transitions, creating this dependability by structuring these other aspects of the college experience:

Time schedules (dependable time slots every term)

Space (all first-year classes in one location, one-stop advising in a single nearby location)

Advising (frequent mandatory meetings)

Social supports (peer cohorts)

Progress (continual monitoring and support)

## Beyond Required Remedial Courses

Despite scarce resources, community colleges often devote enormous resources to remedial courses, which try to repair students' academic deficiencies after they arrive in college. Such courses are not dependably successful, and students pursuing sub-BA credentials can often avoid them.[7] In contrast, Harper College devotes resources to helping local high schools align their standards with the college's and repair student academic shortcomings before they arrive. College remedial classes are often stigmatized, but such courses in high school, presented as "college prep courses," avoid stigma.

Guttman College also takes another approach: incorporating some remedial lessons into college-credit courses. Seeing the practical need for the remedial skills helps students engage in these lessons.

## Beyond Uninformed Choice and Information Overload

Although community colleges encourage students to make their own choices, they often fail to help them make informed choices. Students make poorly informed choices regarding remedial placement tests, course selection, credential alternatives, degree sequences, career alternatives, and job search. Moreover, mistakes lead to time delays, which impose large costs and risks on students, especially disadvantaged youth who cannot afford cost overruns.[8] Instead of relying on students to make (uninformed) choices, colleges can better inform their choices.

Information overload is also a problem. While educators like flexible course schedules, students complain about the difficulty of adjusting work and child care schedules every semester, the frustration of obtaining and interpreting complex information about whether their courses count for their major, and the vexation of trying to figure out whether their major leads to their desired career. Instead of overwhelming students with complex information, structured course offerings provide the optimal choices for their goal, and such offerings are now widely supported.[9] Although we advocated curriculum pathways in our previous book, the research presented in this book advances the conception of pathway procedures.[10] Others have described isolated practices, such as stacking credentials, organizing peer cohorts, and monitoring progress.[11] We agree with these practices, but they can be more effective when integrated into cohesive pathway procedures across all college transitions. Pathway procedures can reduce information overload and make many elements of college predictable and dependable for students—aligned standards, course sequences, time schedules, locations, advising, peer cohorts, and career entry.

Pathway procedures can organize students' experiences and support their progress across the three transitions. They support college entry and college progress by shaping the social context to facilitate and support students in making the right choices and taking the right actions at every stage. "Career courses" inform entering students about various major and career options. "Appetizer courses" let students sample tasks from various careers (such as phlebotomy, medical billing, and medical office assisting). Degree ladders can also structure choices to improve students' advancement toward a degree through incremental successes along the way.

Although college students cherish long summer vacations, taking a long break is risky, as students lose concentration and continuity in their studies and become susceptible to outside pressures. Short vacations reduce the risks of interruptions to students' college momentum.[12]

Pathway procedures can also give students second chances. Instead of labeling poor performance a failure, colleges can encourage students to see failure as ordinary and temporary. Revising the academic calendar to have short makeup terms is a simple reform that has brought major conceptual breakthroughs: these short terms revise our concept of ability by making an initial failure unimportant and second chances readily available, ordinary, and unstigmatized, as has happened at Guttman. Monitoring progress and alerting advisers at the first signs of difficulty are easy interventions. These procedures—in place at both Harper and Guttman—catch mistakes early (when they are easier to fix), reduce the number of mistakes and failures, and increase students' chances of success. Guttman and Harper also report promising early outcomes for pathway procedures that help students make dependable progress and give them helpful peer group support. As students make fewer mistakes, their confidence that college will deliver on expectations increases.[13]

By tradition, community colleges try to maintain choices and electives, and policymakers are reluctant to urge reforms that add structure to college procedures. Even when Bailey, Jaggars, and Jenkins recommend pathways, for instance, they suggest that they are only "default options" that students can choose to ignore.[14] That is a clever use of Richard Thaler and Cass Sunstein's concept of "nudge," but it is risky.[15] If students choose to depart from pathways, they should be warned of the high costs they may incur—losing dependable time schedules, convenient locations, cohort support, and access to required courses when needed. If suitably warned, few students would choose to ignore the default option. That is why Guttman College and many occupational colleges make the "default" option mandatory.

### Beyond Self-Directed Career Entry

Embarking on a career requires many decisions and actions. Although community colleges offer only a few optional workshops on isolated career-related topics, private occupational colleges offer comprehensive career placement services to nearly all students. Career placement offices assist students' career search in many ways—help with writing effective résumés and letters of inquiry as well as job interview techniques, job search strategies, job decisions, and even employer links (chapter 7). Community colleges assume that students can get appropriate jobs on their own, whereas occupational colleges invest in career services that help students get jobs that use their skills and are likely to lead to good future careers.

Similarly, community college students have long had difficulties transferring to four-year colleges, but this process can also be structured.[16] Most community colleges assume that students can cope with this complex problem, but Harper made this the college's responsibility by creating strong incentives for four-year colleges to clarify which credits transfer for various majors and notifying students which colleges recognize their Harper credits. Harper shows that colleges can gather this information, encourage alignment, and build dependable transfer linkages.

## Addressing Students' BA Plans: Making Informed Choices

Although we respect students' choices, the evidence indicates that students' BA plans are often poorly informed. *Uninformed BA plans should not be honored; they should be informed.* With idealistic intentions, policymakers tell all students to get "college-level" academic skills and BA degrees to achieve middle-class earnings and a decent life. This view is far too narrow and often leads to failure, especially for high-risk students. It also prevents students from seeing the many desirable careers they could dependably attain, even on the way to a BA.

The BA focus mistakenly assumes that students' BA plans are informed choices. We even see this mistake among researchers. Bailey, Jaggars, and Jenkins present a thoughtful and thorough analysis of how more students can attain their BA goals, but it has a big omission.[17] Although the authors have extensive knowledge of sub-BA credentials and their potential, sub-BA credentials are rarely considered in their book as goals. The authors justify their BA focus by saying that entering students have BA plans, and community colleges must serve students' stated goals.

We do not agree. Entering students' BA plans are rarely informed choices. In asserting that the BA is the only route to respectable jobs and a living wage, BA-for-all disparages mid-skill jobs, which offer good middle-class careers, many job rewards, and vital services to society. When policymakers claim that the BA degree is "the only sure route out of poverty" and into respectable jobs, they ignore the 25 percent of BAs who earn less than most sub-BAs.[18] While ignoring valuable sub-BA jobs, they also push a one-sided BA goal that leads many students to have no credential even eight years after high school and feel like hopeless failures. Students often "choose" BA plans without understanding their limits or alternatives, and they exaggerate the education requirements for jobs.[19] Even high school teachers of career and technical education (CTE) courses do not understand sub-BA programs and thus cannot offer alternatives to the one-sided BA view.[20] Students report BA plans because they are the only plans they know. That is not informed choice.

Indeed, community colleges rarely provide information about the disadvantages of pursuing a BA degree (the low odds of attaining a degree, timetables of six years or more for a "four-year" degree, sometimes low pay), the advantages of a sub-BA credential (higher odds of attainment, quick timetables, lower obstacles, significant earnings payoffs, nonmonetary job rewards, and options for higher degrees), or incremental success strategies that combine the two goals. Community college students with low test scores should know that BA success is rare (12 percent), that they are three times more likely to successfully attain a sub-BA (37 percent), that sub-BAs deliver significant payoffs, and that using an incremental success strategy permits them to earn a BA later.

When students with low test scores express BA plans, advisers offer vague encouragement. That is not enough. Advisers should also help these students see their backup options, ones with more dependable payoffs. As we have seen, "some college" with no credential and no earnings payoff is the most common outcome for community college students, partly because society encourages them to have BA dreams and says nothing to them about backup options. Before asking students to make uninformed choices, colleges should inform students about alternative options. They can show the pros and cons of BAs and other credentials, help students choose a first goal, help them devise backup options, and create incremental success strategies that combine a sequence of credentials. Encouraging "free choices" without informing students about alternatives does not result in informed choice, and it poorly serves students' needs.

## Why Is the New College Reality Invisible?

BA blinders are the greatest impediment to improving community colleges. Many people fail to see the new college reality and the many alternative options and procedures. New credentials, rules, requirements, and labor market options are often unseen or underappreciated. Even our words are evasive ("developmental education") or misleading ("four-year BAs," "college-readiness"). Educators are vaguely aware of the many alternatives, but they have not figured out how to put them together to meet the needs of youth and society. Social norms and traditions also interfere. Advisers urge young students into programs that put them on track for a BA, and they assume that any students who fail to earn the degree can always return to college later. However, 50 percent do not return, after depleting their money, time, and confidence.[21]

Educators tend to focus on sub-BA disadvantages when compared to a BA rather than on their advantages compared to attaining just "some college," which is a far more common outcome. It seems reasonable to assume that "college" programs require "college-level" academic skills, so educators put heavy emphasis on academic skill requirements. They continue to praise students' free choices even as students' uninformed free choices lead to delays and disappointments. Our capacity to help students is repeatedly undermined by our BA blinders, which prevent us from seeing the problems with traditional procedures and the value of dependable alternatives.

Why do we have a hard time seeing what is in plain sight? We offer five explanations:

1. *Preconceptions:* We acquired preconceptions when we were enrolled ourselves in traditional four-year colleges. Policymakers, educators, and researchers with BA degrees assume that their own experiences

reflect intrinsic attributes of "college." In interviewing staff, we often heard the phrase "in my experience," a natural way to preface advice; however, their experience may not apply to many students today.

2. *Rapid changes in colleges and labor markets:* Our knowledge about college and jobs has become obsolete. In the past fifteen years, the number of certificates and associate degrees awarded has increased by over 75 percent, and these sub-BAs have become not only more valuable but also more often required by jobs.[22] Seeing these radical changes is difficult. Indeed, in our own prior research, we criticized the literature for not noticing the importance of community colleges, but we did not notice that certificate programs were becoming important.[23] It is hard to keep up with a fast-changing reality.

3. *The uncertain implications of complex choices:* Even educators cannot anticipate students' future credential odds and job outcomes, since students move between different community colleges and four-year colleges and experience extended interruptions to their education. To understand outcomes, we need longitudinal studies that follow students into work, but they are rarely done. Administrative data (the National Student Clearinghouse and state employment data) make this possible, but these data are rarely used, and they can't follow 30 to 50 percent of the sample who attend colleges or take jobs out of state.

4. *The narrowing effect of idealism:* Idealism narrows our perceptions. While CFA ideals improve college access, our ideals also distort our perceptions and advice. Seeking to avoid what President George W. Bush called "the soft bigotry of low expectations," educators encourage all students to pursue BA goals.[24] However, this view is shortsighted. "High expectations" feel good, but they can harm students if they are not warned about the disadvantages of BAs and if they receive only disparaging information about sub-BA credentials.

5. *Stereotypes:* With public service ads claiming that a BA can have a $1 million payoff, high schools urge nearly all students to have BA plans. Sub-BA credentials are listed in college catalogs, but they are labeled "adult education," which eighteen-year-olds think does not apply to them. Some sub-BA classes are located in satellite office space, not on a college campus, so they also do not look like "college." Our stereotypes of the college experience may discourage students from considering sub-BAs.

As social scientists, we are intrigued by the complexities and rapid changes of modern society, as well as our own difficulties in distinguishing reality from preconceptions and ideals. However, although our misconceptions underestimate the difficulties, they also reveal some good news—the variety of unseen or underappreciated opportunities and procedures leading to desirable credentials and jobs that are explored in each chapter of this book.

## Who Will Educate the Educators?

The U.S. education "system" is not systematic. As such, it permits flexibility, but also creates enormous confusion and complexity. CFA tells all students to attend college, but it does not specify alternatives or how to choose. By itself, that is not a problem if students could make informed choices, but American education institutions do not provide appropriate information for students' choices.

Throughout this book, we have called for educators to provide students with basic information for making informed choices. However, our interviews in high schools and community colleges indicated that many educators lack good information. How do educators get such information? Who will educate the educators? This study and others like it can inform teachers and administrators about many alternative options and procedures. Our national findings identify new issues in postsecondary education that are rarely recognized, and we have highlighted newly important and valuable credentials that operate by new rules. We hope our study prompts educators to remove their BA blinders and consider these many alternatives.

We would also encourage more and continuing local research, since specific programs and offerings may vary by location and local realities change rapidly. Local research can inform educators, giving them information on how their local education institutions and labor markets are operating and changing so that they can give students information that fits their needs.

It is a cliché that researchers conclude by saying, "More research is needed." The more we learn, however, the more issues we uncover, and that is especially true of research that informs local educators. Local variations are undoubtedly important in their efforts to inform students' choices, and our national findings provide a good overview of the issues that need to be studied locally.

## Conclusion

Fifteen years ago, college for all was merely an ideal. Now it is the new college reality. However, we need to figure out how to make it work for all students and for society. Having convinced nearly all youth to enter college, society must now find a way to guarantee that they are aware of all the alternatives and their payoffs. Some educators may complacently assume that students will eventually see these alternatives, but unfortunately, many students learn about them too late, are not offered second chances, and run out of time, money, and confidence to persist. Some educators confess that they have doubts when they urge low-achieving students to form BA plans, but they cannot describe sub-BA credentials that they do not understand. Meanwhile, idealistic reformers want all students to have the same high goals but neglect to notice that this advice deprives many students of dependable benefits from college and disparages many good jobs that are vital for society.

Community colleges help us see our opportunity ideals in action and have great potential for improving opportunity, reducing inequality, meeting skill shortages, and providing dependable pathways to good jobs. However, when opportunity is tethered to unrealistically high hopes, community colleges create inevitable disappointments and predictable failures.

In each chapter of this book, we have seen that expanding opportunity requires that we look beyond our BA blinders and consider alternative options and procedures to help all students benefit from college. We have discovered that much about the new college reality is often ignored, but of course, part of the problem is limited resources. Resources are allocated based on a fixed formula per student, ignoring program differences in class size, equipment, and other demands.[25] Community colleges are severely short of necessary resources, but we would point out that if some of the reforms we have described require additional funding, many do not. For instance, designing a college website that specifies alternative credentials, their requirements, their potential career outcomes, and degree ladder options has low costs, and such a website may reduce student confusion and mistakes. Further, although pathway procedures (such as dependable time schedules) require planning, they reduce administrative costs by providing dependable demand by a student cohort in a dependable time schedule every week. Mandatory advisory meetings represent an added cost, but if they are held as group meetings, either before or after a class, they add relatively little extra time. Also, we have described many reforms that require nothing more than broadening our views, which, while difficult, is costless.

"Moving the needle," the term for college reforms that aim to make large progress, implies a one-dimensional goal—BA completion—and few reforms have improved students' ability to achieve that goal. Instead of continuing to struggle for gains in BA completion, we contend that big gains for students are more likely if educators see the value of many alternative options and procedures. Reforms should recognize the value of moving *many* needles to increase sub-BA options, new qualifications, new kinds of job rewards, and new procedures for improving completion rates, earnings, and progress to higher degrees. Sub-BA credentials open new job options to students, including jobs that BA graduates cannot get, with various combinations of job rewards. We should recognize these many "needles" and allow students to choose ones that more closely match their qualifications and offer job rewards they value.

Community colleges can provide dependable ways for youth to enter productive jobs that have increased skill needs. Having achieved dependable access, community colleges can now focus on helping students find direction and better prepare themselves for credential completion and subsequent careers. The new college reality described in this book offers many alternatives that can accomplish these goals and improve youths' educational and career success.

Our nation is confronting severe challenges in the face of rapid change of bewildering complexity. Community colleges were not devised to respond to such challenges, but as we have shown, they nevertheless have great potential to do so. However, we will only stifle their efforts by advocating traditional one-size-fits-all procedures and options. We must be willing to depart from deeply held traditions and incorporate new ways of conceptualizing college goals and procedures. This will obviously require greater resources and staff, but the greater obstacle lies in our misconceptions, which prevent us from seeing many valuable alternative options and procedures. To see past our traditional ideas and assumptions—to discard our narrow BA blinders—we must recognize that college for all is far more than simply a nice ideal. To prepare the nation's youth to meet the demands of an increasingly complex world, we must broaden our conceptions so that many more students benefit from the new college-for-all reality and discover multiple pathways to college and career success.

# = Notes =

## Foreword
1. William T. Grant Foundation 1988, 1.
2. Rosenbaum et al. 2015.
3. Turley and Stevens 2015.
4. Gamoran, in press.

## Chapter 1: College for All: New Opportunities Through Community Colleges
1. National Center for Education Statistics 2014.
2. Schneider and Stevenson 1999.
3. National Center for Education Statistics 2008, table 200.
4. Adelman 2003.
5. Laanan 2000.
6. Bailey, Jaggars, and Jenkins 2015, 6.
7. Kirst and Stevens 2015; Roderick, Coca, and Nagaoka 2011.
8. National Center for Education Statistics 2014.
9. College Board, "College Costs FAQs," available at: https://bigfuture.college board.org/pay-for-college/college-costs/college-costs-faqs (accessed April 1, 2017).
10. Deil-Amen 2015; Deil-Amen and DeLuca 2010.
11. Rose 2012.
12. Ahearn, Rosenbaum, and Rosenbaum 2016; Rosenbaum, Deil-Amen, and Person 2006.
13. Roderick, Coca, and Nagaoka 2011; Carnevale, Rose, and Hanson 2012.
14. Bailey and Smith Morest 2006; Bailey, Jeong, and Cho 2010; Bailey, Jaggars, and Jenkins 2015.
15. Bailey, Jaggars, and Jenkins 2015; Rosenbaum, Deil-Amen, and Person 2006.

16. Schneider and Stevenson 1999.

17. Blinder 2006.

18. See table 2.2.

19. Duncan and Murnane 2014; Putnam 2015; Rosenbaum 2012; Schanzenbach et al. 2014.

20. Carter and Reardon 2014; Rosenbaum, forthcoming.

21. Silva 2013.

22. Ibid.; Goldrick-Rab 2016.

23. Armstrong and Hamilton 2013.

24. Grubb and Lazerson 2004.

25. Arum and Roksa 2011; Hacker and Dreifus 2010; Murray 2008.

26. Ahearn, Gable, and Rosenbaum 2016; Stone and Lewis 2012.

27. Ravitch 2013; Rosenbaum 2001.

28. Holzer et al. 2011.

29. Lee 2001.

30. William T. Grant Foundation 1988.

31. Christ Kirkham, "Percentage of Young Americans Living with Parents Rises to 75-Year High," *Wall Street Journal,* December 21, 2016.

32. Settersten and Ray 2010.

33. Symonds, Schwartz, and Ferguson 2011.

34. Hamilton 1990; Lerman 2010; Mortimer and Krueger 2000; Symonds, Schwartz, and Ferguson 2011.

35. Newman and Winston 2016; Schwartz 2014.

36. On public schooling and high school for all, see Trow 1973. On expanded college access, see Cohen and Brawer 2008.

37. Trow 1973.

38. Shavit, Arum, and Gamoran 2007.

39. National Center for Education Statistics 2014, table 303.25.

40. Tom Hanks, "I Owe It All to Community College," *New York Times,* January 14, 2015.

41. Rosenbaum, forthcoming; Cohen and Brawer 2008.

42. Laanan 2000.

43. Kirst and Stevens 2015, 8.

44. We used Google to ask this question in January 2015.

45. Dawn Dugan, "8 College Degrees with the Worst Return on Investment," Salary.com, available at: http://www.salary.com/8-college-degrees-with-the-worst-return-on-investment/ (accessed April 1, 2017).

46. OneGoal, "OneGoal Curriculum," available at: https://www.onegoal graduation.org/about/problem-solution/ (accessed March 22, 2016); College Advising Corps, "Our Results," available at: http://advisingcorps. org/our-impact/our-results/ (accessed February 23, 2015); The Princeton Review, "Find the School of Your Dreams," available at: http://www. princetonreview.com/college-education.aspx (accessed February 23, 2015); Brown 2007; Zasloff and Steckel 2014.

47. Education Trust 2014.

48. See, for example, Massey et al. 2003, 245.

49. Schneider and Stevenson 1999.

50. Ayers 2011; Kahlenberg 2011.

51. Kati Haycock of the Education Trust, quoted in Carr 2013b.

52. Walt Gardner, "'College-for-All' Policy Bad for Students, Bad for Jobs," *Washington Times*, February 10, 2013; Glass 2014; Robert J. Samuelson, "It's Time to Drop the College-for-All Crusade," *Washington Post*, May 27, 2012; Schwartz 2014; Jacques Steinberg, "Plan B: Skip College," *New York Times*, May 16, 2010.

53. Stephan and Rosenbaum 2012.

54. Ahearn, Gable, and Rosenbaum 2016.

55. Goyette 2008.

56. Arum and Roksa 2014; Goldrick-Rab 2016; Silva 2013.

57. GoCollege, "College Prep for Children in Grades K–8," available at: http:// www.gocollege.com/admissions/preparing/childhood/ (accessed April 5, 2017).

58. Meyer 1977.

59. Kirst and Stevens 2015, 11.

60. Ibid., 13.

61. Bragg and Ruud 2012.

62. Jacobson and Mokher 2009.

63. For the earnings payoff for sub-BA credentials, see Grubb 1996, 96. For research on BA payoffs, see Brint and Karabel 1989; Dougherty 1994.

64. Brint 2003.

65. Baum, Ma, and Payea 2013, table 1.1; Carnevale, Jayasundera, and Hanson 2012.

66. Bailey, Jaggars, and Jenkins 2015.

67. Rosenbaum 2002.

68. Bound, Hershbein, and Long 2009.

69. Gamoran 1993.

70.  Rosenbaum, Deil-Amen, and Person 2006.

71.  Ibid., 118, 16.

72.  Bailey, Jaggars, and Jenkins 2015; Venezia and Voloch 2012; Wyner 2014.

73.  Arum and Roksa 2011.

74.  Murray 2008.

75.  Rosenbaum, Deil-Amen, and Person 2006.

## Chapter 2: Alternative Credentials: A Path Around the Usual Opportunity Barriers?

This chapter was written with the assistance of Kelly I. Becker.

1.  Bills 2004, ch. 3; Goldin and Katz 2008.

2.  National Center for Education Statistics 2012, table 301.10.

3.  Kena et al. 2014, 198.

4.  Baum, Ma, and Payea 2013.

5.  Bound, Hershbein, and Long 2009.

6.  Sewell and Hauser 1975.

7.  Kohn and Schooler 1983; Lareau 2011.

8.  DiPrete and Buchmann 2013; Jacob and Wilder 2010.

9.  Dougherty 1994.

10.  Stephan and Rosenbaum 2009.

11.  Tucker 2013.

12.  On the cultural capital requirements of high-status occupations, see Rivera and Ward 2010. On cultural capital and mid-skill jobs, see Lareau 2011.

13.  Adelman 2003.

14.  Authors' (unpublished) calculations from the Education Longitudinal Study (ELS).

15.  Sewell and Hauser 1980.

16.  Like prior research (Adelman 2003), this chapter studies seniors who graduated from high school on time (by June 2004); the ELS data allow us to see outcomes eight years after they left high school. Eighty-six percent of high school seniors graduated on time; the rate is somewhat lower for low-SES students (77 percent). We are not assessing college enrollment for high school dropouts or for those who graduated in later years. For many of these students who did not graduate from high school on time, academic or personal difficulties may have returned to impair their college careers. These students deserve a chance at college, of course, but because they face extra challenges, we believe that they should be treated as a separate group and studied independently.

Tables 2.2 to 2.6 restrict the sample to individuals not enrolled in college in June 2012. This restriction decreases the chance that these students were still working on their degrees and might have graduated in the next year. Earnings tables further restrict the sample to respondents not enrolled in 2011 or 2012, giving them time to establish themselves in the labor market.

17. Sewell and Hauser 1980.

18. Becker et al. 2016.

19. On enrollment immediately after high school graduation, see ACE 2015. On enrollment over the eight years after high school graduation, see Bozick and DeLuca 2005.

20. See, for example, Ayers 2011; Kahlenberg 2011.

21. Rosenbaum, Deil-Amen, and Person 2006; see also chapter 1.

22. See, for example, Goldin and Katz 2008.

23. Carnevale, Jayasundera, and Hanson 2012.

24. Brint and Karabel 1989; see also Grubb 1996.

25. Brint 2003.

26. Carnevale, Jayasundera, and Hanson 2012; Holzer et al. 2011; Jacobson and Mokher 2009.

27. Belfield and Bailey 2011, 55.

28. Ibid., 54.

29. Ibid.

30. Holzer et al. 2011; Vuolo, Mortimer, and Staff 2014.

31. Wyner 2014.

32. See, for example, Belfield and Bailey 2011.

33. Ibid.; Grubb 2002; Marcotte et al. 2005. For research on the earnings of workers under age thirty, see Day and Newburger 2002, fig. 4; Carnevale, Jayasundera, and Hanson 2012.

34. Belfield and Bailey 2011.

35. On the lack of benefits in earning few or no credits, see, for example, Grubb 2002. On students who fail to receive a credential, see Rosenbaum 2001, 77.

36. We use multinomial regression, controlling for SES, test score, race, gender, and BA plans.

37. Sewell and Hauser 1980; Dougherty 1994.

38. Stone and Lewis 2012; Tucker 2013.

39. Merton 1973; Pallas and Jennings 2009.
40. Cook et al. 1975.
41. Meissner, Ahearn, and Rosenbaum 2016.
42. Jacobson and Mokher 2009.
43. Clark 1960.
44. Goffman 1952.
45. Swanson 2002.
46. Rosenbaum 2011a.
47. Carnevale, Rose, and Hanson 2012.

## Chapter 3: Money Isn't Everything: Do Sub-BA Credentials Lead to Nonmonetary Job Rewards?

1. Obama 2013.
2. On earnings payoffs, see Grubb 2002; Carnevale, Jayasundera, and Hanson 2012. For studies examining links between sub-BA credentials and good jobs and career preparation, see Brown 2007; Zasloff and Steckel 2014.
3. On the willingness to sacrifice pay for better training, see Doeringer and Piore 1971; Stern 1978. On young employees' awareness of the earnings-training trade-off, see Ng and Rosenbaum 2015.
4. Hackman and Oldham 1975, 1976.
5. Davidson et al. 1997.
6. Miller 1980.
7. Kalleberg 2011, 7–9.
8. Jencks, Perman, and Rainwater 1988.
9. National Data Program for the Social Sciences 2007.
10. Clark 2005, 2.
11. Goldthorpe 1980.
12. Miller 1980.
13. Marmot 2004, 2.
14. Kanter 1976.
15. Nguyen, Taylor, and Bradley 2001.
16. Borman 1991; Holzer 1996; Moss and Tilly 2001; Silva 2012.
17. Piore 2002.
18. Barley 1996.

19. For one such critique of sub-BA credentials, see Brint and Karabel 1989. For an analysis that ignores sub-BA credentials while focusing on BA degrees, see Carr 2013b.

20. Rosenbaum 2011a 2011b, 2012. The sample consists of 10,582 respondents with high school diplomas who were employed full-time in one job in 2008: 43 percent had no additional credential beyond a high school diploma, 9 percent had a community college certificate, 10 percent had an associate degree, 27 percent had a BA degree, and 11 percent had more than a BA degree. High school equivalency degree holders were excluded because the credential seems to be stigmatized by employers and is associated with lower earnings (Heckman and Rubinstein 2001; Murnane, Willett, and Levy 1995).

21. Since the median earnings is $30,000 a year and many individuals report that amount, the portion "above the median" is actually 46.7 percent.

22. Oreopoulos and Salvanes 2011, 180.

23. Murnane and Levy 1996.

24. Piore 2002.

25. Jencks, Perman, and Rainwater 1988.

26. Rosenbaum 2011a, forthcoming; Belfield and Bailey 2011; Marmot 2004.

27. Ibid.

28. Cummings 2009; Lumley, Kronmal, and Ma 2006; McNutt et al. 2003.

# Chapter 4: Beyond One-Dimensional Qualifications: How Students Discover Hidden Abilities

1. Ayers 2011; ACT 2015; Carr 2013a.

2. Young 1958.

3. ACT 2015.

4. Common Core State Standards Initiative, "What Parents Should Know," available at: http://www.corestandards.org/what-parents-should-know/ (accessed March 22, 2016).

5. Achieve 2009; Conley 2012.

6. Bailey, Jeong, and Cho 2010.

7. On academic achievement and employment outcomes, see Goldin and Katz 2008; Mincer 1974. For analysis of non-academic skills, see Farkas 1997; Heckman, Stixrud, and Urzua 2006; Lindqvist and Vestman 2011; Stone and Lewis 2012.

8. Bills 2004; Heckman, Stixrud, and Urzua 2006; Holzer and Lerman 2007; Lindqvist and Vestman 2011; Moss and Tilly 1996; Neckerman and Kirshenman 1991; Rosenbaum 2001; Wilson 1996; Zemsky 1994.

9. Ayers 2011; Carr 2013b.

10. Bailey, Jaggars, and Jenkins 2015.

11. Rosenbaum 2001; Murnane, Willett, and Levy 1995.

12. For one such case, see Silva 2012.

13. Rosenbaum 2001; Rosenbaum, Deil-Amen, and Person 2006.

14. Carnevale, Jayasundera, and Hanson 2012.

15. Rosenbaum 2001; Rosenbaum, Deil-Amen, and Person 2006. Our sample questions for these faculty included: What degrees or other credentials do you hold, and how long have you held this position? What did you do before you were employed by the community college? What are students' three most common reasons for choosing your program, and what proportion of beginning students in your program need remedial or developmental education in math or reading? What skills do employers want from graduates in this program area, and are grades important in getting a job?

16. See, for example, Grubb and Associates 1999.

17. Tucker 2013.

18. Deming 2015.

19. Baer 1986, 533.

20. Becker et al. 1950.

21. Ingersoll 2004, 116.

22. Cappelli 1992; Zemsky 1994.

23. Shapiro and Iannozzi 1999, table 2.

24. Rosenbaum 2001, ch. 6.

25. Ingersoll 2004.

26. Lerman 2010.

27. Hamilton 1990.

28. On the socialization of physicians, see Becker et al. 1950.

29. For this typical view of low-achieving students, see, for example, Hamilton 1990; Lerman 2010; Steinberg 1996.

30. Bowles and Gintis 1976; Stone and Lewis 2012.

31. Becker et al. 2016; Ng and Rosenbaum 2015.

32. Hamilton 1990, 44.

33. Lerman 2010.

34. On the ineffectiveness of remedial courses, see Bailey, Jeong, and Cho 2010; see also chapter 5. On new approaches to remedial courses, see Bailey, Jaggars, and Jenkins 2015, 119–44.

35. Carnevale, Rose, and Hanson 2012.

36. Silva 2013.

## Chapter 5: The Least Understood Tests in America: How College Procedures Shape Placement Test Results

1. Rosenbaum, Deil-Amen, and Person 2006.
2. Bailey, Jeong, and Cho 2010.
3. Rosenbaum, Deil-Amen, and Person 2006.
4. All respondent names have been changed to protect their privacy.
5. Rosenbaum, Deil-Amen, and Person 2006.
6. Ibid.
7. See, for example, Bailey, Jeong, and Cho 2010.
8. Breneman and Haarlow 1998; Steinberg 1998.
9. Breneman and Haarlow 1998; Steinberg 1998.
10. Mokher 2014; Bailey, Jeong, and Cho 2010.
11. Bailey, Jeong, and Cho 2010.
12. Rosenbaum 2001.
13. National Commission on the High School Senior Year 2001.
14. Rosenbaum, Deil-Amen, and Person 2006.
15. Ibid.
16. National Commission on the High School Senior Year 2001; Rosenbaum, Schuetz, and Foran 2010.
17. Rosenbaum 2001; Kirst and Venezia 2004.
18. Rosenbaum, Deil-Amen, and Person 2006; Venezia, Bracco, and Nodine 2010.
19. Becker et al. 2016.
20. Ayers 2011; Kahlenberg 2011; Kati Haycock of the Education Trust, quoted in Carr 2013b.
21. Bailey, Jeong, and Cho 2010.
22. Entwisle, Alexander, and Olson 1997; Chin and Phillips 2004.
23. Rosenbaum, Cepa, and Rosenbaum 2013.
24. Steve Robbins, personal communication.
25. Mokher 2014.
26. Brown and Niemi 2007.
27. Goldrick-Rab 2006.
28. Lemann 1999.
29. Ibid.
30. Rosenbaum, Deil-Amen, and Person 2006; Venezia, Bracco, and Nodine 2010.
31. Margolin, Miller, and Rosenbaum 2013.

## Chapter 6: Degree Ladders: Procedures That Combine Dependable Credentials and High Goals

1. Cohen and Brawer 2008.
2. Rosenbaum, Deil-Amen, and Person 2006.
3. Spilerman 1977, 561.
4. Grubb 1996, 97.
5. Dadgar et al. 2013; Wyner 2014.
6. Cox 2009.
7. Blau and Duncan 1967; Featherman and Hauser 1978.
8. Rosenbaum 1979, 1984.
9. Mouw and Kalleberg 2010.
10. See, for example, Blau and Duncan 1967; Ross and Reskin 1992.
11. Adelman 2003.
12. Grubb 2002.
13. Spilerman 1977.
14. Schwartz 2004.
15. Rosenbaum, Deil-Amen, and Person 2006.
16. "The structure hypothesis: that community college students will be more likely to persist and succeed in programs that are tightly and consciously structured, with relatively little room for individuals to unintentionally deviate from paths toward completion, and with limited bureaucratic obstacles for students to circumnavigate" (Scott-Clayton 2011, 1).
17. Deil-Amen 2011; Rosenbaum, Deil-Amen, and Person 2006; Scott-Clayton 2011.
18. Dadgar et al. 2013.
19. Gill and Leigh 2004.
20. Carnevale, Jayasundera, and Hanson 2012.
21. Rosenbaum, Cepa, and Rosenbaum 2013.
22. Compare to Becker et al. 2016.
23. Ibid.
24. Cox 2009.
25. Brown 2007.
26. Spilerman 1977.
27. See Deil-Amen 2011.
28. Rosenbaum, Cepa, and Rosenbaum 2013.

# Chapter 7: Beyond BA Blinders: Pathway Procedures Into, Through, and Out of College

This chapter was written with the assistance of Jennifer Stephan.

1. Meyer 1977.

2. Murray 2008.

3. Hoffman et al. 2007.

4. Becker et al. 2016.

5. Stephan, Rosenbaum, and Person 2009.

6. Ibid.

7. Stephan and Rosenbaum 2009.

8. See, for example, Dougherty 1994.

9. Stephan and Rosenbaum 2009.

10. Stephan, Rosenbaum, and Person 2009.

11. Deming, Goldin, and Katz 2012.

12. Stephan and Rosenbaum 2009.

13. We also analyzed graduates' labor market success. Using NELS, which followed the high school class of 1992 until 2000, we compared the earnings of similar students who earned an associate degree or higher. The results suggest that going to an occupational college does not lead to worse earnings outcomes for similar students.

| College Type | N | Mean Earnings 1999 | 95 Percent Confidence Interval |
|---|---|---|---|
| Community college | 734 | $29,481 | $27,324–$31,639 |
| Occupational college | 61 | $28,969 | $25,605–$32,333 |

Although few students attended private occupational colleges in the 1990s, the results suggest that these colleges had higher degree completion rates than community colleges for comparable students, as well as similar earnings. David Deming, Claudia Goldin, and Lawrence Katz (2012) find that for-profits had lower earnings, but that study could not control for academic achievement and was conducted after for-profit college quality had eroded.

14. Bers and Nyden 2000; Shugart and Romano 2008.

15. Bailey, Jeong, and Cho 2010.

16. Tucker 2013; Stone and Lewis 2012.

17. Murray 2008.

18. Horn 1999.
19. Bailey, Jaggars, and Jenkins 2015.
20. Bailey, Jeong, and Cho 2010.
21. Horn 1999.
22. Adelman 2003.
23. On "dependable pathways," see Rosenbaum, Deil-Amen, and Person 2006, 16.
24. Rosenbaum, Deil-Amen, and Person 2006.
25. Ibid.
26. Murray 2008.
27. Moreover, the same might be true for the "academic abilities" that Murray (2008) posits. Four-year-old children who are exposed to word games and complex verbal interaction with adults are acquiring cultural know-how that enables them to learn more than other children from the same experiences, such as watching *Sesame Street* (Cook et al. 1975), and perform better on academic tests that purport to measure "academic ability."
28. Rosenbaum 1986.
29. Stephan, Rosenbaum, and Person 2009.
30. Wyner 2014.
31. Tinto 1993.

## Chapter 8: Innovative Colleges and Improved Transitions

1. Rosenbaum, Deil-Amen, and Person 2006.
2. Ibid.
3. Ibid.
4. Kolenovic, Linderman, and Karp 2013.
5. Brown and Kurzweil 2016, 12.
6. Ibid.
7. Ibid., 12.
8. Rosenbaum, Deil-Amen, and Person 2006.
9. Long and Reilly 2007; Stephan and Rosenbaum 2012.
10. Weissman et al. 2011.
11. Hoffman 2016.
12. Bers and Nyden 2000.
13. Wyner 2014; Bailey, Jaggars, and Jenkins 2015.
14. Jenkins and Cho 2012.

15. Posse Foundation, "About Posse," available at: http://www.possefoundation. org/about-posse (accessed February 23, 2015).
16. Rosenbaum, Deil-Amen, and Person 2006.
17. Wyner 2014.
18. Rosenbaum 1978, 1984.
19. Horn 1999.
20. Stevenson and Stigler 1992.

## Chapter 9: The New College Reality: Alternative Options and Procedures

1. Carnevale, Jayasundera, and Hanson 2012.
2. Ruud, Bragg, and Townsend 2010.
3. Bowen and McPherson 2016, 31.
4. Hoffman 2016.
5. Schneider and Stevenson 1999.
6. Schwartz 2014.
7. Bailey, Jeong, and Cho 2010.
8. Bowen and McPherson 2016, 21.
9. Bailey, Jaggars, and Jenkins 2015; Venezia and Voloch 2012.
10. Rosenbaum, Deil-Amen, and Person 2006.
11. Wyner 2014; Shulock 2007.
12. Jenkins and Cho 2012.
13. Becker et al. 2016.
14. Bailey, Jaggars, and Jenkins 2015.
15. Thaler and Sunstein 2008.
16. Dougherty 1994.
17. Bailey, Jaggars, and Jenkins 2015.
18. Kati Haycock of the Education Trust, quoted in Carr 2013b; Baum, Ma, and Payea 2013.
19. Schneider and Stevenson 1999.
20. Ahearn, Gable, and Rosenbaum 2016.
21. Horn 1999.
22. Kena et al. 2014.
23. Rosenbaum, Deil-Amen, and Person 2006.
24. Newman and Winston 2016.
25. Bailey, Jaggars, and Jenkins 2015.

# References

Achieve. 2009. "What Is College- and Career-Ready?" Washington, D.C.: Achieve (May 1). Available at: http://www.achieve.org/what-college-and-career-ready (accessed April 1, 2017).

ACT. 2015. *The Condition of College and Career Readiness 2015*. Iowa City: ACT.

Adelman, Clifford. 2003. "Principal Indicators of Student Academic Histories in Postsecondary Education, 1972–2000." Washington: U.S. Department of Education, Institute of Education Sciences.

Ahearn, Caitlin, Alexis Gable, and James Rosenbaum. 2016. "Flying Blind: CTE Teachers' Knowledge and Advice for Students in a College-for-All World." Report presented to the Milgrom Program. Chicago: University of Chicago and Northwestern University (November 11).

Ahearn, Caitlin, James Rosenbaum, and Janet Rosenbaum. 2016. "What Educators Should Know About College-for-All Policies." *Phi Delta Kappan* 97(5): 49–54.

American Council on Education (ACE). 2015. "Where Have All the Low-Income Students Gone?" *Higher Education Today* (blog), November 25. Available at: https://higheredtoday.org/2015/11/25/where-have-all-the-low-income-students-gone/ (accessed April 1, 2017).

Armstrong, Elizabeth A., and Laura T. Hamilton. 2013. *Paying for the Party: How College Maintains Inequality*. Cambridge, Mass.: Harvard University Press.

Arum, Richard, and Josipa Roksa. 2011. *Academically Adrift: Limited Learning on College Campuses*. Chicago: University of Chicago Press.

———. 2014. *Aspiring Adults Adrift: Tentative Transitions of College Graduates*. Chicago: University of Chicago Press.

Ayers, Jeremy. 2011. "College for All or College for Some?" Washington, D.C.: Center for American Progress.

Baer, William C. 1986. "Expertise and Professional Standards." *Work and Occupations* 13(4): 532–52.

Bailey, Thomas, Shanna Smith Jaggars, and Davis Jenkins. 2015. *Redesigning America's Community Colleges: A Clearer Path to Student Success*. Cambridge, Mass.: Harvard University Press.

Bailey, Thomas, Dong Wook Jeong, and Sung-Woo Cho. 2010. "Referral, Enrollment, and Completion in Developmental Education Sequences in Community Colleges." *Economics of Education Review* 29: 255–70.

Bailey, Thomas, and Vanessa Smith Morest. 2006. *Defending the Community College Equity Agenda*. Baltimore: Johns Hopkins University Press.

179

Barley, Stephen R. 1996. "Technicians in the Workplace: Ethnographic Evidence for Bringing Work into Organizational Studies." *Administrative Science Quarterly* 41(3): 404–41.

Baum, Sandy, Jennifer Ma, and Kathleen Payea. 2013. *Education Pays 2013: The Benefits of Higher Education for Individuals and Society.* Princeton, N.J.: College Board.

Becker, Howard S., Blanche Geer, Everett C. Hughes, and Anselm Strauss. 1950. *Boys in White: Student Culture in Medical School.* Chicago: University of Chicago Press.

Becker, Kelly Iwanaga, James E. Rosenbaum, Kennan A. Cepa, and Claudia E. Zapata-Gietl. 2016. "Turning the Question Around: Do Colleges Fail to Meet Students' Expectations?" *Research in Higher Education* 57(5): 519–43.

Belfield, Clive R., and Thomas Bailey. 2011. "The Benefits of Attending Community College: A Review of the Evidence." *Community College Review* 39(1): 46–68.

Bers, Trudy H., and Gwen Nyden. 2000. "The Disappearing Student: Students Who Leave Before the Census Date." *Journal of College Student Retention: Research, Theory, and Practice* 2(3): 205–17.

Bills, David. 2004. *The Sociology of Education and Work.* Malden, Mass.: Blackwell Publishing.

Blau, Peter M., and Otis Dudley Duncan. 1967. *The American Occupational Structure.* New York: Wiley.

Blinder, Alan S. 2006. "Offshoring: The Next Industrial Revolution?" *Foreign Affairs* 85(2): 113–28.

Borman, Kathryn. 1991. *The First "Real" Job: A Study of Young Workers.* Albany: State University of New York Press.

Bound, John, Brad Hershbein, and Bridget Terry Long. 2009. "Playing the Admissions Game: Student Reactions to Increasing College Competition." *Journal of Economic Perspectives* 23(4): 119–46.

Bowen, William, and Michael McPherson. 2016. *Lesson Plan: An Agenda for Change in American Higher Education.* Princeton, N.J.: Princeton University Press.

Bowles, Samuel, and Herbert Gintis. 1976. *Schooling in Capitalist America: Educational Reform and the Contradictions of Economic Life.* New York: Basic Books.

Bozick, Robert, and Stefanie DeLuca. 2005. "Better Late Than Never?" *Social Forces* 84: 531–54.

Bragg, Debra, and Collin Ruud. 2012. "Why Applied Baccalaureates Appeal to Working Adults: From National Results to Promising Practices." *New Directions for Community Colleges* 158: 73–85.

Breneman, David, and William Haarlow. 1998. "Remediation in Higher Education: A Symposium Featuring Developmental Education: Costs and Consequences." *Fordham Report* 2(9). Washington, D.C.: Thomas B. Fordham Foundation.

Brint, Steven. 2003. "Few Remaining Dreams: Community Colleges Since 1985." *Annals of the American Academy of Political and Social Science* 586: 16–37.

Brint, Steven, and Jerome Karabel. 1989. *The Diverted Dream: Community College and the Promise of Educational Opportunity in America, 1900–1985.* New York: Oxford University Press.

Brown, Duane. 2007. *Career Information, Career Counseling, and Career Development.* 9th ed. Boston: Pearson.

Brown, Jessie, and Martin Kurzweil. 2016. "Student Success by Design: CUNY's Guttman Community College." New York: Ithaka S+R (February 4).

Brown, Richard S., and David N. Niemi. 2007. "Investigating the Alignment of High School and Community College Assessments in California." San Jose: National Center for Public Policy and Higher Education.

Cappelli, Peter. 1992. "Is the Skills Gap Really About Attitudes?" Philadelphia: University of Pennsylvania, National Center on the Educational Quality of the Workforce.

Carnevale, Anthony P., Tamara Jayasundera, and Andrew R. Hanson. 2012. "Career and Technical Education: Five Ways That Pay Along the Way to the BA." Washington, D.C.: Center on Education and the Workforce, Georgetown Public Policy Institute Civic Enterprises.

Carnevale, Anthony P., Stephen J. Rose, and Andrew R. Hanson. 2012. "Certificates: Gateway to Gainful Employment and College Degrees." Washington, D.C.: Georgetown University Center on Education and the Workforce.

Carr, Sarah. 2013a. "College-for-All vs. Career Education? Moving Beyond a False Debate." Originally published in *Wilson Quarterly.* Reprinted at *The Hechinger Report,* August 19. Available at: http://hechingerreport.org/college-for-all-vs-career-education-moving-beyond-a-false-debate/ (accessed April 1, 2017).

———. 2013b. "Getting Real About High School." *Wilson Quarterly* (Summer). Available at: http://wilsonquarterly.com/quarterly/summer-2014-where-have-all-the-jobs-gone/getting-real-about-high-school/ (accessed April 1, 2017).

Carter, Prudence L., and Sean F. Reardon. 2014. "Inequality Matters." A William T. Grant Foundation Inequality Paper. Stanford, Calif.: Stanford University Graduate School of Education (September).

Chin, Tiffani, and Meredith Phillips. 2004. "Social Reproduction and Child-Rearing Practices: Social Class, Children's Agency, and the Summer Activity Gap." *Sociology of Education* 77(3): 185–210.

Clark, Andrew. 2005. "What Makes a Good Job? Evidence from OECD Countries." In *Job Quality and Employer Behavior,* edited by Stephen Bazen, Claudio Lucifora, and Wiemer Salverda. New York: Palgrave.

Clark, Burton R. 1960. "The 'Cooling Out' Function in Higher Education." *American Journal of Sociology* 65(6): 569–76.

Cohen, Arthur M., and Florence B. Brawer. 2008. *The American Community College.* 5th ed. San Francisco: Jossey-Bass.

Conley, David T. 2012. "A Complete Definition of College and Career Readiness." Portland, Ore.: Educational Policy Improvement Center.

Cook, Thomas D., Hilary Appleton, Ross F. Conner, Ann Shaffer, Gary Tamkin, and Stephen J. Weber. 1975. *"Sesame Street" Revisited.* New York: Russell Sage Foundation.

Cox, Rebecca D. 2009. *The College Fear Factor: How Students and Professors Misunderstand One Another.* Cambridge, Mass.: Harvard University Press.

Cummings, Peter. 2009. "The Relative Merits of Risk Ratios and Odds Ratios." *Archives of Pediatrics and Adolescent Medicine* 163(5): 438–45.

Dadgar, Mina, Andrea Venezia, Thad Nodine, and Kathy Reeves Bracco. 2013. "Providing Structured Pathways to Guide Students Toward Completion." San Francisco: WestEd.

Davidson, Harriet, Patricia H. Folcarelli, Sybil Crawford, Laura J. Duprat, and Joyce C. Clifford. 1997. "The Effects of Health Care Reforms on Job Satisfaction and Voluntary Turnover Among Hospital-Based Nurses." *Medical Care* 35: 634–45.

Day, Jennifer Cheeseman, and Eric C. Newburger. 2002. "The Big Payoff: Educational Attainment and Synthetic Estimates of Work-Life Earnings." *Current Population Reports* P23-210. Washington: U.S. Department of Commerce, U.S. Census Bureau.

Deil-Amen, Regina. 2011. "Socio-Academic Integrative Moments: Rethinking Academic and Social Integration Among Two-Year College Students in Career-Related Programs." *Journal of Higher Education* 82(1): 54–91.

———. 2015. "The Traditional College Student: A Smaller and Smaller Minority and Its Implications for Diversity and Access Institutions." In *Remaking College: The Changing Ecology of Higher Education,* edited by Michael Kirst and Mitchell Stevens. Stanford, Calif.: Stanford University Press.

Deil-Amen, Regina, and Stefanie DeLuca. 2010. "The Underserved Third: How Our Educational Structures Populate an Educational Underclass." *Journal of Education for Students Placed at Risk* 15: 1–24.

Deming, David J. 2015. "The Growing Importance of Social Skills in the Labor Market." Working Paper 21473. Cambridge, Mass.: Harvard University and National Bureau for Economic Research (August).

Deming, David J., Claudia Goldin, and Lawrence F. Katz. 2012. "The For-Profit Postsecondary School Sector: Nimble Critters or Agile Predators?" *Journal of Economic Perspectives* 26(1): 139–64.

DiPrete, Thomas, and Claudia Buchmann. 2013. *The Rise of Women: The Female Advantage in Education and What It Means for American Schooling.* New York: Russell Sage Foundation.

Doeringer, Peter B., and Michael J. Piore. 1971. *Internal Labor Markets and Manpower Analysis.* Lexington, Mass.: Lexington Books.

Dougherty, Kevin J. 1994. *The Contradictory College: The Conflicting Origins, Impacts, and Futures of the Community College.* Albany: State University of New York Press.

Duncan, Greg, and Richard Murnane. 2014. *Restoring Opportunity: The Crisis of Inequality and the Challenge for American Education.* Cambridge, Mass.: Harvard Education Press.

Education Trust. 2014. "College Results Online." Washington D.C.: Education Trust (October 14). Available at: http://www.edtrust.org/issues/higher-education/college-results-online (accessed February 23, 2015).

Entwisle, Doris R., Karl L. Alexander, and Linda Olson. 1997. *Children, Schools, and Inequality.* Boulder, Colo.: Westview Press

Farkas, George. 1997. *Human Capital or Cultural Capital?* Hawthorne, N.Y.: Aldine.

Featherman, David L., and Robert Mason Hauser. 1978. *Opportunity and Change.* New York: Academic Press.

Gamoran, Adam. 1993. "Alternative Uses of Ability Grouping in Secondary Schools." *American Journal of Education* 102: 1–21.

———. In press. "Research for Policy in Higher Education: The Case for Research-Practice Partnerships." In *Advancing Equity, Inclusiveness, and Social Change in Higher Education: How Academics Connect Research, Advocacy, and Policy,* edited by Laura Perna. Baltimore: Johns Hopkins University Press.

Gill, Andrew M., and Duane E. Leigh. 2004. "Evaluating Academic Programs in California's Community Colleges." San Francisco: Public Policy Institute of California.

Glass, Kevin. 2014. "How 'College-for-All' Harms America's Students." *Townhall,* September 14. Available at: http://townhall.com/tipsheet/kevinglass/2014/09/14/how-collegeforall-harms-americas-students-n1891482 (accessed February 23, 2015).

Goffman, Erving. 1952. "Cooling the Mark Out: Some Aspects of Adaptation to Failure." *Psychiatry* 15: 451–63.

Goldin, Claudia, and Lawrence F. Katz. 2008. *The Race Between Education and Technology.* Cambridge, Mass.: Belknap Press of Harvard University Press.

Goldrick-Rab, Sara. 2006. "Following Their Every Move: How Social Class Shapes Postsecondary Pathways." *Sociology of Education* 79(1): 61–79.

———. 2016. *Paying the Price: College Costs, Financial Aid, and the Betrayal of the American Dream.* Chicago: University of Chicago Press.

Goldthorpe, John H. 1980. *Social Mobility and Class Structure in Modern Britain.* Oxford: Clarendon Press.

Goyette, Kimberly. 2008. "College for Some to College for All: Social Background, Occupational Expectations, and Educational Expectations over Time." *Social Science Research* 37: 461–84.

Grubb, W. Norton. 1996. *Working in the Middle: Strengthening Education and Training for the Mid-Skilled Labor Force.* San Francisco: Jossey-Bass.

———. 2002. "Learning and Earning in the Middle, Part I: National Studies of Pre-Baccalaureate Education." *Economics of Education Review* 21: 299–321.

Grubb, W. Norton, and Associates. 1999. *Honored but Invisible: An Inside Look at Teaching in Community Colleges.* New York: Routledge.

Grubb, W. Norton, and Marvin Lazerson. 2004. *The Education Gospel: The Economic Power of Schooling.* Cambridge, Mass.: Harvard University Press.

Hacker, Andrew, and Claudia Dreifus. 2010. *Higher Education? How Colleges Are Wasting Our Money and Failing Our Kids—and What We Can Do About It.* New York: St. Martin's Press.

Hackman, J. Richard, and Greg R. Oldham. 1975. "Development of the Job Diagnostic Survey." *Journal of Applied Psychology* 60(2): 159–70.

———. 1976. "Motivation Through the Design of Work: Test of a Theory." *Organizational Behavior and Human Performance* 16(2): 250–79.

Hamilton, Stephen F. 1990. *Apprenticeship for Adulthood: Preparing Youth for the Future.* New York: Free Press.

Heckman, James J., and Yona Rubinstein. 2001. "The Importance of Non-cognitive Skills: Lessons from the GED Testing Program." *American Economic Review* 91: 145–49.

Heckman, James J., Jora Stixrud, and Sergio Urzua. 2006. "The Effects of Cognitive and Non-cognitive Abilities on Labor Market Outcomes and Social Behavior." Working Paper 12006. Cambridge, Mass.: National Bureau of Economic Research.

Hoffman, Nancy. 2016. "How Guttman Community College Puts Work at the Center of Learning." *Change* (July/August): 14–22.

Hoffman, Nancy, Joel Vargas, Andrea Venezia, and Marc S. Miller. 2007. *Minding the Gap: Why Integrating High School with College Makes Sense and How to Do It.* Cambridge, Mass.: Harvard Education Press.

Holzer, Harry. 1996. *What Employers Want: Job Prospects for Less-Educated Workers.* New York: Russell Sage Foundation.

Holzer, Harry, Julia I. Lane, David B. Rosenblum, and Fredrik Andersson. 2011. *Where Are All the Good Jobs Going? What National and Local Job Quality and Dynamics Mean for U.S. Workers.* New York: Russell Sage Foundation.

Holzer, Harry, and Robert I. Lerman. 2007. "America's Forgotten Middle-Skill Jobs." Washington, D.C.: Workforce Alliance, Urban Institute.

Horn, Laura. 1999. "Stopouts or Stayouts? Undergraduates Who Leave College in Their First Year." NCES 1999-087. Washington: U.S. Government Printing Office for U.S. Department of Education.

Ingersoll, Richard M. 2004. "The Status of Teaching as a Profession." In *Schools and Society,* edited by Jeanne Ballantine and Joan Spade. Belmont, Calif.: Wadsworth.

Jacob, Brian A., and Tamara Wilder. 2010. "Educational Expectations and Attainment." Working Paper 15683. Cambridge, Mass.: National Bureau of Economic Research.

Jacobson, Louis, and Christine Mokher. 2009. "Pathways to Boosting the Earnings of Low-Income Students by Increasing Their Educational Attainment." Washington, D.C.: Hudson Institute Center for Employment Policy.

Jencks, Christopher, Lauri Perman, and Lee Rainwater. 1988. "What Is a Good Job? A New Measure of Labor Market Success." *American Journal of Sociology* 93: 1322–57.

Jenkins, Davis, and Sung-Woo Cho. 2012. "Get with the Program: Accelerating Community College Students' Entry into and Completion of Programs of Study." Community College Research Study Working Paper 32. New York: Columbia University, Teachers College.

Kahlenberg, Richard D. 2011. "Insights and Commentary on Higher Education." *Chronicle of Higher Education,* Innovations (blog), June 9. Available at: http://chronicle.com/blogs/innovations/the-college-for-all-debate/29623 (accessed February 24, 2015).

Kalleberg, Arne L. 2011. *Good Jobs, Bad Jobs: The Rise of Polarized and Precarious Employment Systems in the United States, 1970s–2000s.* New York: Russell Sage Foundation.

Kanter, Rosabeth. 1976. *Men and Women of the Corporation.* New York: Basic Books.

Kena, Grace, Susan Aud, Frank Johnson, Xiaolei Wang, Jijun Zhang, Amy Rathbun, Sidney Wilkinson-Flicker, and Paul Kristapovich. 2014. "The Condition of Education 2014." NCES 2014-083. Washington: U.S. Department of Education, National Center for Education Statistics, Institute of Education Sciences. Available at: http://nces.ed.gov/pubs2014/2014083.pdf (accessed April 1, 2017).

Kirst, Michael, and Mitchell Stevens. 2015. *Remaking College: The Changing Ecology of Higher Education.* Stanford, Calif.: Stanford University Press.

Kirst, Michael, and Andrea Venezia, eds. 2004. *From High School to College: Improving Opportunities for Success in Postsecondary Education*. San Francisco: Jossey-Bass.

Kohn, Melvin, and Carmi Schooler. 1983. *Work and Personality: An Inquiry into the Impact of Social Stratification*. New York: Ablex.

Kolenovic, Zineta, Donna Linderman, and Melinda Mechur Karp. 2013. "Improving Student Outcomes Via Comprehensive Supports: Three-Year Outcomes from CUNY's Accelerated Study in Associate Programs (ASAP)." *Community College Review* 41(4): 271–91.

Laanan, Frankie Santos. 2000. "Community College Students' Career and Educational Goals." *New Directions for Community Colleges* 112: 19–34.

Lareau, Annette. 2011. *Unequal Childhoods: Class, Race, and Family Life*. 2nd ed. Berkeley: University of California Press.

Lee, Linda. 2001. *Success Without College: Why Your Child May Not Have to Go to College Right Now—and May Not Have to Go at All*. New York: First Broadway Books.

Lemann, Nicholas. 1999. *The Big Test: The Secret History of the American Meritocracy*. New York: Farrar, Straus & Giroux.

Lerman, Robert I. 2010. "Expanding Apprenticeship: A Way to Enhance Skills and Careers." Washington, D.C.: Urban Institute.

Lindqvist, Erik, and Roine Vestman. 2011. "The Labor Market Returns to Cognitive and Noncognitive Ability: Evidence from the Swedish Enlistment." *American Economic Journal: Applied Economics* 3(1): 101–28.

Long, Bridget Terry, and Erin Reilly. 2007. "Sending Signals to Students." In *Minding the Gap: Why Integrating High School with College Makes Sense and How to Do It*, edited by Nancy Hoffman, Joel Vargas, Andrea Venezia, and Marc Miller. Cambridge, Mass.: Harvard Education Press.

Lumley, Thomas, Richard Kronmal, and Shuangge Ma. 2006. "Relative Risk Regression in Medical Research: Models, Contrasts, Estimators, and Algorithms." Biostatistics Working Paper Series 293. Seattle: University of Washington.

Marcotte, Dave E., Thomas Bailey, Carey Borkoski, and Greg S. Kienzl. 2005. "The Returns of a Community College Education: Evidence from the National Education Longitudinal Survey." *Education Evaluation and Policy Analysis* 27(2): 157–75.

Margolin, Jonathan, Shazia R. Miller, and James E. Rosenbaum. 2013. "The Community College Website as Virtual Advisor: A Usability Study." *Community College Review* 41(1): 44–62.

Marmot, Michael. 2004. *The Status Syndrome: How Social Standing Affects Our Health and Longevity*. New York: Macmillan.

Massey, Douglas, Camille Charles, Garvey Lundy, and Mary Fischer. 2003. *Source of the River: Social Origins of Freshmen at America's Selective Colleges and Universities*. Princeton, N.J.: Princeton University Press.

McNutt, Louise-Anne, Chuntao Wu, Xiaonan Xue, and Jean Paul Hafner. 2003. "Estimating the Relative Risk in Cohort Studies and Clinical Trials of Common Outcomes." *American Journal of Epidemiology* 157(10): 940–43.

Meissner, Lynn, Caitlin Ahearn, and James Rosenbaum. 2016. "Do Bachelor's Degrees Have Earnings Payoffs for Students with Low Test Scores?" Paper presented to the Midwest Sociology of Education Conference. Bloomington, Ind. (October 21).

Merton, Robert K. 1973. "The Matthew Effect in Science." In *The Sociology of Science*, edited by Norman W. Storer. Chicago: University of Chicago Press.

Meyer, John. 1977. "The Effects of Education as an Institution." *American Journal of Sociology* 83(1): 55–77.

Miller, Joanne. 1980. "Individual and Occupational Determinants of Job Satisfaction." *Work and Occupations* 7(3): 337–66.

Mincer, Jacob. 1974. *Schooling, Experience, and Earnings*. New York: National Bureau of Economic Research.

Mokher, Christine. 2014. "Participation and Pass Rates for College Preparatory Transition Courses in Kentucky (REL 2014-009)." Washington: U.S. Department of Education, Institute of Education Sciences, National Center for Education Evaluation and Regional Assistance, Regional Educational Laboratory Appalachia.

Mortimer, Jeylan T., and Helga Krueger. 2000. "Transition from School to Work in the United States and Germany: Formal Pathways Matter." In *Handbook of the Sociology of Education*, edited by Maureen Hallinan. New York: Kluwer Academic/Plenum Publishers.

Moss, Philip, and Chris Tilly. 1996. "Soft Skills and Race: An Investigation of Black Men's Employment Problems." *Work and Occupations* 23(3): 252–76.

————. 2001. *Stories Employers Tell: Race, Skill, and Hiring in America*. New York: Russell Sage Foundation.

Mouw, Ted, and Arne L. Kalleberg. 2010. "Stepping Stone Versus Dead End Jobs: Occupational Pathways Out of Working Poverty in the United States, 1979–2006." Working paper. Chapel Hill: University of North Carolina.

Murnane, Richard J., and Frank Levy. 1996. *Teaching the New Basic Skills: Principles for Educating Children to Thrive in a Changing Economy*. New York: Free Press.

Murnane, Richard J., John B. Willett, and Frank Levy. 1995. "The Growing Importance of Cognitive Skills in Wage Determination." Working Paper 5067. Cambridge, Mass.: National Bureau of Economic Research.

Murray, Charles. 2008. *Real Education: Four Simple Truths for Bringing America's Schools Back to Reality*. New York City: Crown Press.

National Center for Education Statistics (NCES). 2008. *Digest of Education Statistics*. Washington: U.S. Department of Education, Institute for Education Sciences.

————. 2012. *Digest of Education Statistics*. Washington: U.S. Department of Education, Institute for Education Sciences.

————. 2014. *Digest of Education Statistics*. Washington: U.S. Department of Education, Institute for Education Sciences.

National Commission on the High School Senior Year. 2001. "Student Transitions: The Senior Year of High School: Briefing Paper." Available at: http://www.nacep.org/confdownloads/A_WelcomeSession.doc (accessed April 10, 2017).

National Data Program for the Social Sciences. 2007. *General Social Surveys, 1972–2006: Cumulative Codebook*. James Davis, Tom Smith, and Peter Marsden, investigators. Chicago: University of Chicago, National Opinion Research Center (March).

Neckerman, Kathryn M., and Joleen Kirshenman. 1991. "Hiring Strategies, Racial Bias, and Inner-City Workers." *Social Problems* 38(4): 433–47.

Newman, Katherine S., and Hella Winston. 2016. *Reskilling America: Learning to Labor in the Twenty-First Century.* New York: Metropolitan Books.

Ng, Chenny, and James E. Rosenbaum. 2015. "The Outcomes of Community College Placement." Paper presented to the conference "Looking Ahead: A Forum on Higher Education." Evanston, Ill. (April 25).

Nguyen, Anh Ngoc, Jim Taylor, and Steve Bradley. 2001. "High School Dropouts: A Longitudinal Analysis." Working paper. Lancaster, U.K.: Lancaster University, Department of Economics.

Obama, Barack. 2013. "Remarks by the President in the State of the Union Address, February 12." Washington: The White House. Available at: https://www.whitehouse.gov/the-press-office/2013/02/12/remarks-president-state-union-address (accessed April 1, 2017).

Oreopoulos, Philip, and Kjell G. Salvanes. 2011. "Priceless: The Nonpecuniary Benefits of Schooling." *Journal of Economic Perspectives* 25(1): 159–84.

Pallas, Aaron M., and Jennifer L. Jennings. 2009. "Cumulative Knowledge About Cumulative Advantage." *Swiss Journal of Sociology* 35: 211–29.

Piore, Michael J. 2002. "Thirty Years Later: Internal Labor Markets, Flexibility, and the New Economy." *Journal of Management and Governance* 6: 271–79.

Putnam, Robert D. 2015. *Our Kids: The American Dream in Crisis.* New York: Simon & Schuster.

Ravitch, Diane. 2013. *Reign of Error: The Hoax of the Privatization Movement and the Danger to America's Public Schools.* New York: Alfred A. Knopf.

Rivera, Mario A., and James D. Ward. 2010. "Institutional Racism, Diversity, and Public Administration." In *Diversity and Public Administration: Theory, Issues, and Perspectives*, 2nd ed., edited by Mitchell F. Rice. London: M. E. Sharpe.

Roderick, Melissa, Vanessa Coca, and Jenny Nagaoka. 2011. "Potholes on the Road to College." *Sociology of Education* 84(3): 178–211.

Rose, Mike. 2012. *Back to School: Why Everyone Deserves a Second Chance at Education.* New York: New Press.

Rosenbaum, James E. 1978. "The Structure of Opportunity in School." *Social Forces* 57: 236–56.

———. 1979. "Tournament Mobility: Career Patterns in a Corporation." *Administrative Science Quarterly* 24(2): 220–42.

———. 1984. *Career Mobility in a Corporate Hierarchy.* New York: Academic Press.

———. 1986. "Institutional Career Structures and the Social Construction of Ability." In *Handbook of Theory and Research for the Sociology of Education,* edited by John G. Richardson. New York: Greenwood Press.

———. 2001. *Beyond College for All: Career Paths for the Forgotten Half.* New York: Russell Sage Foundation.

———. 2002. "Beyond Empty Promises: Policies to Improve Transitions into College and Jobs." Paper presented to "Preparing America's Future: The High School Symposium Conference." U.S. Department of Education, U.S. Chamber of Commerce. Washington, D.C. (April 4).

Rosenbaum, James E., Kennan Cepa, and Janet Rosenbaum. 2013. "Beyond the One-Size-Fits-All College Degree." *Contexts* 12(1): 49–52.

Rosenbaum, James E., Regina Deil-Amen, and Ann E. Person. 2006. *After Admission: From College Access to College Success*. New York: Russell Sage Foundation.

Rosenbaum, James E., Janet Rosenbaum, Caitlin Ahearn, and Kelly Becker. 2015. *The New Forgotten Half and Research Directions to Support Them*. New York: William T. Grant Foundation.

Rosenbaum, James E., Pam Schuetz, and Amy Foran. 2010. "How Students Make College Plans and Ways Schools and Colleges Could Help." Working paper. Evanston, Ill.: Northwestern University, Institute for Policy Research.

Rosenbaum, Janet. 2011a. "Do Degrees Matter? Health Disparities Between Bachelor's and Associate Degree Holders with Similar Job Quality." Paper presented to the International Conference on Health Policy Statistics. Cleveland, Ohio (October 7).

———. 2011b. "When Do Health Impairments and Family Instability Not Hurt Community College Completion?" Paper presented to the American Public Health Association. Washington, D.C. (November).

———. 2012. "Degrees of Health Disparities: Health Status Disparities Between Young Adults with High School Diplomas, Sub-Baccalaureate Degrees, and Baccalaureate Degrees." *Health Services and Outcomes Research Methodology* 12(2/3): 156–68.

———. Forthcoming. "Predicting Educational Attainments of Young Adults from Their Health Status During College: A Longitudinal Study of Students in Community College and Four-Year College." *Community College Review*.

Ross, Catherine E., and Barbara F. Reskin. 1992. "Education, Control at Work, and Job Satisfaction." *Social Science Research* 21: 134–48.

Ruud, Colin, Debra D. Bragg, and Barbara K. Townsend. 2010. "The Applied Baccalaureate Degree: The Right Time and Place." *Community College Journal of Research and Practice* 34(1/2): 136–52.

Schanzenbach, Diane W., Patricia M. Anderson, Kristin F. Butcher, and Hilary W. Hoynes. 2014. "New Evidence on Why Children's Food Security Varies Across Households with Similar Incomes." Discussion Paper 4. Lexington: University of Kentucky, Center for Poverty Research.

Schneider, Barbara, and David Stevenson. 1999. *The Ambitious Generation: America's Teenager, Motivated but Directionless*. New Haven, Conn.: Yale University Press.

Schwartz, Barry. 2004. *The Paradox of Choice: Why More Is Less*. New York: HarperCollins.

Schwartz, Robert B. 2014. "The Pursuit of Pathways: Combining Rigorous Academics with Career Training." *American Educator* 38(3): 24–41.

Scott-Clayton, Judith. 2011. "The Shapeless River: Does a Lack of Structure Inhibit Students' Progress at Community Colleges?" Working Paper 25. New York: Columbia University, Teachers College, Community College Research Center.

Settersten, Richard, and Barbara Ray. 2010. *Not Quite Adults: Why Twenty-Somethings Are Choosing a Slower Path to Adulthood, and Why It's Good for Everyone*. New York: Bantam.

Sewell, William H., and Robert M. Hauser. 1975. *Education, Occupation, and Earnings: Achievement in the Early Career.* New York: Academic Press.

———. 1980. "The Wisconsin Longitudinal Study of Social and Psychological Factors in Aspirations and Achievements." *Research in Sociology of Education and Socialization* 1: 59–99.

Shapiro, Daniel, and Maria Iannozzi. 1999. *The Benefits to Bridging Work and School: Results of the 1997 National Employer Survey.* Philadelphia: University of Pennsylvania, National Center for Postsecondary Education.

Shavit, Yossi, Richard Arum, and Adam Gamoran. 2007. *Stratification in Higher Education: A Comparison Study.* Stanford, Calif.: Stanford University Press.

Shugart, Sanford, and Joyce C. Romano. 2008. "Focus on the Front Door of the College." *New Directions for Community Colleges* 144: 29–39.

Shulock, Nancy. 2007. "Rules of the Game: How State Policy Creates Barriers to Degree Completion and Impedes Student Success in the California Community Colleges." Denver, Colo.: Education Commission of the States.

Silva, Jennifer. 2012. "Constructing Adulthood in an Age of Uncertainty." *American Sociological Review* 78(4): 505–22.

———. 2013. *Coming Up Short: Working-Class Adulthood in an Age of Uncertainty.* New York: Oxford University Press.

Spilerman, Seymour. 1977. "Careers, Labor Market Structure, and Socioeconomic Achievement." *American Journal of Sociology* 83(3): 551–93.

Steinberg, Laurence. 1996. "Psychosocial Factors in Adolescent Decision Making." *Law and Human Behavior* 20(3): 249–72.

———. 1998. *Beyond the Classroom: Why School Reform Has Failed and What Parents Need to Do.* New York: Simon and Schuster.

Stephan, Jennifer L., and James E. Rosenbaum. 2009. "Permeability and Transparency in the High School–College Transition." In *AERA Handbook on Education Policy Research,* edited by Gary Sykes, Barbara Schneider, and David N. Plank. Washington, D.C.: American Educational Research Association.

———. 2012. "Can High Schools Reduce College Enrollment Gaps with a New Counseling Model?" *Educational Evaluation and Policy Analysis* 35(2): 200–219.

Stephan, Jennifer L., James E. Rosenbaum, and Ann E. Person. 2009. "Stratification in College Entry and Completion." *Social Science Research* 38: 572–93.

Stern, David. 1978. "Willingness to Pay for More Agreeable Work." *Industrial Relations* 17(1): 85–90.

Stevenson, Harold W., and James W. Stigler. 1992. *The Learning Gap: Why Our Schools Are Failing and What We Can Learn from Japanese and Chinese Education.* New York: Summit Books.

Stone, James R., III, and Morgan V. Lewis. 2012. *College and Career Ready in the 21st Century: Making High School Matter.* New York: Teachers College Press.

Swanson, Christopher. 2002. "Cooling-Out and Warming-Up: The Role of the Postsecondary Institutional Environment in Managing Ambitions." Chicago: University of Chicago, National Opinion Research Center.

Symonds, William C., Robert Schwartz, and Ronald F. Ferguson. 2011. *Pathways to Prosperity: Meeting the Challenge of Preparing Young Americans for the 21st Century.* Cambridge, Mass.: Harvard University Graduate School of Education, Pathways to Prosperity Project.

Thaler, Richard, and Cass Sunstein, 2008. *Nudge: Improving Decisions About Health, Wealth, and Happiness.* New Haven, Conn.: Yale University Press.

Tinto, Vincent. 1993. *Leaving College: Rethinking the Causes and Cures of Student Attrition.* 2nd ed. Chicago: University of Chicago Press.

Trow, Martin. 1973. *Problems in the Transition from Elite to Mass Higher Education.* Berkeley, Calif.: Carnegie Commission on Higher Education.

Tucker, Marc. 2013. "What Does It Really Mean to Be College and Work Ready?" Washington, D.C.: National Center on Education and the Economy.

Turley, Ruth N. López, and Carla Stevens. 2015. "Lessons from a School District–University Research Partnership: The Houston Education Research Consortium." *Educational Evaluation and Policy Analysis* 37: 65–155.

U.S. Census Bureau. 2012. "PINC-03: Educational Attainment—People 25 Years Old and Over, by Total Money Earnings, Work Experience, Age, Race, Hispanic Origin, and Sex." Washington: U.S. Census Bureau. Available at: https://www.census.gov/data/tables/time-series/demo/income-poverty/cps-pinc/pinc-03.2012.html (accessed April 1, 2017).

Venezia, Andrea, Kathy Reeves Bracco, and Thad Nodine. 2010. "One-Shot Deal? Students' Perceptions of Assessment and Course Placement in California's Community Colleges." San Francisco: WestEd.

Venezia, Andrea, and Daniel Voloch. 2012. "Using College Placement Exams as Early Signals of College Readiness." *New Directions for Higher Education* 158: 71–79.

Vuolo, Mike, Jeylan T. Mortimer, and Jeremy Staff. 2014. "Adolescent Precursors of Pathways from School to Work." *Journal of Research on Adolescence* 24(1): 145–62.

Weissman, Evan, Kristin F. Butcher, Emily Schneider, Jedediah Teres, Herbert Collado, and David Greenberg. 2011. "Learning Communities for Students in Developmental Math: Impact Studies at Queensborough and Houston Community Colleges." *National Center for Postsecondary Research,* February. Available at: http://postsecondaryreadiness.org/wp-content/uploads/2014/10/learning-communities-for-students-in-developmental-math.pdf (accessed April 10, 2017).

William T. Grant Foundation. Commission on Work, Family, and Citizenship. 1988. *The Forgotten Half: Pathways to Success for America's Youth and Young Families.* New York: William T. Grant Foundation.

Wilson, William J. 1996. *When Work Disappears: The World of the New Urban Poor.* New York: Alfred A. Knopf.

Wyner, Joshua. 2014. *What Excellent Community Colleges Do.* Cambridge, Mass.: Harvard Education Press.

Young, Michael. 1958. *The Rise of the Meritocracy.* London: Thames and Hudson.

Zasloff, Beth, and Joshua Steckel. 2014. *Hold Fast to Dreams: A College Guidance Counselor, His Students, and the Vision of a Life Beyond Poverty.* New York: New Press.

Zemsky, Robert. 1994. "What Employers Want: Employer Perspectives on Youth, the Youth Labor Market, and Prospects for a National System of Youth Apprenticeships." Philadelphia: National Center on the Education Quality in the Workforce.

# Index

191